CORONALOGY:
Multidisciplinary Academic Analysis in Perspective of Covid-19

Edited by
Sefer DARICI
Ayşe Meriç YAZICI

FOREWORD

In the aftermath of the pandemic crisis, people sought new answers. The complexity of the situation encountered brought new questions along with anxiety and fear. In a very short time, the world faced big changes. Looking ahead, what are individuals, companies, supply chains, technology, communication, individual relationships, and sustainability going to look like? What's it going to take for this new system to succeed? Which challenges are there to come?

There are quite important questions in these hard days that need to be answered. In this book, experts in their field tried to answer these questions. The chapters of this book, each containing valuable research, convey useful information from each other. It also seeks answers to questions in our minds regarding the uncertainty of the future.

The book aims to contribute to the new paradigm of sense-able COVID-19 from an analytical perspective of different disciplines, to define and relate that kinds of multi-disciplines are able to provide users with the relation of contextual services, to relate and analyze their dynamics and to react accordingly, in a seamless exchange of information during pandemic terms.

In this context, this book's main aim is to understand the complexities of society's pandemic beginning from information that is theoretically accessible from various viewpoints, through a multidisciplinary approach and in multiple contexts, both indoors and outdoors. Also, this book examined what will be changes and transformations after COVID-19 too.

Sefer DARICI
Ayşe Meriç YAZICI

EDITORIAL STAFF

Assist. Prof. Murat Adil SALEPÇİOĞLU- IAU Corporate Governance and Sustainability Application and Research Center Manager
muratsalepcioglu@aydin.edu.tr

GRAPHIC DESIGN

İsmail Cemre DAĞLI
i.cemredagli@gmail.com

ISBN 978-83-66675-15-5 Print
e-ISBN (PDF) 978-83-66675-15-2 Online
e-ISBN (EPUB) 978-83-66675-17-9 Epub

CONTENTS

Foreword

    Sefer DARICI
    Ayşe Meriç YAZICI

CHAPTER 1. Change and Transformation in the Financial System and Institutions After the Pandemic..........................1

    Serhat YANIK

CHAPTER 2. The Future and Sustainability of Financial Markets after the Covid-19 Crisis..............................22

    Cüneyd Ebrar LEVENT

CHAPTER 3. Post-COVID-19: The Great Reset and Senism............................48

    Erdal ŞEN

CHAPTER 4. Macroeconomic Results of the Effects of Covid-19 Pandemic on the Supply Chain............................68

    Erdem BAĞCI

CHAPTER 5. The Prevention Paradox of the COVID-19 Crisis in Germany. Science Communication in Times of Uncertainties.................................85

Lutz PESCHKE

CHAPTER 6. Hybrid-Covid Process Management: The New Economy and Sustainable Network Organization Approach - A New Model Design...110

Murat Adil SALEPÇİOĞLU
Turgay CEYHAN

CHAPTER 7. Developments in Cost Systems During the Industrial Revolutions and Cost Calculation at Smart Factories.........................144

Mustafa ÇANAKÇIOĞLU

CHAPTER 8. The Role of Nanotechnology for Antimicrobial Agents..................170

Figen ÖZYILDIZ
Elif Alyamaç SEYDİBEYOĞLU
M.Özgür SEYDİBEYOĞLU

CHAPTER 9. A Comparative Study of Privacy Policies and Data Protection During the COVID-19 Pandemic Within Different Countries....................................186

Seldağ Güneş PESCHKE
Ömer Fatih SAYAN

CHAPTER 10. The Impacts of Outbreaks on External Trade and Macroeconomic Structure: The Case of Covid-19 Pandemic in Turkey..197

Ali Osman BALKANLI

CHAPTER 11. An Alternative Method of Growth for Turkish Companies: A Discussion over the Defense Industry.........................218

Tuncay Turan TURABOĞLU

CHAPTER 1

Change and Transformation in the Financial System and Institutions After the Pandemic

Serhat Yanık
{syanik@istanbul.edu.tr}

Professor, Istanbul University, Faculty of Political Sciences, Department of Business Administration, Istanbul/Turkey

Abstract

In recent years, rapid changes in technology have led to significant destructive and creative effects in the economy, business life and social life. Issues such as the development of financial technologies, digitalization, blockchain, cryptocurrencies, the use of artificial intelligence have started to change the entire economy and financial processes. In addition, the COVID-19 pandemic that has made us face a crisis that reshaped all our life habits, changing the economies and the business models, has brought these changes in another phase. In the foreseeable future, it is observed that fintech ecosystem will be exposed to serious structural changes and lead to development of new business models. In the current study, financial institutions and markets before the pandemic and financial transformation after the pandemic are comparatively examined. Also, new financial concepts and regulations such as fintech, regtech, cryptocurrencies, artificial intelligence, blockchain, and their roles in the financial markets are explained.

Keywords: Covid-19 Pandemic, digitalization, fintech, regtech, cryptocurrency, blockchain.

Introduction

The world has always been in a constant state of change. People have been pressed to make a major choice between being part of or resisting to change. They have often tended to take the easier path in a disillusion that they can prevent change rather than taking the challenging course of changing. In the past, such changes have gone beyond the lifetime of an individual. A good example may be electricity. It took many years after its invention to ensure that it is widely used. However, the digital transformation of the last 20 years marks a magnitude of change which would span thousands of years in the past. It is safe to say that this is just the beginning and there is so much more to come.

The technology shift of the recent years had a destructive and creative impact on economy, business life, social life and everything else. This impact had its toll also on the finance industry, even in the form of reshaping it. The industry as a whole as well as the economy and financial processes were affected by the developments in financial technologies, blockchain applications, cryptocurrencies and artificial intelligence. These developments of the past few decades have a major impact on the finance industry and the Covid-19 pandemic carried the change to another level as of the end of 2019. As a result of the pandemic, certain new practices were introduced and accepted by the business community and the people. This resulted with certain positive outcomes but also highlighted certain structural problems in the financial and political system. This paper focuses on the change and transformation in the financial systems and institutions triggered by the pandemic as well as possible trends in the future.

Defining the Future: Before the Pandemic and Financial Transformation

With the financial crises in recent years, there has been huge changes in the financial system, institutions, tools and markets. After 2000, we experienced more connections between national economies and industries, macroeconomic instabilities and a process of globalization which resulted with more competition in the local and global markets. The finance industry had a major role in these developments. The major areas affected by the transportation include the organization of financial institutions, operating mechanisms of financial markets, new financial tools and financial technologies (Fintech) (Szyszka, 2012: 3-7).

Transformation of Financial Institutions

The process of digitalization and globalization changed the operations of traditional financial institutions. Increased money supply and the financial markets resulted with new types of crises. The financial crises in Mexico, Thailand, Russia, Brazil and other countries in the 1990s were the result of high debt, high current deficit and speculations. Turkey experienced major financial crises in 1994, 2000, 2001, 2008 and 2018. These crises triggered major changes in financial institutions (Çekin, 2019: 3). There was a major transformation of financial and public institutions, new institutions were established, and business models of current institutions were changed. As mentioned earlier, basic reasons of the need for such change included financial crises, globalization, speculative attacks and the transformation of the digital media.

The major element of the financial markets in Turkey is the banking industry (Çekin, 2019: 3). In the last 20 years, the importance of the investment banks increased. The size of funds held and made available by these institutions may exceed the budgets of many countries. Investment banks had a major role in developing emerging markets by transferring funds from developed economies to the individual and corporate banking systems of emerging markets. The share of insurance market, speculative funds and risk evasion funds increased dynamically. Non-bank financial institutions which emerged after 1980s and focused on high-risk loans triggered uncontrolled growth of markets. This resulted with an increase in the frequency of economic crises (Çekin, 2019: 10).

As a result of the fragilities of the economy and the financial markets, we experienced financial crises in 1994 and 2001 and a banking crisis in 2000. As of 1999, there were 81 banks in Turkey and the number decreased to 48 as a result of the mergers and failures following the crises in 2000 and 2001. Banking Regulation and Supervision Agency (BDDK) was established in September 2000 as a result of these crises and with the purpose of supervising the banking industry. With the 2000s, crises and digital transformation resulted with the emergence of many other institutions and business systems. Some of them are listed below.

- Banking Regulation and Supervision Agency (BDDK)
- Risk Center
- Electronic Funds Transfer System (EFT)
- TL Transfer System Between Banks
- TL Transfer System Between Customers
- Electronic Transfer of Securities System (EMKT)
- Bankalararası Kart Merkezi A.Ş. (BKM)
- İstanbul Takas ve Saklama Bankası A.Ş. (TAKASBANK)
- Merkezî Kayıt Kuruluşu A.Ş. (MKK)
- Garanti Ödeme Sistemleri A.Ş. (GÖSAŞ)
- Paycore Ödeme Hizmetleri Takas ve Mutabakat Sistemleri A.Ş. (Paycore)
- Derivatives Exchange (VOB)

The institutions listed above were established to provide the control mechanisms required for the financial system, build trust, facilitate digital operations, and ensure speed and cost savings.

Transformation of Financial Markets

The economy and finance entered into a new era with the crisis in 2008. Central banks used monetary policies to manage the value of money and stabilize prices in an effort to bring a solution to the financial crisis. Central banks played a major role in expanding the money supply and the monetary base. They attempted to boost the economy and reduce unemployment through low interest rates, increased prices and a low foreign trade deficit. During the pandemic, a monetary expansion was implemented. Low-income individuals and SMEs were supported through stimulus packages and other measures. In addition to the crises, the money supply and the liquidity increased as a result of the digital transformation of the economy, improvements in payment systems and active participation of financial brokers. These resulted with the emergence of a new approach to the financial markets. They are now more liberal, easy to enter, faster, safer thanks to technology and accessible to all segments of the society as well as all business lines. With the internet, financial markets became 24/7 available and it became easier for the users to perform transactions. The stock exchanges make more use of digital tools and are less dependent on people. Prices and trading volume increased in all asset categories. Derivatives markets, Islamic finance, lease certificates, sukuks and many other markets and practices emerged.

In recent years, goods are used in the markets as speculative tools like other financial assets. Increased demand for raw materials from developing economies, especially the Chinese economy, increased the volatility in the prices of goods. Investors invested in crude oil and copper using the cheap money provided by public institutions with the hopes of more growth. Certain new financial tools accessible to all kinds of investors were introduced. The derivatives markets also triggered major changes. In the last twenty years, derivatives were used for speculative purposes rather than risk evasion. The trading volume in the derivatives markets reached 10 times of the volume of the underlying assets before the crisis (Szyszka, 2012: 5-9).

New Finance Products and Institutions Based on Financial Technologies

Financial technologies were used to create many new products and services. Some of these services were offered to meet the needs and demands of customers and some were naturally made available with the technological improvements. In either case, they are widely used. Some of them are listed below:

- Virtual money (Bitcoin, Lindencoin)
- Electronic money (from electronic money institutions)
- Smart card
- Electronic cheque
- EFT (electronic funds transfer)
- Electronic invoice
- Crowd funding
- Digital wallet
- Digital banking
- Electronic insurance
- Digital credit comparison
- Credit rating services (findeks)
- Virtual credit card
- 2D-code

Evolution of Financial Technologies: Fintech, Cryptocurrencies, Artificial Intelligence, Blockchain

The major development which will have a huge impact on the future of the finance industry is the emergence of new finance technologies. Recent financial crises and the underlying reasons required the need for the restructuring of the financial system and businesses. Public authorities and regulators imposed new regulations on financial institutions in a number of areas including transparency, information flow and protection of confidential information. They also introduced limitations on financial institutions and their customers through fiscal requirements. Furthermore, the increased competition between financial institutions and the developments in mobile communication increased the need for financial technologies. There are now more companies which offer new solutions for individuals and companies (KPMG, 2020). Like the rest of the world, major improvements were experienced in Turkey. We now have finance technologies, cryptocurrencies, artificial intelligence, machine learning and blockchain applications.

Fintech: Cornerstones of Fintech Revolution

It should be no surprise that digital technologies had an impact on financial institutions. However, it was a surprise that the demands and expectations of the finance industry guided, even created the companies which develop these technologies. Many ideas are created to solve a problem and fintechs are built on this concept. In this sense, we can talk about three major elements of the transformation process. These are: changes in the macroeconomic regulations, fast evolution of technology and the changes in expectations (Arslanian and Fischer, 2019: 26-27).

The rules of finance are shaped by the economic crises and traumatic experiences. As a result of the crises in 2000s and financial manipulations, regulatory authorities focused on the safety and stability of the financial system. With the increased regulatory burden, financial institutions were forced to allocate certain resources for risk management and compliance. This helped fintech companies emerge and develop. Technological evolution is a good environment for fintech companies to prosper. This was triggered also by the improvements in mobile (3G, 4G, 5G, 6G), computers (Quantum Computers) and software (e.g. establishment of a technology company by a financial institution) as well as competition. The major issue is whether this process is triggered to meet the demands of the financial system (Fintech) or the technologic developments are adapted to the financial system (Techfin). In essence, this process was in the form of a spiral and gave rise to the fintech ecosystem. Another issue with an impact on this process is the change in customer expectations. The improvements in and widespread use of digital technologies forced banks and other financial institutions to adapt these technologies. This process was triggered especially by the younger generations who embrace these developments. This was more apparent in Turkey and other countries with a younger population. It is obvious that this is a rising trend and will be even more effective with the improvements in digital literacy.

Organizational Models for Fintech Companies

A huge share of the economy consists of financial services. Therefore, it is an area of attraction for many companies and initiatives. There are now innovative companies focused on better products and services, low costs and improved customer experience. In this sense, leading industries for fintech companies are payment systems, asset management companies, insurance and banking. Fintech companies operate in payment systems (fund transfer services, mobile POS etc.), banking (Digital Wallet, banking infrastructure, card systems, application providers, data providers, etc.), corporate finance, insurance (sales services, agency and broker services, bank assurance, etc.), crowd funding (reward-based, share-based, donation-based) and cryptocurrencies (trading, etc.) (FinTech Istanbul, 2020). What these industries have in common is that they are subject to strict regulations. This area, named RegTech, has a major influence on fintech companies. Fintech companies always follow up and adapt to rules and regulations introduced by regulatory authorities.

Fintech companies will have a major role in the future of the finance industry. In a sense, the evolution of these institutions and the finance industry will have an effect on each other. It is possible that we will see fintech companies integrated with financial institutions in the future and these will be supported, even encouraged by regulatory authorities.

Blockchain

Blockchain technology is evolving and it is destructive for the financial system. The areas of use of blockchain are grouped under 3 categories. These are Blockchain 1.0, cryptocurrencies, Blockchain 2.0, smart agreements, Blockchain 3.0 government, health, science, art and finance services (Frizzo-Barker, et al., 2020).

Blockchain technology is an electronic payment system essentially developed to solve security gaps in maintenance, use and transfer of digital data (especially double payment in digital currencies). In simple terms, blockchain is a distributed database for management of encrypted data on an easy-to-access network protected against security breaches (Yavuz, 2019: 16). A data block created on a blockchain network is connected to the previous block to form a complete data chain from the first to the last block. The system prevents any modification. Blockchain technology is at the forefront with the emergence of cryptocurrencies in financial markets. This is a form of distributed database technology and some of its features are as follows (Iansiti and Lakhani, 2017):

- Parties of blockchain transactions have access to the complete database and the date but cannot control them.

- The communication is between multiple parties rather than on a central system.
- All transactions are open to all and the parties can choose whether or not to be anonymous.
- The records are chain-connected and cannot be changed back.

Blockchain technology will probably reshape the financial services industry. It is used in many areas including international trading, banking, insurance, crowd funding and individual retirement funds. Distributed Book Technology, Know Your Customer Process, smart agreements, DLT, BIGA (gold-based digital asset platform) are also used in Turkey. This resulted with faster and safer transactions, less fraudulent operations and less losses and costs in the finance system (Yavuz, 2019: 22-23). Use of blockchain in the finance industry ensured faster ID confirmation through digital IDs, less costs in international transfers, faster transactions, more efficient results in credit rating as compared to traditional methods, prevention of modification of logs and more efficiency through smart agreements (Durbilmez and Türkmen, 2019: 38-39). Use of smart agreements in the insurance industry helped prevention of insurance fraud (Roriz and Pereira, 2019: 214).

A major benefit of the blockchain technology is transparency. Security of logged data, prevention of modification and safe access to such data resulted with major changes in the finance industry. Many financial applications will probably be built on this technology in the future. What matters here is the maintenance of public benefit. Manipulative transactions by individuals and institutions in the finance industry damage public benefit. Blockchain will obviously provide huge benefits in this area (Schinckus, 2020).

Artificial Intelligence & Machine Learning

AI automation automates standard and simple tasks like data entry, cash transfers and data logging and helps the whole finance industry, especially banking. AI automation currently optimizes the whole process from offering financial products to processing loans through robot technologies and functions as the interface between machines and people. AI makes the computers smarter (Moloi and Marwala, 2020: 1). AI is used in many areas in the finance industry, including the following.
- Real-Time Data Processing
- Increased Efficiency
- Cost Savings
- Improved User Experience
- New Business Areas

Use of AI in the finance industry results from financial demands, competition and profitability, financial data and technologic improvements. Areas of improvement include development of insurance services, algorithmic trade, detection of fraud and money laundering, text mining and credit rating.

As a result, the finance industry is in a shared evolution with technology and AI. Use of AI in financial systems is growing exponentially. In recent years, use of digital and AI technologies in the finance industry resulted with Digital CVV, digital wallets, wearable payment devices, no-vault shopping, cash withdrawal without any contact with the ATM, mobile ATMs and Internet branches (Tadapaneni, 2020). Most of the service providers in this area offer robot-consultancy services.

Machine learning and AI has a certain impact on the lives of many individuals and is a part of our culture. Machine learning is defined as a subset of data science which uses statistical models to create insights and make estimations (Emerson et al., 2019). The financial services industry made huge steps in the machine learning process. The level of achievement in machine learning in finance depends on an efficient and good infrastructure, gathering of good data sets and implementation of proper algorithms. In the finance industry, transactions can be monitored, and services can be improved through machine learning. Machine learning helps customers optimize costs, improve customer experience and scale services. With the improvements in technology, machine learning will play a major role in the future of finance services (Yılmaz, 2019).

Cryptocurrencies (Digital Money)

Another major change in the financial system is the emergence of cryptocurrencies (Nakamoto, 2008). The idea was conceptualized for the first time in 2008 by the Japanese author Satoshi Nakamoto in "Bitcoin: A Peer-to-Peer Electronic Cash System". Digital currency is a large topic. In this section, we will focus only on the future impact of digital currencies. Traditionally money is printed and circulated by the public authority. Where deemed necessary by the public authority, money supply can be increased or decreased. With the revocation of gold-standard monetary system, governments used their power to supply money more frequently. The bank money and printed money reached huge amounts as compared to the amount of gold. Huge supply of money is among the reasons of recent economic crises.

Cryptocurrencies are supplied to the financial markets through digital encryption without any central authority. There are currently many cryptocurrencies available and they include Bitcoin, Ethereum, Ripple, Tether and Litecoin. The emergence and development of cryptocurrencies resulted with certain characteristics different from the traditional financial system. Some of these characteristics are as follows:

- Cryptocurrencies are encrypted.
- A cryptocurrency is not managed by a central authority.
- Your personal information is not needed to transfer cryptocurrency. The wallet address will be enough.
- Personal information is confidential, but the transfers made using wallets are accessible to all on a blockchain.

- A global legal framework is still not available for cryptocurrencies.
- Cryptocurrency transactions cannot be cancelled or reversed.

Increased money supply during the pandemic resulted with the money losing value against certain assets. The money supply was increased all around the world as an economic and social measure. The increased supply results with an inflationary pressure. Due to such effects which were experienced during former crises, money loses its position as a value store to other assets. In this sense, cryptocurrencies are used in recent years as a value store rather than a value transfer tool.

Furthermore, cryptocurrencies are also used in the informal economy and the world of crime. This resulted with various occasions of fraud and proved that there is still progressed to be made in cryptocurrencies. The system is fast and secure in essence and ID information is not required for transactions. This confidentiality of the sender and the receiver as well as the lack of any central government authority means that the transactions cannot be tracked, and this creates a risk of cryptocurrencies being used for drug sales, arms sales and money laundering (Yurtsever, 2013). A digital currency system with regional and global rules may be required in the future (Dibrova, 2016: 43). The recent fluctuations in digital currency rates and the distrust against traditional monetary policies resulted with gold, silver and other precious metals being the choice of asset to store value. A recent research on digital currencies suggests that it would be wise to add a certain amount of cryptocurrency to the portfolio for risk diversification (Gilbert and Loi, 2018: 115). This trend will increase with regulations.

Another important issue is that cryptocurrency mining causes great energy consumption on a global scale. Renewable energy resources are not yet used in many countries. This has a negative impact on the environment (Schinckus, 2020).

Destructive and Creative Effects of the Pandemic on the Financial System and Institutions and Possible Financial Results

The pandemic emerged as an unexpected crisis in Turkey and in the world. This was unexpected for businesses and they face damages and losses as well as a risk of survival. The risk continues as of now and the magnitude of the devastating effects of the process is unclear.

The pandemic had an impact on all countries. This is not like any economic or social crises we experienced before. No war, pandemic or economic crisis was as global as this one and had an impact on such a large population. Therefore, we do not have previous experience on which to build our estimates about the outcome.

The pandemic resulted with a limitation on the movement of goods and people, a delay or stoppage of the manufacturing process, curfews, closure of shops, a sharp decline in the services and trade and an increase in the unemployment rate. The growth rate declined, unemployment rate increased, investments are delayed, and inflation increased on a global scale. Money supply was increased to support economic and social life and social and economic stimulus plans were introduced. How the process will continue is unclear but there is an expectation that things will be back to normal within a year. One of the few positive effects of the pandemic is the environmental detox. Interruption of the manufacturing processes resulted with a decrease in gas and heat emission and less pollutants had a refreshing impact on the environment. This is a major opportunity in terms of increasing environmental awareness.

Businesses are under similar conditions. Manufacturing was interrupted, certain companies stopped, and stores were closed. There were problems in the supply of raw materials and logistics processes. Taxes were delayed and employees were supported through economic support programs. These action plans assume that the crisis will be over in the short term and they help although they are conclusive. Many businesses are in trouble due to fixed costs and insufficient cash flow. The critical issue is the uncertainty of the process. Some companies and managers have resorted to solutions which may have a negative impact on the economy in a state of panic.

Despite many unfavorable conditions, the pandemic started to create its own economic and social nature with certain good results. Awareness increased on a number of issues including the digital economy, a philosophy of life and production focused on people, environment and income inequality. Many governments increased the money supply and social and economic stimulus packages were introduced. The packages and the money supply are generated and collected through the financial system.

Restrictions on travel resulted with the internet and other digital channels being used more in the provision of goods and services. Companies looked for ways to make use of online market opportunities and customers started using these processes more. It is now clear that we need the rules and mechanisms which emerged with the digital transformation. This transformation will take time and new business models will be developed on a national and international level.

It is obvious that this crisis will not end easily, but we should remember that crises come with their opportunities. Managers look for new markets and distribution channels after the shrinking markets. It is safe to say that awareness on digital channels is at peak. In this sense, digital channels are accepted by the people and businesses which are ready for this have increased their market shares. It is clear that the new economy will be shaped during the post-pandemic era. Possible financial results of the pandemic may include the following:

- More companies may go bankrupt.

- Possible mergers and acquisitions.
- Investments in technology countries will increase.
- Interest in and awareness on fintech companies will increase.
- Home-office will expand, and a suitable ecosystem will rise.

The balance sheets of companies will be affected by the problems in sales and manufacturing processes. The activity cycle will slow down during and after the pandemic. Many companies could not reduce costs proportional to the decrease in sales and were faced with serious damages and losses. Therefore, many companies will experience a major decline in profitability. The companies will take loans or delay them to balance cash flow. This process will result with an increase in financing costs.

Post-Pandemic Process and the Financial Transformation Ahead

A major change in the finance industry is experienced by the banks and insurance companies. There are also major changes in financial regulations. This section will focus on areas of change which will have an impact on the finance industry in the short- and long-term. We will then review possible changes in banking and insurance, regtech and the effect of algorithmic transactions on finance.

Issues and Trends of Transformation in the Financial Industry

It is believed that the pandemic will end with the vaccine. But it is clear that its certain effects will continue to last. It has triggered or accelerated a process which will have a major impact on social life. The change triggered by the pandemic has economic, social and psychological aspects. The financial impact of the process is not only on businesses but also on all segments of the society. Major changes in the finance industry are as follows.

- Digital is more important. Individuals make more use of digital tools and businesses change their business models and sales strategies accordingly.
- Businesses are more willing for home office and flexible working hours. Home office, remote education and remote services will require the need for suitable financial solutions.
- Income inequality is more important and social and financial solutions to address these issues will be prominent.
- The level of social awareness on the significance and adequacy of health services is higher. It is obvious that new methods will be implemented on this issue. The finance industry will act accordingly. Provision of health services will result with a new era in health financing.
- Finance institutions will experience major changes. Traditional business models will be left, and institutions will provide integrated financial solutions. Banks, insurance companies and other companies will be affected.
- Islamic finance is currently on the rise. It is safe to assume that Islamic fintech will also develop and become more prominent.

- The pace of technological development will probably be faster as compared to financial solutions. Therefore, it is possible that techfin will be more prominent than fintech.
- Digital technologies prevented fraud in many industries but also created new possibilities of fraud due to its nature. At this point, use of fintech solutions will help develop this industry. Software solutions based on AI, machine learning and other algorithmic analyses will be developed.
- Emergence of AI in our lives will result with a more personal financial services experience. Custom finance and other services will be used on a wide scale. Analyses based on individual genetic history and custom products are already in use by the banking and insurance industries.
- New and dynamic solutions will be developed in payment systems. We now pay for home deliveries with credit cards, but this will be replaced with new financial tools.
- There will be several ethical issues. Digital and technological applications will create various ethical issues and approaches. Certainly, various ethical rules will be required for robots and software.
- The concept of money will probably change. Digital currency is the result of the distrust for the financial system in the last 30 years. Wider use and standardization of digital currency will take the financial system to a new phase (crises, fraud, risk applications, etc.).
- Risk management will be very important. The pandemic added to the recent financial shocks which are the result of financial crises. The perception of risk is high both for businesses and individuals and the concept of risk evaluation is changing. All parties are encouraged to become aware of risks and take measures against them. Major changes are expected in risk management methods, products and approach.
- The concept of sustainability will be very important for businesses and societies in the future. The most important area of application for businesses is the corporate governance approach and rules. It is safe to say that corporate governance will go beyond public companies and used by all businesses.
- There will be major changes in public management. The change expected after the pandemic can be explained shortly as follows. Public financing methods, public enterprises and business models of companies which do business with the government will change and public and private organizations will be much more similar. In a sense, public and private life will be more transparent.
- New and alternative financing methods will be used. Crowd funding applications may be a good example.
- Quantum computing technology is a major change itself. Beginning with the 1950s, computers were improved, and they are now at a level we did not dream of in the 1980s. This had a huge impact on the financial system. We

have strong mobile and home devices and we can make financial transactions this way. Quantum computers will make a huge mark in the future.

Banking in the Future

The banking industry experienced a major shift with the technological developments in early 2000s. This was also a period of major crises and strict regulations. The emergence of fintech companies and new actors which offer new financial solutions started to threaten the role of the banks within the financial system. Considering banking as a single-track process will prevent understanding its possible evolution in the future.

Banks operate in a vast number of areas. Various subcategories include individual banking, corporate banking and investment banking. The trends listed above will have different effects on these subcategories and the process of change will progress differently.

Individual banking refers to banking services offered to individuals. This is a service area for a huge number of people and will be affected vastly by the digital transformation. The use of digital banking in this area is on the rise. As displayed in Table 1, *the number of individual customers who use digital banking increased by 21.8% annually as of March 2020. The number of corporate customers which use digital banking increased by 17.5% annually as of March 2020.* With the impact of the pandemic, these figures are expected to increase.

Table 1. Number of Digital Banking Customers

Number of Customers (MS)	MARCH 31, 2019 (Thousand People)	March 31, 2020 (Thousand People)	Difference	%
Active Digital Individual MS	44,303	53,981	9,678	21.8
Active Digital Corporate MS	1,994	2,343	349	17.5
Active Total Digital MS	46,297	56,324	10,027	21.7
MS Only Internet	4,000	3,154	-846	-21.2
MS Only Mobile Banking	33,000	43,061	10,061	30.5
MS Mobile Banking and Internet	7,347	7,766	419	5.7

The Banks Association of Turkey, March 2019 and March 2020 - Digital, Internet and Mobile Banking Statistics. Retrieved from: https://www.tbb.org.tr/Content/Upload/istatistikiraporlar/ekler/1289/Dijital-Internet-Mobil_Bankacilik_Istatistikleri-Mart_2020.pdf. Retrieved date: 13 July 2020.

As of January-March 2020, the volume of transactions performed via banking reached TL 1.5 trillion, with a total of 111 million transactions. EFT, TL transfers and F/X transfers reached TL one trillion, with a total of 56 million transactions. This segment has the largest share (67 percent of all financial transactions). Investment transactions reached TL 364 billion, with a total of 17 million transactions. Total number of transactions performed via internet decreased by 9 million and total transaction volume increased by TL 40 billion as compared to the previous period (The Banks Association of Turkey, 2020).

Table 2. Financial Transactions in Internet Banking

	October-December 2019		January-March 2020
	Number of Transactions (Million)	Transaction Volume (Billion TL)	Number of Transactions (Million)
Money transfers	66	1,066	56
Payments	30	62	28
Investment transactions	13	286	17
Credit card transactions	8	23	7
Other financial transactions	4	55	4
Total	**120**	**1,492**	**111**

The Banks Association of Turkey, March 2019 and March 2020 - Digital, Internet and Mobile Banking Statistics. Retrieved from: https://www.tbb.org.tr/Content/Upload/istatistikiraporlar/ekler/1289/Dijital-Internet-Mobil_Bankacilik_Istatistikleri-Mart_2020.pdf. Retrieved date: 13 July 2020.

As of January-March 2020, stock exchange transactions reach TL 125 billion, with a total of 11 million transactions. The volume of F/X transactions reached TL 69 billion, with a total of 2 million transactions.

Table 3. Investment Transactions in Internet Banking

	December 2019		March 2020		Net Change	
	Number of Transactions (Thousand)	Transaction Volume (Billion TL)	Number of Transactions (Thousand)	Transaction Volume (Billion TL)	Number of Transactions (Thousand)	Transaction Volume (Billion TL)
Investment Funds	1,543	60	1,583	65	39	5
Foreign Currency Transactions	2,308	68	2,143	69	-165	2
Time Deposits	724	46	769	54	45	8
Stocks *	7,740	87	10,784	125	3,044	37
Repurchase Agreements	84	5	82	5	-2	1
Bonds and Bills	82	2	88	2	6	0
Gold	482	4	780	13	298	9
VIOP **	216	14	364	29	148	15
Total	**13,179**	**286**	**16,592**	**364**	**3,413**	**78**

* *Number of actual stock transactions*
** *Derivatives Exchange*

The Banks Association of Turkey, March 2019 and March 2020 - Digital, Internet and Mobile Banking Statistics. Retrieved from: https://www.tbb.org.tr/Content/Upload/istatistikiraporlar/ekler/1289/Dijital-Internet-Mobil_Bankacilik_Istatistikleri-Mart_2020.pdf. Retrieved date: 13 July 2020.

In January-March 2020, loans offered through internet banking channel reached 3,015,000,000, with a total number of 127,000. 37,000 insurance policies were sold in the same period.

As is obvious many new technologies, some of which are listed above, has a huge impact on banking. Banking is changing and transforming. Traditional banking applications are being replaced with new ones with a fast pace. The pace of such change is increasing. The basic elements of the change are as follows (The Banks Association of Turkey, 2020):

• Banking is being digitalized fast, alternative channels diversify and they are used on a wider scale.
• New finance technologies allow faster, easier and less costly banking transactions through non-bank institutions. This resulted with big technology companies turning into financial institutions and compete with banks.
• Banks also go through a fast change with open banking applications.
• General banking services are replaced by custom products and services. AI is widely used here.
• New regulations especially on protection of confidential information require banks to use RegTech solutions to meet the requirements. There will be more improvements in this area.

- New channels are available to offer banking services on social media platforms.
- These new finance methods are developed out of the banks and the need for banks decrease to a certain extent. Change will continue in the future with new technologies and financing methods. Some examples are crowd funding platforms, digital payment and e-cash, international funds transfer, individual and corporate loans, per-to-peer (P2P) credit platforms.
- Quantum computing has a capacity to change the world and it will have a huge impact on banking.
- We will see banks operating only in the virtual world, without a physical location. Many solutions will be developed with external resources.
- The use of AI in banking will increase, the number of employees will decrease, and their qualifications will change.
- The banks will have less branches and employees. In the future, less transactions will be performed through branch offices. It is even possible that branch offices will disappear over time (Yurtsever, 2012).
- In addition to banks, virtual banks will be established by major telecommunication companies, technology companies, tourism companies etc. to offer banking services. These companies will collaborate to establish virtual banks.
- The banks will be more of a technology company than a financial institution. Various institutions will collaborate to fund R&D in this area.

European governments support technology companies in an effort to create more competition in financial services through fast and customer-focused solutions. The also impose regulations to support technology initiatives (Esen, 2020). This process is called open banking and started in Europe in 2015. The process started in Turkey in 2020 where third-party initiatives were allowed to combine their accounts in various banks and transfer funds (Law on Payment and Securities Settlement Systems, Payment Services and Electronic Money Institutions; 2013).

Insurance in the Future

Technologic improvements will obviously affect the insurance industry. In a major industry where big data is used for risk management, IT improvements are adapted to the business with a fast pace. Here we have "Insuretech" companies which combine insurance and finance technologies.

Insurance industry will experience innovations based on technological improvements in terms of risk definition and management. Digital insurance has reached a certain pace. Big data will help accurate pricing of any risk. It is also possible that the concept of open insurance will emerge.

Table 4. Premiums by Method of Sales (Million TL)

Branch	Tele-Sales	E-Commerce	Traditional	Total
NON-LIFE TOTAL	112.3	49.6	27,234	27,396
LIFE TOTAL	216.8	613.3	4,880	5,710
GRAND TOTAL	329.1	662.9	32,115	33,107

May 2020 Premiums by Method of Sales (Million TL), Turkish Insurance Association. Retrieved from: https://www.tsb.org.tr/resmi-istatistikler.aspx?pageID=909. Retrieved Date: 14 July 2020.

As of May 2020, a huge share of insurance sales was made through traditional sales channels. However, sales through tele-sales and e-commerce channels are increasing. Sales through e-commerce almost doubled as compared to the previous year (TL 308.7 million).

In insurance, expectations include use of AI, use of roboadvisory and similar applications in investment management, use of VR in training (Yazıcı, 2020), better and improved use of digital sales channels and even disappearance of traditional agency offices.

Possible dynamics in the future include the emergence of new insurance products, collaboration with technology companies and use of preventive and protective measure to prevent damages. The industry also uses many software products to prevent fraud. Technology is not a threat to the insurance industry and helps development and improvement of processes. In Turkey, the insurance industry is expected to take the leading position in the finance industry.

Regtech

In recent years, regulatory authorities and public institutions impose new rules and request short-term reports. However, system developments are needed to meet these requirements and institutions are faced with challenges in meeting them (Yurtsever, 2020). Regulation technologies will improve significantly in this area in the future.

Regtech is defined as the regulation technologies applicable to finance. The fintech ecosystem is in collaboration with the industry to develop solutions required by financial institutions to meet the requirements of the regulations. The process of offering technological solutions by fintech companies is called regtech. In other words, regtech is a control and application mechanism operated by the software to ensure compliance. Companies can routinely adapt compliance standards, meet requirements and minimize operational risks arising from reporting requirements (Demirdöğen, 2019: 313). There is a vast portfolio of solutions and software from holistic governance, risk and compliance (GRC) software to custom solutions. A major concept related with legal compliance is the concept of real-time compliance.

Algorithmic and High-Frequency Trading (HFT)

"Algorithmic trading" can be defined as using programs based on mathematical algorithms to place orders and financial transactions based on various scenarios. High-frequency trading (HFT) is the use of software-based algorithms to determine trade strategies. HFT is a fairly new concept as compared to traditional financial transactions but has reached a significant volume in a short time. In USA, where largest financial markets of the world are located, HFT accounted for 60 percent of the market in 2017. The share in the UK was 77 percent in 2010 (Ersan and Ekinci, 2016). The share of these transactions in Turkey is smaller as compared to USA and other finance centers but this will probably increase in the future. Various fluctuations all around the world (like flash crash sales wave) created attention to the issue and various regulations were introduced (Kirilenko and Lo, 2013). Various regulations like breakers were introduced to prevent negative effects of algorithmic trading on the markets and losses suffered by small investors. These technologies are used also in Turkey and the regulations should be introduced to limit possible side effects of these in the future. Otherwise, algorithmic trading may cause crises in the future.

Conclusion

Each and every crisis will come to an end. What matters is what it takes from us. We are now on the brink of an era which will change our daily routines, reorganize life, change economies and transform business models. This transformation will end well. A transformation is usually a challenging process resulting with certain sacrifices. COVID-19 pandemic crisis will be no different. In this sense, various financial applications will have to change.

The fintech ecosystem will be marked by major structural changes and collaborations, new business models will emerge and banks, insurance companies and financial institutions will work closely. Fintech companies are more agile than financial institutions and they will force these institutions to change. Countries which fail to transform digitally will be left behind. Young people should be educated on digital finance technologies and applications. Major drivers to use finance technologies include direct performance of transactions and the perception of benefit. This gives an idea on areas to focus. Financial and digital literacy should both be improved.

References

Arslanian, H., and Fischer, F. (2019). The Future of Finance: The Impact of FinTech, AI, and Crypto on Financial Services. Hong Kong. Palgrave Macmillan Publishing.

Çekin, S. E. (2019). Türkiye'de Finans Sisteminin Yapısı ve Dönüşüm Gereksinimi. İstanbul. Seta Yayınları.

Demirdöğen, Y. (2019). Essential Regulations for the Fintech Ecosystem

(Regtech). Suleyman Demirel University Visionary Journal. 10 (24). 311-321. https://doi.org/10.21076/vizyoner.574621.

Dibrova, A. (2016). Virtual Currency: New step in Monetary Development. 5th International Conference On Leadership, Technology, Innovation And Business Management. 229. pp. 42-49. Procedia - Social and Behavioral Sciences. https://doi.org/10.1016/j.sbspro.2016.07.112.

Durbilmez, S. E., and Türkmen, S. Y. (2019). Blockhain Technology and its State in the Financial Services Sector in Turkey. Research of Financial Economic and Social Studies (RFES). 4 (1). 30-45. https://doi.org/10.29106/fesa.509254.

Emerson, S., Kennedy, R., O'Shea, L., and O'Brien, J. (2019). Trends and Applications of Machine Learning in Quantitative Finance. 8th International Conference on Economics and Finance Research (ICEFR 2019). SSRN: https://ssrn.com/abstract=3397005.

Ersan, O., and Ekinci, C. (2016, December). Algorithmic and High-Frequency Trading in Borsa Istanbul. Borsa Istanbul Review. 16 (4). 233-248. https://doi.org/10.1016/j.bir.2016.09.005.

Esen, U. (2020). The Future of Open Banking. Retrieved July 13. 2020. from Softech 2020 Technology Report: https://softtech.com.tr/en/softtech-technology-report-2020/

FinTech Istanbul. (2020, January 7). Turkish Fintech Ecosystem Map v5.0. FinTech Istanbul: https://fintechistanbul.org/.

Frizzo-Barker, J., Chow-White, P. A., Adams, P. R., Mentanko, J., Ha, D., and Green, S. (2020). Blockchain as a disruptive technology for business: A systematic review. International Journal of Information Management. 51. 1-14. https://doi.org/10.1016/j.ijinfomgt.2019.10.014.

Gilbert, S., and Loi, H. (2018). Digital Currency Risk. International Journal of Economics and Finance. 10 (2). 108-123. https://doi.org/10.5539/ijef.v10n2p108.

Iansiti, M., and Lakhani, K. R. (2017). The Truth About Blockchain. Retrieved from Harward Business Review: https://hbr.org/2017/01/the-truth-about-blockchain.

KPMG. (2020, February). Pulse of Fintech H2 2019. Retrieved from https://assets.kpmg/content/dam/kpmg/xx/pdf/2020/02/pulse-of-fintech-h2-2019.pdf.

Kirilenko, A. A., and Lo, A. W. (2013). Moore's Law versus Murphy's Law: Algorithmic Trading and Its Discontents. Journal of Economic Perspectives. 27 (2). 51-72. https://doi.org/10.1257/jep.27.2.51.

Law on Payment and Securities Settlement Systems, Payment Services and Electronic Money Institutions. ((2013, June 27). Official Gazette (Nr: 28690). Retrieved July 7, 2020, from https://www.tcmb.gov.tr/wps/wcm/connect/de4fb4cc-19c4-47fe-a9cb-

9ef0397a8923/1.+LAW.pdf?
MOD=AJPERES&CACHEID=ROOTWORKSPACE-de4fb4cc-19c4-47fe-a9cb-9ef0397a8923-m3fw3yI.

Moloi, T., and Marwala, T. (2020). Artificial Intelligence in Economics and Finance Theories. Springer Nature Switzerland AG.

Nakamoto, S. (2008). Bitcoin: A Peer-to-Peer Electronic Cash System. Retrieved July 27, 2020. from Bitcoin.org: https://bitcoin.org/bitcoin.pdf.

Roriz, R., and Pereira, J. L. (2019). Avoiding Insurance Fraud: A Blockchain-based Solution for the Vehicle Sector Vehicle Sector. Procedia Computer Science. 164. 211-218.
https://doi.org/10.1016/j.procs.2019.12.174

Schinckus, C. (2020, November). The Good, the Bad and the Ugly: An Overview of the Sustainability of Blockchain Technology. Energy Research & Social Science. 1-10. https://doi.org/10.1016/j.erss.2020.101614.

Szyszka, A. (2012). Systemic Changes in the Financial World and the Search for the New Paradigm of Finance. In B. M., L. F., V. d. F., A. R., & L. D.T., New Paradigms in Banking, Financial Markets and Regulation? (pp. 1-25). SUERF - The European Money and Finance Forum.

Tadapaneni, N. R. (2020, May). Artificial Intelligence in Finance and Investments. International Journal of Innovative Research in Science. Engineering and Technology (IJIRSET). 9 (5). 2792-2795.

The Banks Association of Turkey. (2020, April). March 2019 and March 2020 - Digital, Internet and Mobile Banking Statistics. Retrieved July 13, 2020. from
https://www.tbb.org.tr/Content/Upload/istatistikiraporlar/ekler/1289/Dijital-Internet-Mobil_Bankacilik_Istatistikleri-Mart_2020.pdf.

Yılmaz, V. (2019). Finansmanı Öğrenen Makineler. 4th International Symposium on Innovative Approaches in Social, Human and Administrative Sciences. 4. pp. 187-192. Samsun: SETSCI Conference Proceedings. https://doi.org/10.36287/setsci.4.8.035.

Yavuz, M. S. (2019). Digital Transformation in Economy: A Review of Blockchain Technology and Application Areas. Research of Financial Economic and Social Studies (RFES). 4 (1). 15-29. https://doi.org/10.29106/fesa.498053.

Yazıcı, S. (2020). Insurance and Finance Technologies. Retrieved July 13, 2020. from Softech 2020 Technology Report: https://softtech.com.tr/en/softtech-technology-report-2020/.

Yurtsever, G. (2012, July 1). İnternet Bankacılığı Kullanımı Hızla Artıyor. Retrieved July 7, 2020. from Turcomoney: https://www.turcomoney.com/haber-detay.php?hid=internet-bankaciligi-kullanimi-hizla-artiyor.

Yurtsever, G. (2013, December 31). Sanal Para Bitcoin, Gerçek Paranın Yerini mi Alıyor? Retrieved June 27, 2020. from Turcomoney:

https://www.turcomoney.com/sanal-para-bitcoin-gercek-paranin-yerini-mi-aliyor.html.

Yurtsever, G. (2020, July 1). Regülasyon Teknolojilerinin (Regtech) Önemi Artıyor. Retrieved July 13, 2020. from Turcomoney: https://www.turcomoney.com/regulasyon-teknolojilerinin-regtech-onemi-artiyor.html.

CHAPTER 2

The Future and Sustainability of Financial Markets after the Covid-19 Crisis

Cüneyd Ebrar Levent
{cuneydebrarlevent@gmail.com}

Assist. Prof., Istanbul Aydin University, Anadolu BİL Vocational School - Accounting and Tax Practices Program, Istanbul/Turkey

Abstract

This study aims to examine the future and sustainability of financial markets after the Covid-19 crisis. The study covers the dates from early 2020 to June 30, 2020. Trend and comparative analysis methods were used. The extreme value method was preferred to calculate intraday volatility. It was determined that the stock markets with different dynamics in the crisis period acted as if they were a single market. In addition, it was found that the uncertainty and panic caused by the crisis surpassed even the 2008 global financial crisis. High volatility in the financial markets is expected to continue in the near future as significant uncertainties regarding the pandemic and the economy remain. Apart from that, Covid-19 also had negative effects in the context of social and environmental sustainability. It is highly likely that all this will have a negative impact on the national economies, companies and financial markets.

Keywords: Financial markets, sustainability, Covid-19, stock market, risk, volatility.

Introduction

The Covid-19 pandemic has caused a major crisis in global markets. The biggest reason for this was that, unlike many previous crises, it occurred without any economic symptoms. When the virus first occurred in just one person in Wuhan, China, at the end of 2019, no one had predicted that this mysterious virus would soon lead to an economic, financial and social devastation.

The virus infected about 10,000 people at the end of January, and 98.7% of those cases were in China (Worldometer, 2020). Most of these cases occurred in Hubei province. Therefore, China started implementing strict isolation and quarantine measures. Global markets did not react to this instantly because it was perceived as a regional epidemic like SARS. In February, when it became apparent that the number of cases and deaths was increasing exponentially, global companies operating in China decided to stop their operations in this country. Initial awareness in global financial markets also took place in this period, the stock prices of the companies that stopped Chinese operations or were significantly dependent on China began to drop. Due to the fact that China was one of the world's most important oil importers, oil prices also fell sharply (IEA, 2020). The decline in oil prices caused Russian and Mexican currencies to depreciate, whose economies rely heavily on oil.

The outbreak also spread rapidly to countries outside of China, and the number of cases and virus-related deaths increased. World Health Organization declared Covid-19 as a pandemic on March 11 (WHO, 2020). The center of the "pandemic" changed direction, the number of confirmed cases in the US, Italy and Spain surpassed China as of the end of March. Health systems collapsed in Europe and the US. This forced countries that considered Covid-19 to be the Chinese virus and did not take the virus seriously at first, to implement unprecedented harsh measures. Lockdowns and restrictions began to be imposed in many countries around the world. As a result, many production and service operations stalled to a large extent globally. Worldwide stock markets fell dramatically in the first half of March, recalling the 2008 global financial crisis.

While stock markets crashed in this period, the Dollar Index increased, and wide fluctuations occurred in commodity markets. There was significant capital outflow from the markets in developing countries. Some of the investors turned to gold and developed countries' bonds as safer financial assets.

Many countries took various measures to reduce the impact of the pandemic on the economy. Some of the central banks, including the FED, decided to cut policy rates. In some countries, the application of negative policy rates is still in force. In addition, it was promised that rescue packages for companies and some sectors would be given. Many countries provided aid, incentives, or sent checks to citizens affected by the pandemic, or imposed a ban on laying-off of workers.

If Covid-19 triggered a financial crisis, the first bottom point of this crisis is March 18, 2020 (we do not yet know if there will be second, third and other bottom points). After that date, equity markets around the world started to increase. Although the number of confirmed total Covid-19 cases exceeded 10 million, the financial markets recovered a significant portion of their losses by the end of June. The big shock in the commodity and foreign exchange markets was also overcome. Lockdowns have been lifted on national scale, and both social life and financial markets have returned to "new normal".

In this context, this study aims to discuss the future and sustainability of financial markets after the Covid-19 pandemic. In the study, not only a country or an index, but also the markets are examined from a global perspective. After Covid-19, the effects of the pandemic on financial markets has begun to be investigated and the literature has been evolving. In this respect, this study aims to contribute to the existing literature.

The study covers from January 1, 2020 to June 30, 2020. The financial effects of the pandemic have been handled in three periods considering the impact it has created. The first period called Phase 1 covers the period between January 1 and February 29. The period between March 1 and March 18, in which the major shock is experienced in the financial markets, is analyzed as Phase 2. The future and sustainability of financial markets are discussed in a separate section, considering March 18 and beyond. Trend and comparative analysis methods are mainly used in the study.

The study also examines the social and environmental dimensions of sustainability, which are the other two pillars of sustainability in addition to economics. That section discusses social and environmental sustainability after the pandemic and its impact on financial markets. The last section includes conclusion and recommendations.

Financial Crises and Covid-19 Case

The title of the study refers to "Covid-19 crisis". Could we consider the fluctuations, sharp movements, and panic in the financial markets after the pandemic as a financial crisis? What are the characteristics of financial crises? Would it be wrong to compare the Covid-19 crisis with the 2008 global financial crisis? In this section, the answers to these questions will be sought, the definitions of financial crisis in the literature will be analyzed, and it will be discussed whether what we are experiencing is a financial crisis.

Financial Crises

The word "crisis" generally means great danger, difficulty, depression, and failure. Not every difficulty or problem encountered can be called a crisis, the crisis covers or affects more a period than a momentary or temporary situation. From an economic perspective, the crisis often occurs in an unexpected moment and catches the affected unprepared. The economic environment and the current negativities help to predict the occurrence of a crisis, even the crisis indicators are mentioned in the literature (Nelson, 1990; Arndt & Hill, 2000; Reisen, 1999; Edison, 2003), but it is almost impossible to predict the exact date of the crisis.

In the financial context, a crisis is an unexpected and damaging situation that seriously disrupts the stability of the financial system. The main function of financial institutions in the economic system is to realize the transfer between those who have funds and those who need funds. Financial institutions have to generate profit while continuing their operations. Within the system, there is an interminable conflict between financial institutions and borrowers, while financial institutions also compete among themselves. On the real sector side, firms struggle to grab an intense market share. It is inevitable that this economic environment will produce problems and conflicts. However, this challenge cannot be called a financial crisis. As mentioned above, a financial crisis is far beyond all this and occurs unexpectedly.

Almost all of the crises experienced in the last century stem from the failure or deficiencies in the financial system in one way, and there may be adverse selection and moral hazard in origin. Having examined the crisis issue in this respect, Mishkin, (1992) described the financial crisis as *"a disruption to financial markets in which adverse selection and moral hazard problems become much worse, so that financial markets are unable to efficiently channel funds to those who have the most productive investment opportunities"*. In particular, Enron case and the 2008 Global Financial Crisis can be cited as examples of adverse selection and moral hazard.

Kindleberger and Aliber (2005) stated that financial crises should be handled in a wider perspective as well as moral hazard. They emphasized that crises include a combination of factors such as sharp declines in asset prices, failures of both financial and non-financial firms, and excessive movements in the foreign exchange market. This definition of crisis exactly describes the 2008 global financial crisis. The process that started with asset prices, then the crisis spread to financial and then non-financial institutions, and eventually all markets collapsed.

Each financial crisis has different dynamics. Therefore, the reason of the crises should not be attributed to a single factor. Before some crises, it is observed that factors such as deregulation and hot money stimulated the economy and increased growth rates, and then brought great destruction. In this context, Kaminsky and Reinhart (1998) stated that financial crises occurred when the economy entered to recession after a long boom in economic activity fueled by credit creation and fluctuations in capital inflows.

Minsky (1972) focused on the fact that financial crises were caused by cash need and debt. According to Minsky, financial crises take place *"because units need or desire more cash than is available from their usual sources and so they resort to unusual ways to raise cash."* As a result of all this, the author stated that financial and non-financial units could withdraw from financial markets for a variety of reasons, as a result, the usual way of doing business might change, business connections might deteriorate, and prices in the market might be affected.

Financial crises, as in the Covid-19 outbreak, are always thought to occur with an external impact. The devaluation of Thai Baht (1997), debate between the President and Prime Minister in Turkey (2001), the subprime loans announcement from Freddie Mac (2007) or the collapse of Lehman Brothers (2008) are thought to cause crises. Furman, Stiglitz, Bosworth and Radelet (1998) disagreed with this conception and stated that *"financial crises are not strictly exogenous; in many cases the slowdown itself, or the very factors that led to it, have helped to cause a financial crisis."* Extraordinary events take place at first in the chronology of crises. However, when the anatomy of the crises is examined, it is seen that there are hundreds of wrong decisions and failures behind the crises. The 2020 crisis has occurred in this context with an external impact (Covid-19) that differs from other crises in the past 50 years. However, it should be taken into consideration that the devastation caused by the crisis in the coming months or years will still be related to internal factors. For the most accurate evaluation of the future, we should examine the origin and the aftermath of the nearest past crisis (2008 Global Financial Crisis).

2008 Global Financial Crisis vs Covid-19 Crisis

The 2008 crisis has been regarded as the most important crisis that shaked the world economy after the Great Depression in 1929. It would have been predicted that structural problems in the US and Europe would at least be a "problem", but it was not easy for most to know that this would turn into a global crisis and cause collapses. In the US, mortgage loan interest rates dropped significantly after 2001. Thousands of people who were almost incapable of paying back were given loans at low interest rates. It was of course anticipated that this would have economic consequences. It was not surprising that derivative instruments "engineered" and generated from these loans would also cause a chain reaction to the non-payment of loans.

Crises may resemble each other in certain respects, but each crisis should be evaluated with the period and conditions it occurs. However, the 2008 crisis provides several clues to understanding the Covid-19 crisis, just like the effect of the 1997 Asian crisis on the 1998 Russian crisis. Behind the 2008 crisis, it is necessary to examine Enron and dot.com crises in depth. It was impossible for Enron's auditor Arthur Andersen not to know the real situation of the company. The CEO of Lehman in 2008 and the executives of hundreds of large companies that went bankrupt in 2008 also predicted that their companies were not financially sustainable. The crisis and the collapse did not occur suddenly like in the pandemic, approaching step by step. The crises after 2000 gave birth to Sarbanes-Oxley Act (2002) and Dodd-Frank Wall Street Reform and Consumer Protection Act (2010) in the United States. In countries other than the United States, important regulations entered into force on financial markets and the sustainability of the economic system. Discussions in the aftermath of the global crisis were about getting rid of derivative instruments and toxic assets whose contents were unclear. There was consensus that excessive risk-taking by firms and executives would threaten the financial system.

But after a while all this was forgotten, equity markets hit the records, structural reforms were either canceled or postponed. Firm risks did not decrease and on the contrary, they increased even more through borrowing. Global markets were caught with great risks, unprepared for the Covid-19 pandemic. The most striking similarity of the two crises is that they had not learnt from previous experiences.

Covid-19 and Financial Markets
First phase

When the outbreak first emerged in China, western countries considered the outbreak (which was not called a pandemic at the time), as a disease that would never spread to them like SARS, MERS or Ebola. Therefore, US and European stocks continued to rise with enthusiasm. The only issue of concern was that a problem from production and supply chains would arise. Some countries even started making plans to replace China in the supply chain. In the context of financial markets, China was the first country to be affected by the outbreak as expected. Chinese financial markets acted as the epicenter of both physical and financial contagion (Corbet, Larkin, & Lucey, 2020).

Figure 1 provides a trend analysis of the three most important stock indices of the Far East. Dow Jones Industrial Index (DJI) is also included in the chart for comparison. Shanghai Composite Index in China, the place of the outbreak, fell more than 10% between January 22, 2020 and February 3, 2020. However, neither in South Korea (KOSPI) nor in Japan (NIKKEI), there was a significant decrease in the first phase of the outbreak, as in China. DJI was close to the end of the rapid rise that started in 2009, but did not yet react significantly in this period.

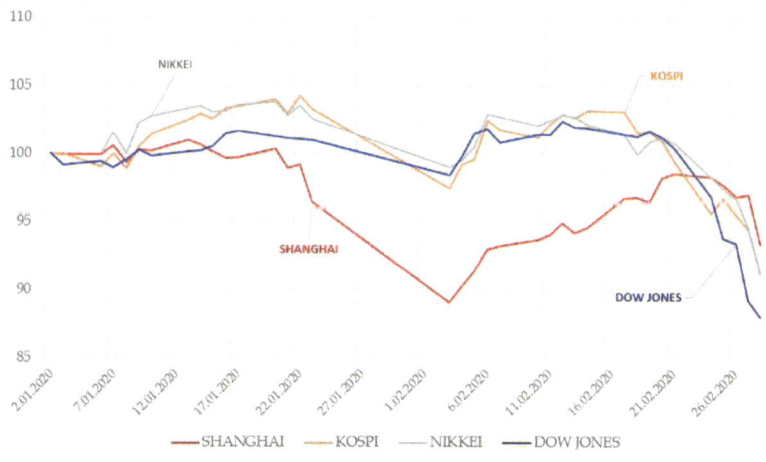

Fig. 1. Trend analysis of far east indices and Dow Jones Industrial Index

The virus was also transmitted to the US financial markets on February 21, after which the DJI fell significantly. Moreover, as of February 28, the number of total confirmed cases in the USA was 63, and a death due to virus had not yet occurred (Worldometer, 2020). NIKKEI and KOSPI indices also suffered losses, but it is clear that the most significant loss in the first phase of the outbreak compared to the beginning of 2020 was in DJI (Figure 1).

In this phase of the outbreak, European indices experienced declines similar to Dow Jones. In the first two months of 2020, DAX (Germany), FTSE 100 (UK), CAC 40 (France), IBEX 35 (Spain) and FTSE MIB (Italy) each fell by 11, 13, 12, 10 and 8 percent, respectively. What is noteworthy here is that these indices, which have a significant weight especially in global markets, acted in correlation with DJI. This result has also been found in several studies in the literature (Ali, Alam, & Rizvi, 2020).

The effects of the outbreak began to appear in markets other than equity markets in the first phase. There were serious fluctuations especially in commodity markets. However, the main effect of the outbreak on the markets took place in March.

Second phase (March 1 - March 18, 2020)

The most important effect of the Covid-19 outbreak on financial markets was between March 1, 2020 and March 18, 2020. The number of total confirmed cases, which was 14,553 at the beginning of February, increased to 88,586 on March 1. Total death toll from COVID-19 increased 10 times as compared to February and reached 3,050. The outbreak had actually crossed China's borders for a long time, but it took March for the rest of the world to be aware of it. The World Health Organization announced Covid-19 as a "pandemic" on March 11, as the number of cases and deaths grew exponentially. In March, European countries were the center of the pandemic. The best solution the world had for this pandemic other than treatment and vaccination was to force people to stay at home and close the borders. Millions of people were imprisoned at home, economic activities around the world stopped to a large extent. The panic mentioned in the previous section, which describes the characteristics of financial crises, took place during this period. The fear and the reaction of the financial markets to all these were not matched even to those in the 2008 crisis (Table 1).

Table 1 shows the values of the VIX index in previous high volatility events and crises. VIX, also known as the fear index, is an index of fear and stress in the financial markets. With the bankruptcy of Lehman Brothers, the index rose above 30, which is considered as the critical threshold, and reached its peak at 80.06 during the global financial crisis. In the following years, it rose above 40 in various crises (such as the European debt crisis, US debt crisis and Chinese currency crisis). However, the panic and fear that ensued after the Covid-19 pandemic pushed the VIX index above the level of the 2008 crisis.

Table 1. Previous high volatility events

Crisis Event	Event Date	VIX at Event Date
Covid-19	16.03.2020	82.69
US/China trade war	24.12.2018	36.07
China currency crisis	24.08.2015	40.74
US debt crisis	8.08.2011	48.00
European debt crisis	7.05.2010	40.95
Global financial crisis	27.10.2008	80.06
Global financial crisis (Lehman Brothers collapse)	15.09.2008	31.70

Adapted from the data for event dates and VIX index from Wang, Yao and Bonne (2020) and Marketwatch (2020).

The panic and collapse in the second phase occurred not only in the US stock markets but in the markets in Europe, Asia and developing countries. Table 2 shows the total number of Covid-19 cases and changes in the stock market indices. Total cases in the US increased 92 times between March 2 and March 18, while the Dow Jones Index (DJI) fell by 25% in just 13 trading days. During this phase, the number of Covid-19 cases in Italy, where the pandemic was first intensified in Europe, reached almost half that of China, while the FTSE MIB index also fell by 30%. Total cases rose exponentially in Britain, Germany, France, and Spain, with the main indices of those countries dropping dramatically between 24% and 30%.

Table 2. Main indices and total Covid-19 cases in the second phase

Country	Index Code	2.03.2020		18.03.2020		Change %
		Total Cases *	Index Close	Total Cases *	Index Close	Cases %
US	DJI	100	26,703	9,330	19,899	9230%
UK	FTSE100	38	6,655	2,376	5,081	6153%
Germany	GDAXI	165	11,858	12,327	8,442	7371%
France	FCHI	191	5,334	9,134	3,755	4682%
Italy	FTMIB	2,038	21,655	35,731	15,120	1653%
Spain	IBEX	120	8,742	14,769	6,275	12208%
Japan	N225	274	21,344	914	16,727	234%
S.Korea	KOSPI	4,335	2,003	8,413	1,591	94%
China	SSEC	80,151	2,971	80,928	2,729	1%
India	NSEI	6	11,133	169	8,469	2717%
Indonesia	JKSE	2	5,361	227	4,331	11250%

Brazil	BVSP	2	106,625	529	66,895	26350%
Mexico	MXX	6	42,167	93	35,533	1450%
Russia	IMOEX	3	2,766	147	2,113	4800%
Turkey	XU100	0	107,310	191	85,577	-----

*Total Covid-19 cases numbers are retrieved from Worldometer (2020).

In China, the country where the outbreak began, the number of daily cases began to be controlled in the first half of March. Therefore, the reaction of Chinese stock exchanges in this phase was less than that of other countries. Japan and South Korea were able to better control the Covid-19 outbreak with the experience of outbreaks in previous years. However, equity markets in these countries also fell by more than 20% in correlation with DJI.

The impact of the pandemic on emerging markets was at least as damaging as in developed countries' indices, in spite of the fact that the virus was not yet widely spread these countries. The rate of drop was 24% in Nifty 50 (India), 19% in JKS (Indonesia), 24% in MOEX (Russia) and 20% in XU100 (Turkey) and there was panic and fear in these countries. The biggest loss was at the Brazilian Stock Exchange, which was down by 37%. It should be emphasized that the total number of Covid-19 cases did not reach 3-digit numbers at that time in any of these countries.

These results in Table 2 show that financial crises have a virus-like contagion effect. Globalization and the integration of its markets accelerate the devastation. Although the progress of the pandemic is unknown, the second phase of the crisis examined in this section gives signs of how the financial markets will be fragile in the medium and long term. The economic consequences of the pandemic in the coming months are likely to cause collapse in financial markets, as in this phase.

Financial Sustainability of Markets
Market reaction: V-shaped financial recovery or bubble?

As explained in the previous section, there were significant decreases in financial markets in the first and second phases. Especially after the 20th of March, the equity markets in many countries around the world increased after the shocking decline. At the beginning of this rise, analysts were evaluated it as a temporary reaction of the markets, and they predicted that within a few weeks the indices would fall harder, as in the 2008 crisis. However, when the March to June period is analyzed, it is seen that none of the major indices dropped under the lowest point in March 18.

Figure 2 provides trend analysis results of the US, German, UK, Spain and Italy indices of 2020 January - June period. The DJI index was chosen because it has the potential to affect all stock markets around the world. Germany, on the other hand, was preferred because it is the strongest economy in the EU, and Britain was included in the chart as it is one of the most important financial markets in Europe. The reason for the inclusion of Spain and Italy was due to the fact that they had a fragile economy and they were relatively more affected from the pandemic. As of June 30, 2020, it is seen that the US and German equity markets recovered most of the losses they suffered in March. In UK and Italy, they got over the initial shock, but they could not catch the performance as in the beginning of 2020. It is obvious that Spain, whose economy is mostly based on tourism, lagged far behind the other four markets.

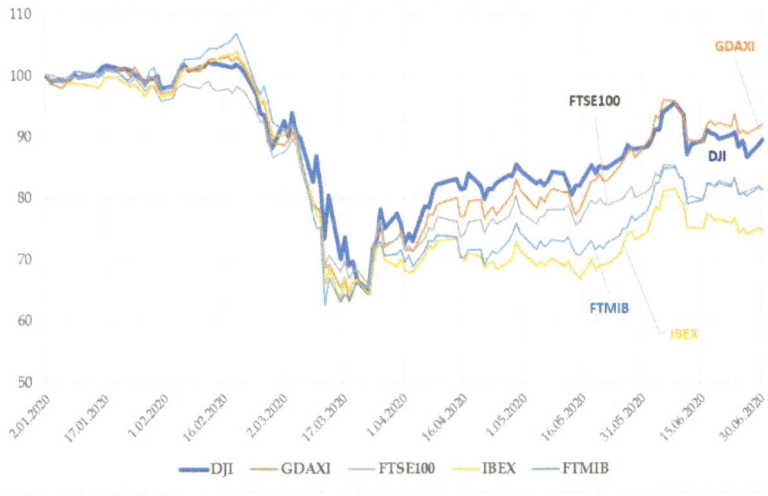

Fig. 2. Trend analysis of European Indices and Dow Jones Industrial Index

Table 3 gives information to help analyze the changes in both indices and total cases by country comparatively. In the period of March 19 - June 30, the center of the pandemic shifted to Europe, US, and then to Russia, South America and India. Severe restrictions (such as full lockdown, closing borders or partial quarantine and curfew) were imposed in all of the countries in the table. Restrictions largely stopped production, consumption also decreased dramatically, except some critical products. Despite all this, a wide "V-shaped" increase and recovery was observed in all stock indices on the list. Whether the V shape is actually a recovery or a bubble for the future of financial markets requires extensive scrutiny with economic indicators.

Table 3. Main indices and total Covid-19 cases after the second phase

Country	Index	19.03.2020		30.06.2020		Change %
		Total Cases *	Index Close	Total Cases *	Index Close	Cases %
US	DJI	13,929	20,087	2,727,357	25.813	19480%
UK	FTSE100	2,957	5,152	282,432	6.170	9451%
Germany	GDAXI	15,320	8,610	195,832	12.311	1178%
France	FCHI	10,995	3,856	164,801	4.936	1399%
Italy	FTMIB	41,054	15,467	240,578	19.376	486%
Spain	IBEX	18,077	6,396	296,351	7.231	1539%
Japan	N225	943	16,553	18,593	22.288	1872%
S.Korea	KOSPI	8,565	1,458	12,800	2.108	49%
China	SSEC	80,967	2,702	83,512	2.985	3%
India	NSEI	194	8,263	585,792	10.302	301855%
Indonesia	JKSE	309	4,105	56,385	4.905	18148%
Brazil	BVSP	640	68,332	1,408,485	95.056	219976%
Mexico	MXX	118	35,144	220,657	37.716	186897%
Russia	IMOEX	199	2,276	647,849	2.743	325452%
Turkey	XU100	359	85,195	199,906	116.525	55584%

* Total Covid-19 cases are retrieved from Worldometer (2020).

The increase in indices can be partially explained by the control of the epidemic for European countries, China, Japan and South Korea, as economies began to return to the new-normal. Nevertheless, even in these countries, the fact that the number of daily cases in the pandemic still has not fallen below 100 as of the end of June highlights that the threat continues.

In developing countries, the progress of the pandemic is even more frightening for the future. The total Covid-19 cases in Brazil has exceeded 1.4 million, in India and Russia more than 500 thousand, and there are no signs of a decline. In the financial context, international investors have reduced their portfolio in the capital markets of these countries or there has been no new capital inflow. Nonetheless, main indices of stock markets increased in Brazil by 39%, in Turkey by 37% and in India by 25%, much more than expected. In Turkey, the Borsa Istanbul 100 Index climbed for a 13th consecutive day, a record for its longest-ever rally (Bloomberg, 2020).

The increases of market capitalizations might be explained separately for each country, associated with different causes and expectations, and market analysts do it already. Various justifications can be made for each market. For the US, "the money injected into the market will level the economy" (expectation), or "German economy will be Europe's only undisputed force after the Covid-19" (forecast), or "thousands of new Turkish domestic investors have revived the markets" (cause of the rise). However, none of them fully explain the global rise in the quarter. When developed and emerging markets are evaluated together, Figure 2 and Table 3 highlight the following facts about the future and sustainability of markets:

1-Even before the pandemic spread, markets in developed countries moved together, and continued after this pandemic.

2-When the important movements in the trend graphs are analyzed, it is seen than equity markets are acting in correlation depending on DJI in sharp rises and decreases.

3-Markets react similarly to critical news such as news of vaccine research works, second wave concern in the pandemic, oil prices.

4-Market cycles have intensified for the reason that the markets affect each other excessively (US markets, futures markets, Asian markets, European markets, US markets ...). It is estimated that this will happen until the pandemic disappears completely from the world.

Commodity Markets: What does the negative price mean?

Covid-19 pandemic has seriously affected commodity markets as well as stock markets. It can even be said that this impact is more severe than stock markets. S&P GSCI index dropped 48% from the beginning of 2020 until April 21. After this date, it increased by 42.5% by taking back some of the losses like other indices. Commodity markets are more associated with the real economy than stock markets, and this increase can be explained by the fact that the Chinese economy has partially overcome the effects of the pandemic and has resumed commodity purchases. China is one of the major importers of oil, coal, and fertilizers, especially copper and iron. Like other metals and agricultural products, China's weight is also high in commodities, and China's purchasing strategies play an important role in price movements.

Gold, which always has a special importance in commodities, is not a metal price of which is manipulated only by the purchase of a single country. It is often seen as a safe haven for investment in crises and uncertainties. Gold demonstrated its characteristic in the Covid-19 pandemic process. However, what is surprising is that in the middle of March, when the financial markets collapsed and the price of gold had pushed the $ 1700 limit, it went below $ 1500 in a week (Figure 3). Notwithstanding the fact that it rose in the following days, if the crisis of Covid-19 origin will continue, that case will be an important indicator that we should consider the possibility of such movements.

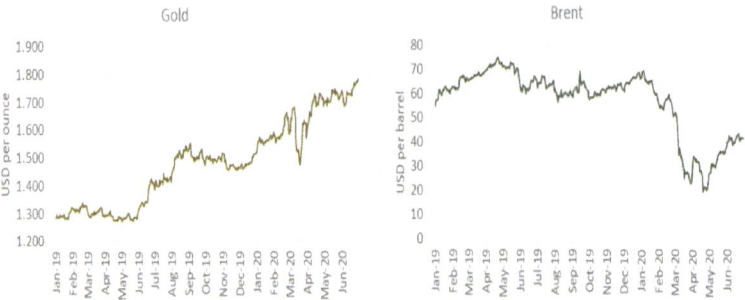

Fig. 3. Gold and Brent crude oil prices

Figure 3 also represents the performance of Brent crude oil from January 2019 to June 2020. The price of Brent oil, which was in the $55 - $75 (per barrel) band throughout 2019, declined below $25 on April 1 and then to the $20 limit towards the end of April as the pandemic's effects on the economy increased. But, Brent oil jumped in June and exceeded $40. This increase means the price of Brent oil doubling in a short time, which is very striking in terms of showing the fluctuation in commodity markets.

Coronavirus cut oil prices down, but these prices were not expected to drop to an unimaginable level in the WTI (West Texas Intermediate) crude oil futures markets. For the first time in history, prices fell below zero per barrel to -37.63 dollars on April 20, 2020 (Figure 4). The fall in oil prices after the Covid-19 crisis was effected by the global supply problems and the dispute between OPEC countries had an impact. A negative price, however, means much more.

Speculators have always existed in futures markets and will continue to be important market players in the future. In the past, prices had risen or fallen due to speculators. Even in times of a crisis, tensions and disagreements between countries are excellent opportunities for speculators to fluctuate the markets. However, it could never have been predicted that the price of a critical commodity such as oil would fall below zero. A negative price means that the producer or contract owner pays extra money to the buyer. Cohen (2020) as explained as follows:

*"Oil traders and speculators rarely have the physical capacity to hold the crude they buy, despite being legally bound to take it by their contract. Under normal circumstances, these contracts (typically 10,000 barrels in size) can be sold to other speculators, or wound down over time. **But in this instance, there was no one willing to buy May's expiring contact.**"*

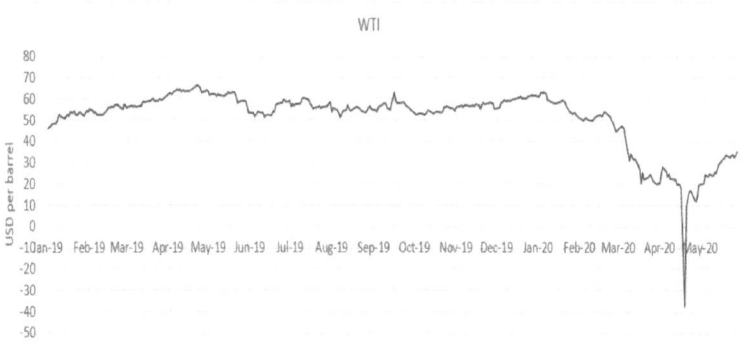

Fig. 4. WTI crude oil prices

The Covid-19 crisis, and all this, has changed entrenched beliefs in commodity markets, which are an important part of financial markets. We have learned that the risk of a commodity can be infinite and its price may also have a value below zero. This has been a key milestone for the sustainability of financial markets and for understanding what we will face in future crises. The absence of a buyer and the lack of storage space are side factors, the main reason for this is the unpredictability of the future in financial markets, that is, uncertainty. This issue is discussed below.

Uncertainty and volatility

While being in crises, everyone wants to learn the answers to these two basic questions: "When will we get rid of this crisis?" and "When will everything go back to the way it was?" It was not possible to find the exact answer to the first question in any crisis. Because it is not possible for some units to get rid of the crisis, while for others, the recovery occurs in different time periods. But what is certain is that the crises occur suddenly, but the recovery does not happen immediately. It may take a long time. To the second question, the answer is absolutely no, because it is never possible to return to the old situation after any crisis. In fact, in the financial context, what these questions mean is when the uncertainties in the crisis environment will decrease. Each financial crisis process contains many uncertainties, and the intensity of these uncertainties is decisive for the destructive effect of the crisis.

The difficulty of the predictability of the near future lies behind the Covid-19 outbreak turning into a crisis in terms of financial markets. Some of these uncertainties can be listed as follows:
- How much of the virus will spread to the world,
- Whether the virus will mutate, whether the first wave has been completed, whether there will be second, third etc. sequential waves,
- Whether there will be mass deaths in these waves,

- Possibility of restrictions, closing borders, curfews such as the period between March and May,
- When an effective and definitive vaccine against the virus will be introduced, if yes, how long it will take to manufacture, distribute, vaccinate,
- When will the concepts such as "social distance" and "mask usage" will be completely removed from our lives,
- Whether the economic programs, packages, aid and incentives implemented by developed countries will work,
- Which sectors or companies will be saved (by governments), which ones will be left to die (bankrupt, collapse etc.) like in 2008,
- Whether to help developing or underdeveloped countries,
- Whether the change in consumption habits will be permanent,
- What percentage of global economy and national economies will shrink (or grow) in 2020, 2021, 2022,
- What shape of the recovery will be, V, W, U, L etc.
- How the problems such as unemployment and decrease in consumption will affect financial markets,
- Whether the crisis will cause social and political unrest in various countries and its impact on financial stability,
- How 2020 Q2, Q3, Q4 (quarter) financial statements of the companies will be like,
- Whether the companies' investment and growth (or contraction) strategies will change,
- Whether a panic or collapse like March 2020 will recur in the financial markets,
- What measures regulators will take in financial markets (such as leverage limitation or short selling ban),
- Whether there will be negative pricing again in commodity markets such as WTI case,
- Whether the outbreak is really exaggerated or not, whether there is a scare scenario.

The list of uncertainties can be extended further. For stock or commodity traders, the combination of all uncertainties can be interpreted as prices might move sharply in both directions. This situation causes excessive volatility in financial markets. Since high volatility is a signal of uncertainty that increases due to economic, financial or political reasons, it can also be used to predict a financial crisis (Danielsson, Valenzuela, & Zer, 2018).

In Figure 5, the daily volatilities of some selected indices for the year 2020 are given. Parkinson's (1980) Extreme Value Method was used to calculate the volatility of the indices. It is observed in the DJI index that volatility reached its peak in March, but did not stagnate in April, May and June. In March, when panic was high, Germany's DAX index was found to be more volatile than DJI.

BOVESPA index of Brazil, which is one of the developing countries, had about 6 times higher volatility than DJI. Turkey's XU100 index is lower than the maximum value volatility than in the other three countries. However, it is observed that it was still significantly affected by the pandemic.

These four graphs highlights that the fluctuation in the financial markets after the pandemic increased the range between the high and low values of the asset prices. The increase in this range makes it difficult to predict the future price of the asset, indicating the risk of that asset. In this case, it causes anxiety in investors aiming for long-term investment and thus withdrawing from the markets until stability is achieved. The biggest problem in terms of sustainability of financial markets is that the market is only left to day-traders.

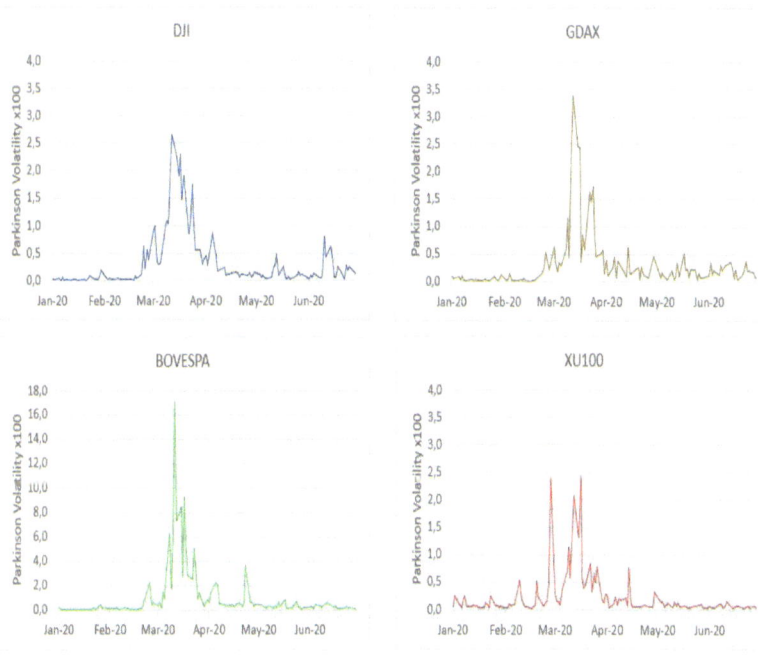

Fig. 5. Intraday volatility of selected indices

VIX

Another indicator showing the fluctuation and panic caused by the Covid-19 pandemic in the financial markets is the VIX index mentioned in the previous section. The VIX index (Chicago Board Options Exchange CBOE Volatility Index) was created by CBOE (Chicago Board of Trade) in 1993. In the technical context, VIX index is the "risk-neutral" expected stock market variance for the US S&P500 contract and is computed from a panel of options prices (Bekaert & Hoerova, 2014). Although VIX is applied to option prices, it is mainly used as a barometer in determining the degree of fear in financial markets (Whaley, 2009), therefore it is also called the "Fear Index".

The reason why VIX got the name of fear index in financial markets is that investors in the market also express their hesitation from investment by fearing volatility. The fact that a high VIX index indicates that the uncertainty is high. The value of the VIX increases during the sharp decline in the markets or the sudden rise after that decline. Although it is not a general rule, VIX values from 20 to 30 are accepted as normal values in the markets. If VIX is above 30, it is interpreted that there are significant uncertainties in the market, that is, volatility. Figure 5 shows the values of the VIX index between July 2008 - June 2020.

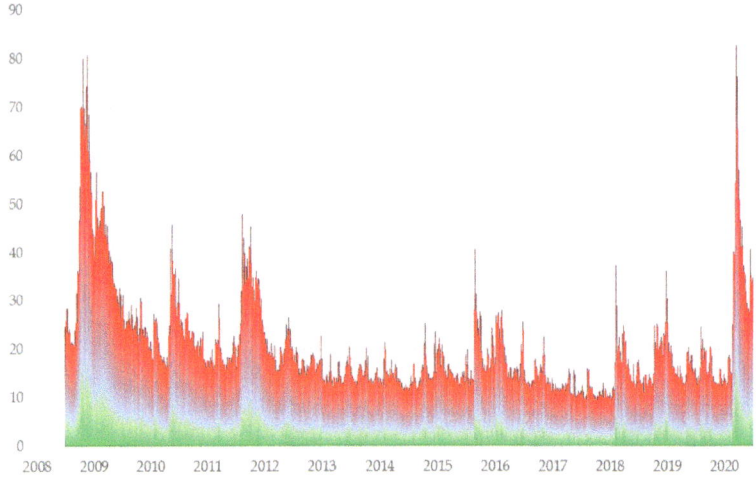

Fig. 6. VIX IndexCBOE (2020) and Yahoo Finance (2020)

The highest value of VIX was 80.06 until 2020 and this value was observed in the global financial crisis. As seen in Figure 5, this value was exceeded in the Covid-19 pandemic and the index hit its record value of 82.69 on March 16, 2020. This demonstrates that the Covid-19 crisis actually caused greater effects even than the global crisis and has the potential to create greater fluctuations in the future.

Despite the rise in stock markets and the recovery in commodity markets, the VIX index average of June 2020 is still above the critical level of 30. This means that uncertainties regarding the future of financial markets continue, and it indicates that we will experience a fluctuating process due to economic growth even if there would be positive developments with the vaccine or the control of the pandemic.

Social ve Environmental Sustainability

In the parts up to this point, this study has focused on the "economic sustainability" of financial markets. However, sustainability has two other pillars besides the economy, which are social and environmental sustainability. The pandemic actually caused more severe environmental, social, health and safety risks than the economy. All these risks create damage that is hard to repair for companies, labor and society. It would be a big mistake to consider that social and environmental impacts will not be reflected in the financial markets that are the subject of this study.

Social Sustainability

The data on Covid-19 cases presented in the previous sections show that the complete disappearance of the pandemic from the world will not happen in a short time. For this reason, companies should make human-oriented adjustments, including those listed on stock markets. What is meant is not just distributing masks, protective equipment or anti-bacterial, but for some industries, all work flow charts and rules will have to be reorganized. In addition, working environments, employees' working hours will have to be reorganized. It is a risk even just one employee is infected. As before, it is no longer possible to cover up or ignore it. All these are issues that need to be considered both in terms of social sustainability and economy.

The issue of cleaning and hygiene, which is included in the occupational health and safety standards and also in the social sustainability criteria (Levent, 2018), has become more important and is now added to the working subjects of the company managers. This issue, which was formerly referred to only as "cleaning expenses" from an accounting perspective, will become a critical issue both to protect employees' health and to reassure customers, after the pandemic.

To provide this assurance, companies should develop an action plan adapted to their operations against the Covid-19 pandemic. The design, implementation, sustainability and supervision of these plans also require critical preparations. For example, how to act if a worker shows symptoms in a department? How will the treatment be followed? How will communication with the authorities be ensured? Will the department be completely quarantined, or will production be halted? What measures should be taken to prevent employees from hiding their symptoms in order not to lose their jobs? All this requires a truly complex and detailed design as well as flexible plans according to the developments.

The issue of security, which is vital for human health, will also create a significant financial cost. For all these measures, companies will be against changing their resource allocation preferences. In addition, risk may arise in the company, suppliers and distribution channels, or operations may partly or completely stop. Another possibility is that lockdown measures can return for whole country or locally, as experienced in April and May. In this case, how to deal with the economic loss that will occur without harming the rights and interests of the employees is an important problem for both companies and governments. This is where social and economic sustainability intersect.

Environmental Sustainability

Besides causing death of thousands, the pandemic will also have permanent environmental consequences on a global scale. Everyone focused on the human health and economic dimensions of the pandemic at the first stage. This is of course necessary, but neglecting the environmental dimension is a serious threat to the future.

One of the reasons of ignoring environmental concerns is that the pandemic causes positive results in terms of climate change and environmental pollution in the short term. Several studies conducted during the early stages of the pandemic revealed evidences confirming this. Muhammad, Long, and Salman (2020) revealed the decrease in NO_2 concentrations before and after lockdown with satellite photographs in USA, China, Italy, France and Spain. In another study, Zambrano-Monserrate, Ruano, and Sanchez-Alcalde (2020) stated that PM 2.5 concentrations were lowered in China, Germany, France, Italy and Spain. The authors emphasized that in their studies covering the early stages of the pandemic, positive results were also obtained on the increase of water quality on the beaches and environmental noise reduction.

Bashir, et al. (2020) analyzed the association between Covid-19 and climate indicators in New York City. In the study, it was found that average temperature, minimum temperature and air quality were significantly related to the Covid-19 pandemic. In another study, the effects of emission reductions due to reduced anthropogenic activities in China during the pandemic on air pollution were investigated (Wang, Chen, Zhu, Wang, & Zhang, 2020). As a result of the research, it was concluded that the decrease in anthropogenic emission due to delays in transportation and industry contributed to the reduction of PM2.5 concentrations.

With the spread of the Covid-19 around the world, research on air pollution has also expanded to cover more countries. During the lockdown period, compared to the same period of 2019, PM2.5 concentrations decreased by 31% in Los Angeles, 25% in New York, 9% in London, 60% in Delhi, 34% in Mumbai, 44% in Wuhan and 54% in Seoul (Australian Academy of Science, 2020).

In the period when curfew was imposed, production decreased and transportation was canceled, there was less gas emission and less industrial wastewater discharge. However, this was due to restrictions, not pandemics. With the end of restrictions all over the world, everything has returned to the pre-pandemic situation in terms of environmental pollution. Yunus, Masago, and Hijioka (2020) demonstrated with evidence that pollution concentrations decreased in the lockdown period in India. But they stressed that with the opening of industries, tourism activities and other businesses, pollutants will return to freshwater again.

In the context of environmental sustainability, it can easily be said that air pollution caused by individuals will increase with restrictions, especially in developed countries. Due to the pandemic, people are expected to prefer their own private vehicles instead of public transportation.

In other countries, more critical problems are foreseen. The pandemic is expected to cause poverty in a significant proportion of developing countries, particularly in all undeveloped countries. This will lead to the use of products that are harmful to the environment, especially in heating. Thus, it indicates that the decrease in pollutants during the lockdown period will be replaced by an increase.

The United Nations Environment Program states that global warming after the pandemic is expected to bring disasters such as different outbreaks, extreme weather events, droughts, and flooding (UN Environment, 2020). They predict that diseases passed from animals to humans, zoonoses such as COVID-19, will continue to rise, as the world continues to see unprecedented destruction of wild habitats by human activity. In addition to social effects, all of these are likely to have a negative impact on national economies, companies and financial markets.

Another possible problem is wasting food products. During the lockdown period, it was observed that people bought excessive food products during their stay at home, and threw away a significant portion without consuming them. Despite the possibility of restrictions coming back, it seems that in some people, individual food storage has become a permanent habit. While this increases the value of food and supermarket shares in the financial markets (Gelski, 2020), it is alarming in terms of environmental sustainability.

Another negativity caused by pandemics in terms of environmental sustainability is the increase in the consumption of disposable products. The consumption of plastic products, most of which are harmful to the environment, has increased especially after the pandemic. Especially, the widespread use of disposable plastic products or excessive plastic bags and packaging contributes only to the market values of packaging companies.

Financial markets are concerned with the economic dimension of sustainability, as in every crisis. Governments are also concentrating mostly on the survival of companies. So the possibility of loosening regulations or weakening controls on environment, solid wastes, wastewater discharge and air pollution, which are seen as a cost for companies, is the biggest threat to environmental sustainability. In the short term, the pandemic is not expected to have a positive impact on the development of sustainable financial investments, which is not already popular.

Conclusion

Financial markets are affected by various political, social and cyclical factors, as well as companies, sectors and macroeconomic events. Prices in the markets reflect not only current conditions, but also future expectations. Events such as political tensions, war, terrorism and outbreak that could not be predicted earlier have the potential to directly affect the prices of financial assets. Some of them cause temporary movements, while others cause a long-lasting effect or even a crisis. Therefore, it is not bewildering that a global pandemic such as Covid-19 caused a crisis in the markets.

Without doubt, it was unpredictable that when the virus first appeared in China, it would spread to all countries of the world in six months and infect more than 10 million people, affecting everyone's lifestyle in some way. The reason for this collapse in the financial markets was that the world faced an unexpected, unpredictable and unidentified attack. Medically, there was inadequate virus related information, about how the virus transmitted, in what environments it could live, what destruction it could make in the human body. Now we know at least the name of the virus and some genetic characteristics. Treatment methods have been developed, vaccine research studies have been continuing in hundreds of laboratories. We have learned how soap and mask have a vital effect on our lives. Uncertainty was also the case for financial markets. The coronavirus was ignored in January and February, then it was seen that the virus spread everywhere in March. So uncertainty peaked, and the crisis scenarios that the financial markets (also the world) would disappear started to be discussed. The issue of how people can survive overshadowed the issue of how we can sustain the future of companies and the economy. As of May and June, we have more data to discuss on the future of financial markets, like we know more about the virus.

In this context, this study aimed to examine the future and sustainability of financial markets after the Covid-19 crisis. The first reaction of the markets after the Covid-19 outbreak led to the comparison of this crisis with the 1997 Asian crisis. However, when the virus spread and turned into a pandemic and caused a great collapse in the global markets, this time it was compared with 1929 and 2008. Therefore, in this study, firstly, the definitions and characteristics of financial crises are examined, and the similarities and differences of the Covid-19 crisis especially with the 2008 crisis are revealed. Then, the evolution and phases of the Covid-19 crisis were analyzed in two phases. In equities markets, March 18, 2020 was a turning point in terms of the crisis. After this date, almost all stock markets in the world have risen similar to the "V" form. The study analyzed both the rise in the markets and the progress of the pandemic together.

Commodity markets, as well as equity markets, reacted sharply to the pandemic. The study also explored excessive movements in commodity markets, revealing "uncertainty" and "volatility", which are common aspects of the two markets.

The most important difference of this study from other studies after Covid-19 is that it has examined the impact of the pandemic not only in the financial dimension but also in the context of social and environmental sustainability, which are the other two pillars of sustainability. The social and environmental damage caused by the outbreak is expected to be seen more clearly in the coming period. The study also reveals these impacts from the multidisciplinary perspective of the concept of sustainability.

One of the features of financial crises is that it causes sharp movements in the markets. This is different from daily temporary movements and lasts for an uncertain period. Movements in the crisis should not be evaluated only in the direction of decline. In crises, sharp drops and rises may occur one after the other, as in the 2008 crisis. Research findings revealed that this occurred not only in the post-March period but also in the entire first six-month period. However, we do not know whether the short-term effect of the pandemic in the financial markets is over. Consequently, there is a possibility that sharp downward or upward movements may continue in the coming periods.

The spread of excessive movements in the market from one country to another, just like the virus, is a common occurrence in crises. After Covid-19, the markets experienced this situation, the movements in the China equity markets spread first to neighboring countries, then the US and the whole world. Research findings reveal that in the second phase of the crisis - even the stock markets of countries with Covid-19 cases below 200 - fell close to 20%, hence the contagion effect. Another point to be emphasized is that in this crisis, it is determined that even stock markets with different dynamics act as a single market. In the research, this situation is clearly demonstrated in the trend analysis of DJI, GDAX, FTSE100, IBEX and FTMIB indices. These markets moved with high correlation even in June, when the effects of the crisis diminished.

Besides the stock markets, important events also occurred in the money and debt markets. Most of the central banks lowered interest rates, in some developed countries policy rates were dropped to even below zero. The fact that real interest rates were negative in many countries before Covid-19 and in the pandemic process made borrowing attractive. Not only companies and individuals, but governments also increased their debt. All these can be considered as the signals of different crises that may occur in the global economy and financial markets in the years ahead.

When the crises of 1929, 1997 and 2008 are analyzed, it is seen that there was an interaction between capital markets, commodity markets, asset prices and exchange rates. The same was true for the 2020 Covid-19 crisis. After the pandemic, there were major fluctuations in oil and then other commodity prices, eventually the stock prices slumped. All this also affected the foreign exchange market.

This study emphasized that the covid-19 pandemic was a crisis in financial and economic terms. The reason for this is actually very clear. The uncertainty caused by the crisis and the state of panic in the first two phases were so severe that it even surpassed the 2008 crisis. Despite the increases in stocks as reaction, great anxiety prevails the markets. In the study, this issue is presented with both VIX index findings and intraday volatility analysis. Decreasing volatility in June is expected to increase further, especially with the announcement of companies' 2020 financial report results.

If an estimate will be made about the future of financial markets, markets should not be examined in one dimension. When markets are handled only with indices such as DJI, DAX, FTSE100, it can be concluded that there is no crisis in the world as of June 2020 and what happened in March may be evaluated as a temporary fluctuation. In this way, such an evaluation is a big mistake, it means to forget bubbles in the stock markets and the great enthusiasm in the markets before 2008 crisis. Those who are trying to predict the post-Covid-19 period are recommended to consider both the results of this study and the following words of Paul Krugman:

"...Whenever you consider the economic implications of stock prices, you want to remember three rules. First, the stock market is not the economy. Second, the stock market is not the economy. Third, the stock market is not the economy. That is, the relationship between stock performance -largely driven by the oscillation between greed and fear - and real economic growth has always been somewhere between loose and nonexistent..." (Krugman, 2020)

This pandemic demonstrates that a stop that is not due to financial markets can also affect the real sector. Demand contraction in the global context in the economy was not caused by a pandemic, due to the tough but necessary measures to control the pandemic, an unpredictable demand reduction occurred in many sectors. There was a sudden stop in the world, especially between March and May. Operations continued in some sectors such as food and technology, some sectors waited for the restrictions to end, while others preferred the way of digitalization by changing traditional business methods. As of early June, many countries entered a period called "the new normal". We do not know whether there will be new sub-crises as a result of this normalization in the coming period, and that each sub-crisis will result in "new-new normal" or "new-new-new normal". The most certain thing about the future and sustainability of financial markets is that uncertainty and volatility will be part of the markets.

References

Ali, M., Alam, N., & Rizvi, S. (2020). Coronavirus (COVID-19) - An Epidemic or Pandemic for Financial Markets. *Journal of Behavioral and Experimental Finance, 27*.

Arndt, H., & Hill, H. (2000). *Southeast Asia's Economic Crisis: Origins, Lessons, and the Way Forward.* Singapore: Institute of Southeast Asian Studies.

Australian Academy of Science. (2020). *What impact will COVID-19 have on the environment?* Retrieved from https://www.science.org.au/curious/earth-environment/what-impact-will-covid-19-have-environment

Bashir, M., Ma, B., Bilal, B., Komal, B., Bashir, M., Tan, D., & Bashir, M. (2020). Correlation between climate indicators and COVID-19 pandemic in New York, USA. *Science of The Total Environment, 728*, 1-4.

Bekaert, G., & Hoerova, M. (2014). The VIX, the variance premium and stock market volatility. *Journal of Econometrics, 183*(2), 181-192.

Bloomberg. (2020). *Locals Replace Foreigners in Turkey's Record Stock Market Rally.* Retrieved from https://www.bloomberg.com/news/articles/2020-06-05/locals-replace-foreigners-in-turkey-s-record-stock-market-rally

CBOE. (2020). *Vix-Index - Cboe.* Retrieved from http://www.cboe.com/vix

Cohen, A. (2020). *Oil Plummets Over 300% To Almost -$40 A Barrel In Historic Collapse.* Retrieved from Forbes: https://www.forbes.com/sites/arielcohen/2020/04/20/oil-plummets-over-300-to-almost40-a-barrel-in-historic-collapse/#1bd156d0931b

Corbet, S., Larkin, C., & Lucey, B. (2020). The contagion effects of the COVID-19 pandemic: Evidence from gold and cryptocurrencies. *Finance Research Letters*, https://doi.org/10.1016/j.frl.2020.101554.

Danielsson, J., Valenzuela, M., & Zer, I. (2018). Learning from History: Volatility and Financial Crises. *The Review of Financial Studies, 31(7)*, 2774-2805.

Edison, H. (2003). Do indicators of financial crises work? An evaluation of an early warning system. *International Journal of Finance & Economics, 8*(1), 11-53.

Furman, J., Stiglitz, J., Bosworth, B., & Radelet, S. (1998). Economic Crises: Evidence and Insights from East Asia. *Brookings Papers on Economic Activity, 1998*(2), 1-135.

Gelski, J. (2020). *Supermarket stocks trend higher as coronavirus spreads.* Retrieved from Food Business News: https://www.foodbusinessnews.net/articles/15648-supermarket-stocks-trend-higher-as-coronavirus-spreads

IEA. (2020). *Oil Market Report - February 2020.* Retrieved from https://www.iea.org/reports/oil-market-report-february-2020

Kaminsky, G., & Reinhart, C. (1998). Financial Crises in Asia and Latin America: Then and Now. *The American Economic Review, 88*(2), 444-448.

Kindleberger, C., & Aliber, R. (2005). *Manias, Panics, and Crashes: A History of Financial Crises* (Fifth Edition ed.). New Jersey: John Wiley & Sons, Inc.

Krugman, P. (2020). *Crashing Economy, Rising Stocks: What's Going On?* Retrieved from The New York Times: https://www.nytimes.com/2020/04/30/opinion/economy-stock-market-coronavirus.html

Levent, C. E. (2018). Determination of social sustainability level with quantitative indicators: a research on non-metallic mineral companies listed on Borsa Istanbul. *Journal of Business, Economics and Finance, 7*(3), 295-308

Marketwatch. (2020). *CBOE Volatility Index*. Retrieved from https://www.marketwatch.com/investing/index/vix

Minsky, H. (1972). Financial stability revisited: the economics of disaster. *Board of Governors of the Federal Reserve System, Reappraisal of the Federal Reserve Discount Mechanism, 3*, 95-136.

Mishkin, F. (1992). Anatomy of a financial crisis. *Journal of Evolutionary Economics, 2*, 115-130.

Muhammad, S., Long, X., & Salman, M. (2020). COVID-19 pandemic and environmental pollution: A blessing in disguise? *Science of The Total Environment, 728*.

Nelson, J. (1990). *Economic Crisis And Policy Choice: The Politics Of Adjustment In The Third World: The Politics of Adjustment in Less Developed Countries.* Princeton: Princeton University Press.

Parkinson, M. (1980). The Extreme Value Method for Estimating the Variance of the Rate of Return. *The Journal of Business, 53(*1), 61-65.

Reisen, H. (1999). Domestic Causes of Currency Crises: Policy Lessons for Crisis Avoidance. *IDS Bulletin, 30*(1), 120-133.

UN Environment. (2020). *COVID-19: Four Sustainable Development Goals that help future-proof global recovery*. Retrieved from https://www.unenvironment.org/news-and-stories/story/covid-19-four-sustainable-development-goals-help-future-proof-global

Wang, J., Yao, J., & Bonne, G. (2020, 3 5). *The coronavirus market impact spreads globally*. Retrieved from MSCI: https://www.msci.com/www/blog-posts/the-coronavirus-market-impact/01732620365

Wang, P., Chen, K., Zhu, S., Wang, P., & Zhang, H. (2020). Severe air pollution events not avoided by reduced anthropogenic activities during COVID-19 outbreak. *Resources, Conservation and Recycling, 158*, 1-9.

Whaley, R. (2009). Understanding the VIX. *The Journal of Portfolio Management, 35*(3), 98-105.

WHO. (2020). *World Health Organization*. Retrieved from WHO Director-General's opening remarks at the media briefing on COVID-19 - 11 March

2020: https://www.who.int/dg/speeches/detail/who-director-general-s-opening-remarks-at-the-media-briefing-on-covid-19---11-march-2020

Worldometer. (2020). *Covid-19 Coronavirus Pandemic*. Retrieved from https://www.worldometers.info/coronavirus/

Yahoo Finance. (2020). Retrieved from https://finance.yahoo.com

Yunus, A., Masago, Y., & Hijioka, Y. (2020). COVID-19 and surface water quality: Improved lake water quality during the lockdown. *Science of The Total Environment, 731*, 1-8.

Zambrano-Monserrate, M., Ruano, M., & Sanchez-Alcalde, L. (2020). Indirect effects of COVID-19 on the environment. *Science of The Total Environment, 728*, 1-4.

CHAPTER 3

Post-COVID-19 Era: The Great Reset and Senism

Erdal Şen
{sen@senizm.com, erdals@aydin.edu.tr}

Associate Professor., Istanbul Aydin University, Faculty of Economics and Administrative Sciences, Department of Business Management, Florya/İstanbul

Abstract

Development in all areas in the world has caused especially important and transformative results in the last fifty years. In particular, the effects of science and technology on production and consumption factors and processes are becoming more and more effective. As the effectiveness of information and communication technologies increase, production, presentation, consumption and management forms are also transformed with technological developments. This phenomenon, also defined as digitalization, reveals new processes and results in the context of the liberal-capitalist governance model of the world. Within this context, economic, political, diplomatic, military, administrative, socio-cultural and individual dimensions are transformed. With the advent of the COVID-19 pandemic, the process that affected the whole world and caused the transformation of globalization through digitalization until the beginning of 2020 is evolving in a hugely different direction. The aim of this study is to define the process that has emerged especially with the COVID-19 pandemic and reshaping the whole world in terms of individual, society, institution and system dimensions and to evaluate it in the light of "The Great Reset" and with the theoretical basis of the "Senism" approach.

Keywords: COVID-19, Digitalization, New Normal, New Management, The Great Reset, Senism.

What we know is a drop, what we don't know is an ocean.
Isaac Newton

Introduction

Since the world existed, there have been very important breakpoints in known history. These fractures have paved the way for the emergence of many results that can be evaluated as positive or negative over time. The rapid and effective development of new information, communication and production technologies that emerged especially with the active use of the internet since the mid-1990s has deeply affected management, governance and economy all over the world. The fast and effective changes and transformations of new technologies, and the continuation of digital transformation, enable the emergence of various effects on many concepts, especially the transformation of management, governance, economy, finance, politics, social and cultural dimensions all around the world. E-commerce, digital services, artificial intelligence, algorithms, augmented reality, blockchain technology, robotics and autonomous robots, 3D printing, Cyber Physical Systems, Smart Factories and machine learning, Internet of Things, databases and cloud applications and all digital services started to be the foundations of the digital world. The world is experiencing the beginning of the digital revolution in these years. The meaning and practices of the "Digital Revolution" will become even more visible within coming years. From this point of view, globalization may have to update today's situation, which is based on neo-liberal policies, with the benefits of digitalization. On the other hand, issues about sustainability of the system has got lots of remaining issues and questions to be answered.

In the period that the world is passing through, the effect of digitalization in the process of sustainability and the test of globalization is examined. With the COVID-19 pandemic, this test of the whole worlds citizens, institutions and systems is taken to a whole new dimension. The new type of Coronavirus emerged in late 2019 stands out as one of the most important factors affecting today's world. With this health crisis, the COVID-19 pandemic has profoundly affected the whole world in areas such as health, economy, social, cultural and business life. This is one of the most important issue at this point and needs to be evaluated in depth is the medium and long-term effects in today's world. In this regard, the short, medium and long-term consequences of the pandemic crisis are very important. At the same time, another important evaluation method is the analysis of micro and macro dimensions. Pandemic has realized different cause-and-effect relationships in many different areas. It can be predicted that this change and transformation will continue in the future. One of the most important building blocks for this is the possible effects of the "Digital Revolution" on both globalization in today's world and the individual who gains relative importance day by day. At this point, it can be said that in the future, the interaction of possible effects in the field of COVID-19 and Social Sciences with the individual, which is a common variable of all structures, concepts, practices and processes, will be valuable (Şen, 2020b: 254). From the change and transformation experienced and to be experienced with the COVID-19 pandemic, how it will evolve in which areas constitutes the basic areas and infrastructure. As a general framework, this infrastructure; reveals the future of systems, institutions, societies and individuals as a very important field of study (Şen, 2020a: 176).

The restructuring and change in the world, especially after the Second World War, is of great importance. After the Second World War, in the last 75 years, one of the important breaking points is the information and communication technologies that have changed, transformed and developed especially with the internet since the mid-1990s. At the same time, production, consumption, communication, interaction and sharing factors, methods and processes continue in a deep transformation. The new type of coronavirus has been effective all over the world at a time when this change, transformation and differentiation is felt at the highest level and many positive and negative phenomena are being discussed. Novel Coronavirus is not the only and unique fact or variable for the possible future results. On the other hand current problems of the whole world has been much more seen and questioned with this crisis period. In the continuation of this process, in the post-COVID-19 period, it can be predicted that many new political, climatic, inter-country and diplomatic crises will arise, especially for economic reasons (Şen, 2020a: 197-202; Şen and Batı, 2020: 81; Duygun and Şen, 2020: 59-63; WEF, 2020b).

World Economic Forum is starting The Great Reset initiative to improve the state of the world. According to WEF, there is an urgent need for global stakeholders to cooperate in simultaneously managing the direct consequences of the COVID-19 crisis (WEF, 2020a).

The First Wave of the Novel Coronavirus: COVID-19

Many concepts and phenomena related to the new type of Coronavirus COVID-19 outbreak, which emerged in Wuhan, Hubei, People's Republic of China, in the last months of 2019 and was declared pandemic by the World Health Organization on March 11, 2020, have begun to be discussed (WHO, 2020). At the same time, with the initial process of this crisis and its spread to different regions around the world, both business life, social life and education systems have been subjected to exceptionally large and effective changes in a noticeably short time. In the first months of this process, technical discussions and health sector practices in the field of medicine were mainly discussed (Duygun and Şen 2020: 60), and with the beginning of June, the topics that were most emphasized and researched worldwide began to stand out as future scenarios about digitalization, innovation, data, economy, justice and all relevant variables. Although COVID-19 is a health-related pandemic, the period of this pandemic crisis and after it started to affect all the world, actually it showed that it contains transformational changes and clues of a new system.

Digitalization and new digital technologies, globalization, sustainability, climate change, polarization, human rights, internet, data, information, knowledge management, governance, stakeholder management, chip technologies, monitoring systems, social scoring systems, new normal, change management, emotional management, behavioral economy, the role of individual and all the relationships and interactions between individual, groups, society, institutions and systems are started to be discussed much more deeply and effectively. This is not only about a virus threating the health of the citizens of the world. It's much more than that; one of the most important features of this crisis is very fast and effective change realized within this period was the trigger, the indicator, the cause and also the result of the COVID-19 pandemic crisis (Şen, 2020a: 192-202; Şen and Batı, 2020: 81-82).

Globalization and Digitalization

Globalization is conceptually included in the paper on the distribution and use of resources around the world written by W. Foter in 1833. It can be said that the studies conducted by Garett Hardin in 1968 are the basis for the formation of the current globalization phenomenon (Karabıçak, 2002: 116). Multiple thoughts can be mentioned about explaining the concept of globalization. In fact, the different point of these thoughts is that they deal with globalization in a holistic or narrow context.

According to Peter Dicken (1992: 1) globalization is a more advanced and complex concept than internationalization and it enables the flow of goods and services to increase within the borders of the country and region and enables the functional integration of nations in order to increase the distribution of economic activities in the international environment.

Defining globalization with a holistic approach, Giddens explains it as an increasingly balanced integration of interdependence of economic, social, technological, cultural and political areas (Aydeniz et al., 2012: 1016).

Economic globalization represents the integration of national economies with international economies such as trade, foreign investment, short-term capital flows (through firms and multinational firms), the international transition of workers and people in general, and technology flows etc. Apart from holistic definitions, there are definitions that evaluate globalization in a narrow scope (Bhagwati, 2004: 3). Rugman and Moore (2001) made the first of these definitions: Globalization is the production and distribution of products with similar products and quality worldwide (Yeşil, 2010: 26).

Common sub-dimensions of many different definitions of globalization stand out as economical, technological, social, cultural, political, environmental, diplomatic, military, management and individual (Şen and Batı, 2020: 75; Schwab and Malleret, 2020:24). However, one of the most important consequences of globalization in neo-liberal terms stands out as increasing individualism (Şen, 2020a: 178). This individualism resulting with being self-centered and with the effect of the interaction among internet and all digital technologies it is creating a strong basis of "meism" (Şen, 2017b: 251-253). The relevant dimensions of globalization are also critical concepts for the world after digitalization and COVID-19 in the light of similar variables within the historical paradigm shifts (Şen 2020a: 178; Schwab and Malleret, 2020:20).

Digitalization adds value to the ecosystem and customers starting from the organizational structures of companies, brands and structures to adapt to the digital age and develops business processes. In addition, this process provides convenience in increasing the knowledge and capabilities of firms, new ways of doing business and thinking and transitions (Mert, 2019: 221).

Digitalization is the activity of transforming digitalized resources into operational structures that will add value to new growth, income and company. Digitalization is to create customer experiences by introducing new business models, combining information, resources and digital technologies with a new regulation, to reveal new products and services and to organize technology according to these sources for the effective use of corporate resources (Accenture Digitalization Index, 2016: 12).

Companies have to keep pace with digitalization in order to ensure that changing consumer behaviors, technology development speed and digitalization increase, business models, products and services, customers' experiences are positive and their way of doing business are improved (Mert, 2019: 221).

Digitalization develops approaches that will affect all sectors and firms for the country's economy and it is difficult to maintain organizational activities without applying these approaches. Digitalization plays an important role in the future plans, programs, policies and strategies, development, investment and applications of companies (Fırat and Fırat, 2017: 10).

With digitalization, each institution is obliged to implement change management in leadership policies and strategic management processes, but this rate of change varies according to the sector in which the business operates and the role of the sector in digitalization. When digitalization begins, company managers and employees should carry out their work in a coordinated manner and ensure digital transformation in their work. The provision of digital transformation is through the knowledge, skills and vision of the top manager and leader. Only the leader in the position of top manager can initiate the digital transformation process and the leader should change the business model and strategic management process according to digitalization (Mert, 2020: 51).

Although globalization has many different definitions and dimensions, the most up-to-date issue that needs to be evaluated and considered is its affinity and relationship with digitalization. With the onset of the COVID-19 pandemic, the overwhelming weight of digitalization has begun to affect all dimensions of globalization. Although this transformation originates from data, information and knowledge management, it deeply affects all individuals, structures, processes, institutions, organizations and systems (Şen, 2020a: 176; WEF, 2020a).

At this point, the importance of the individual should increasingly come to the fore, and its role and importance in this revolutionary process should be thoroughly evaluated. Also importance and critical effect of leadership must be taken into consideration about all the management issues and practices within the function of the leadership for business world and for politics; in the area of political and corporate governance.

Big Data and Knowledge Management: Paradigm Shift

Data, information and knowledge management are the terms that are being more and more important with the use of information and communication technologies since mid's of 1990's. These are important for the organizations and especially for the firms to be effective, efficient, and productive. The relative competition that can be told for the consumers to benefit from is a new question to be answered after the COVID-19 period. As the data, information and knowledge management started to be critical factors for management's success and sustainability, the power of the global digital companies took an important place in the area of management of the individuals digital presence, firms success, governments elections. This power may result with digital imperialism of the global firms all over the world (Şen, 2020a:188).

Information management is the publication, production, selection and evaluation of regulated and systematic information in creating value and achieving a strong competitive advantage in the market (Buckman, 2004: 17). Information management is the provision, sharing and use of information that includes learning processes and management information systems in organizations (Harrison and Kessels, 2004: 39). Knowledge management is a method that ensures the protection and regulation of the information existence of an organization. Knowledge management is an approach that constitutes the learning organization. A learning organization is an organization where its employees obtain, share, create information or transfer this information to practice through various decisions (Güçlü and Sotirofski, 2006: 351). Information management is a process that assists organizations in problem solving, active learning, strategic planning and decision making, transfer, finding, selection, regulation and publication of information (Rooney and McKenna, 2010: 308).

Information management practice takes place by acknowledging and understanding the value of knowledge and information as a strategic tool, having a management team willing to implement information management, being willing to change and having the power to do so, trying hard to be the best, being willing to attract the attention of employees in the information management process, believing that employees have sufficient potential, acknowledging openness for sharing information and information (Kalseth and Cummings, 2001:165-166).

Companies that can stand against uncertainty, adapt quickly to change, produce information and maintain old-new information can continue their lives. Companies are becoming increasingly knowledge-based in order to achieve sustainable competitive advantage (Tiwana, 2001: 37). The need for knowledge-based activities also made the companies to depend more on the technology producing digital firms. The ones that has got the data in their hands has the potential power for the management. At this context, information management is the main source for decision-making processes and facilities.

Jennex expressed information management as to make the organization more effective, the experience gained from previous decisions should be applied immediately or to future decisions (Jennex, 2007). According to Bhatt (2001) information management includes an understanding of the production, validation, presentation, distribution and implementation of information and the process of learning, reflecting, forgetting and re-learning information for the construction of the core capabilities of the organization, the maintenance and renewal of the built capability (Bhatt, 2001).

Big Data is the potential strategic management key for all institutions and systems. After COVID-19 pandemic crisis started, the importance of data, information and knowledge management has been so obvious for all the stakeholders of the world.

From Shareholder Capitalism to Stakeholder Capitalism: Global, Political and Corporate Governance

Governance is one of the main terms that all management activities of organizations, structures and systems. It can be defined within political, public, corporate or global level. Corporate governance is one of the most prominent results by interacting in a similar way to the areas of political governance and by establishing and managing the structures aimed at ensuring the active participation of the members in the governance processes in all sub-processes. Politically and institutionally important players of governance: "Individual, Societies, Institutions and Systems". Digitalization database management, blockchain technology, robotic production, artificial intelligence and similar applications and health, population policy, education, justice, economy, tax, employment, social responsibility activities, transportation, are increasingly being used in all different areas such as tourism at macro and micro level (Şen, 2020a: 193; Schwab and Malleret, 2020: 20).

In the COVID-19 period, stakeholder management stands out as the most powerful and up-to-date method of creating added value for systems, institutions and/or individuals (Şen, 2020a: 193; Schwab and Malleret, 2020: 185). Environmental and social governance (ESG) principles must be realized with the interaction of the individual. Global, political and corporate governance must be adopted according to individual perspective. Sustainable Development Goals (SDG) are the most important bases for stakeholder management for the future (Şen ve Batı, 2020: 78).

Although the concept of social score is also used as a citizenship score, the use of the term "social score" is more appropriate since this system has an application area that cannot be restricted only by the use of national states. In this context, it can also be predicted that there may be a system that can be used by creating unique models in all social areas (Şen, 2018: 885).

The posts that social media users share in their "virtual space" that make the individual traceable can be an evidence of how rapid applications such as "Social Score" will dominate different areas of life and emerge as another vital result of digital transformation that utilizes ICTs to monitor humans and interpret their data (Şen, 2020a: 182, Şen et al., 2018: 162-163). In response to COVID-19, this can be viewed in China's approach of utilizing its social credit system as a tool to fight against the virus. In Shanghai, Yunchuan, and Rongcheng cities, individuals who contributed to research and development of products/ or services that are beneficial against COVID-19 their social credit score was increased and were put on the " red list" however, those who withheld information such as their potential exposure to COVID-19 were blacklisted, and received a decrease in their scores (Koty, 2020).

Those with high scores in the social rating system will be in contact with those with high scores like themselves and will have privileges (VIP class for home, ticket, hotel and car rental services without easy credit, deposit). Those who receive low scores will be punished and deprived of them (Lam, 2016; Xiangrong, 2015). This social dramatization is expected to lead to significant changes and consequences in economic, social, cultural and individual areas.

Digital Revolution, New Normal and The Great Reset

The current COVID-19 pandemic has made the world become familiar to a "new normal" (Hall et al., 2020) and deal with new circumstances, such as the multiple states of lock-down and self-isolation, which resulted in an increase in the need for digital transformation of human interaction (O'Leary, 2020). In the aspect of management change, implementation of new systems includes a development of technical solutions and redefinition of job activities, interactions, configurations, and power relationships within an organization, however end users might reject this application leading to loss of performance improvements (Dalcher and Shine, 2003). However, COVID-19 is making the whole globe change its traditional strategies to more innovative and agile ones in order to preserve its ability to continue operating in such global widespread challenges; in other words making the world shift to a "new normal" (Şen and Tarabah, 2020). By which, IT is playing a significant role in mostly all aspects of the COVID-19 pandemic, including "temporal, organizational, and societal" (Agerfalk, et al., 2020) and specifically in how organizations adjust to the "new normal" (Davison, 2020; O'Leary, 2020). In this matter, the pandemic might result in the beginning of a "new era" and a "new society", that is more digitalized and resilient to natural hazards and disasters (Bragazzi, 2020). As organizations worldwide have had to alter their work patterns (Davison, 2020; Richter, 2020) and their workspaces in compliance with the social distancing requirements (Leidner, 2020; Nguyen et al., 2020; O'Leary, 2020; Papagiannidis et al., 2020), thus during the pandemic some organizations have had to adopt new information technology systems and some had to entirely rethink their business model, move to online products and services and engage in new business channels to those removed as a result of the pandemic (Carroll and Conboy, 2020). The integration of digital technology into pandemic policy and response have not only helped in maintaining low mortality rates within the countries who have had quickly deployed digital technologies to facilitate surveillance, testing, planning, contact tracing, quarantine, and clinical management in the aim of containing the virus (Whitelaw et al., 2020), but it also resulted in enabling people to work from home with a "new" office culture, work timings, virtual meetings, virtual offices, virtual clinics and extensive written communications (Javaid et al., 2020). These rapid changes and transformations in employment and work have direct implications for the economy and may lead to permanent shifts that last past the pandemic (Brynjolfsson et al., 2020). By which, COVID-19 is considered to be a product of the technological and digital revolution that has transformed the world over the past century (Keesara et al., 2020), and these new technology-driven practices will now result in a "new normal', and since planning for, embedding, integrating, and implementing technology to simplify new norms is significantly challenging, organizations will have to normalize these technology-driven practices and the utilization of technology in the aim of accomplishing their goals (Carroll and Conboy, 2020). The problems that the world faces are constantly changing, overriding the habits of the past, forming new rules and behaviors are the basis of the new normal (Ertuna, 2009: 6).

In today's globalized world, many of challenges are imposed such as transformation, rapid changes, industry revolutions making the world to develop agile and innovative responses and strategies in order to adapt to such challenges. In other words, utilizing what is already known in the "traditional normal" in a contemporary way in order to adapt to the "new normal". The basis of this paradigm shift is the digital revolution that is taking place after the mids of 1990's.

There are different definitions and perspectives for "The New Normal" and for "The Great Reset". According to World Economic Forum at the end of July 2020; the cooperation of global stakeholders is an urgent need for managing today's consequences of the COVID-19 crisis. "To improve the state of the world, the World Economic Forum is starting The Great Reset initiative" (WEF, 2020a; Schwab and Malleret, 2020: 246-250).

At this point of view, World Economic Forum defends that "our systems need a reset". Many variables will be effective in this transformation, and there are plenty of questions to answer. In this context, one of the most important questions is whether "the great reset" will be with the structure and rules of the establishment. The main reason for this is that humanity is so lagging in solving basic problems despite all this development and progress. Besides the basic principles of governance such as transparency, accountability, fairness and responsibility; Stakeholder management, common sense and cooperative philosophy should form the basis of "The Great Reset" approach. This foundation should only be laid with the individual at the center and by redefining all concepts, processes, structures, institutions and systems according to the individual (Şen, 2020a: 193; Schwab and Malleret, 2020: 24).

It is still debated whether the change that occurred during the initial period of the COVID-19 pandemic is of nature or human origin. According to the "Cyclic Balance and Value Model", which was developed in 2017, nature and/or human are involved in the initial stage of change and/or transformation (Şen, 2017a: 148). In this context, the pandemic initiation period and how the future process will affect the change is an especially important factor. The world is currently in the period when change and/or transformation begins to take place. The most important outputs related to this process are seen as how the value will emerge, at what points the balance will occur and how "The Great Reset" will occur at the end of this cycle. In this process, change and transformation management within the scope of the "Cyclic Balance and Value Model" is of vital importance in this respect.

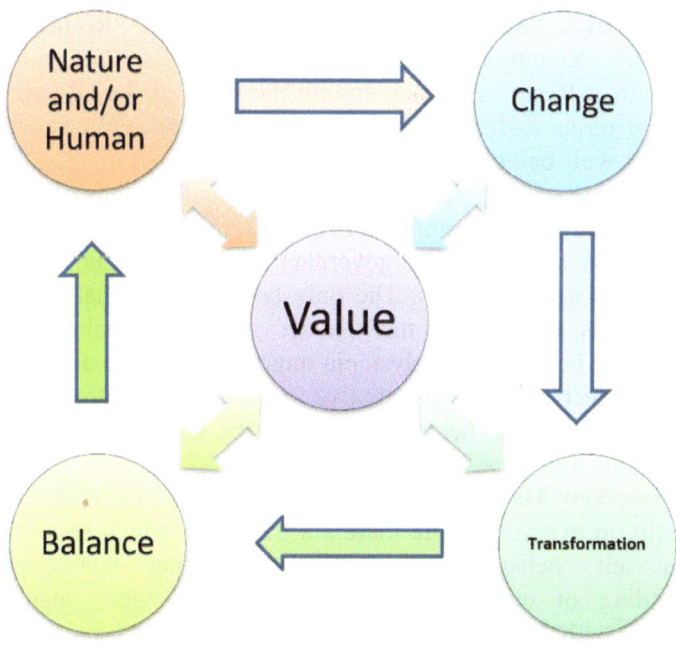

Fig. 1. CBVM - Cyclic Balance and Value Model (Şen, 2017a: 148).

The most obvious indicator of change and transformation are terms and concepts that include new and begin with re-. All concepts including being "new" and/or starting with "re-..." may have much more importance in this reset period. For example, "New Normal", "New Management", "New Applications", "New Admissions", "New Economic and Financial Systems" "New Currencies", "New Paradigm", "New Political Structures and Systems".

On the other hand terms and concepts starting with "re-" can be exampled as; "Re-set", "Re-establishment", "Re-create", "Re-start", "Re-begin", "Re-define", "Re-structure", "Re-design", "Re-measure", "Re-analyse", "Re-evaluate", "Re-estimate", "Re-examine", "Re-establish", "Re-do"; "Re-build", "Re-form", "Re-act", "Re-open", "Re-elevate", "Re-educate", "Re-skill", "Re-cover", "Re-enact", "Re-collect", "Re-emerge", "Re-change", "Re-enforce", "Re-elect", "Re-enter", "Re-enable", "Re-classify", "Re-allocate", "Re-assume", "Re-adapt", "Re-attempt", "Re-brace", ""Re-cement", "Re-challenge", "Re-ally", "Re-alter", "Re-argue", "Re-earn", "Re-embody", "Re-embrace", "Re-emerge", "Re-emit", "Re-emphasize", "Re-energize", "Re-enforce", "Re-engage", "Re-engrave", "Re-enjoy", "Re-enlarge", "Re-erect", "Re-evoke", "Re-execute", "Re-exhibit", "Re-experience", "Re-explain", "Re-explore", "Re-expose", "Re-express", "Re-incorporate", "Re-introduce", "Re-lay", "Re-mark", "Re-formation", "Re-emergence", "Re-listen", "Re-cycle", "Re-arousal", "Re-emphasis", Re-imagine etc.

"The Great Reset" approach and all the basis of the "Re-set" must include all of these terms and concepts and these must be realized for the wellness, welfare and well-being of all individuals one by one, all over the world. This can also be done with all the tools, techniques and systems of digital revolution. All systems, societies, institutions, organizations and individuals must be taken as stakeholders and the good governance must be reached for reaching the desired results and outcomes. The only critical point that must be taken into consideration is, at the end of this "Re-set" not to "Re-enslave" the stakeholders of the world. The risk of the dystopia must be evaluated and must be managed with the collective and contributive way. Z Generation's ideas, feelings, perception, attitude and behaviors must be the guideline of "The Great Reset" within the new age.

Senism, New Management and Individual

Mostly, in everyone's life there's a transition which results in reformation of own self, behaviors, perceptions; in other words, rebuilding the understanding of one's self or reforming the "Sen" inside of "me" in compliance with the "new normal" that is imposed on or chosen by the individual. Although "change" is a reality that cannot be accepted immediately, humans usually have the tendency to adapt to any "new normal" passing through several phases. This tendency or ability to prepare for, anticipate, respond, and adapt to vital changes in order to survive in , grow, and adapt to the new normal is not only seen on an individual level but also on a societal and organizational levels as well (Şen, 2020a: 181-183). In other words, this "New Normal" includes "The New Management" philosophical approach starting from self-management of individual, to corporate level, society level and the system level.

During the COVID-19 period, social distancing can be seen as a multi-sided public health measure that involves many practices, stakeholders, and consequences in the form of remote work, online social activity, and remote education, and the "adaptation" side is captured by how individuals have managed to adapt their livelihood into virtual settings according to these aspects (Kwon et al., 2020).

In this matter, the resilience of a population during a pandemic depends on how society members cope with their anxiety and fears in which is beneficial on the individual level, and on the societal level through better management of the pandemic (Schimmenti et al., 2020).

In response to COVID-19 a lot of terms have gained new meaning, making the world adapt accordingly. By which in the current and past few months of the COVID-19 crises, it's obvious that technological advancements such as Industry 4.0 and ICTs have been gaining increased acceptance, importance, and utilization whether on the organizational or individual levels, which can be seen in the use of technology in knowledge management strategies, governance of corporation, and in the innovative methods that are used to fight against the virus (Şen and Tarabah, 2020). COVID-19 has increased the importance of digitalization more than ever before, as on the individual level this can be seen in the increase of individual's interest and awareness about perceiving digital technologies as a key solution to adapt to the new normal that was imposed on them, which resulted in an increase in the number of technologies' inactive and new users. Besides, on the organizational level it can be seen in remote working, distance learning, and digital technology utilization in many sectors and mainly in the health sector. By which, ICT's role is going beyond facilitating business activities to protecting the whole world and humanity. The ability to adapt to this new normal and utilize what is already known in a new and innovative way is determining the effectiveness of societies and organizations in surviving the new era that is resulted by COVID-19. Nevertheless, COVID-19 has addressed the issue on how the world will interact with the individual and vice versa, how fear will be used in management and processes, how corporations will be governed, and how nations will respond to the crisis and utilize the modern approaches in order to save the whole globe, and what "new normal" will occur during and post the COVID-19 crisis.

Despite of many challenges imposed on individuals for centuries, COVID-19 is considered one of the hardest challenges that the world has ever experienced. As every individual is being distant of "Sen" inside of "Me" (Şen,

2000: 10), "the self-actualization" has changed its identity in some way. Senism is the theory for understanding the actualization and/or realization of individual by defining, measuring and analyzing "Sen in me" (Şen, 2016: 117). All the internal and external variables must be taken into consideration to define the Sen of an individual. It is unique for every one of the humanity and all variables may be rational or emotional based (Şen, 2020a: 201). By which, the "Sen" inside of "Me" that has shapes "Me"; thoughts, feelings, perception, attitude and behavior. When considered from this perspective, globalization and digital revolution were the main two variables that directly and / or indirectly affect the formation and development of "Sen". For example, every identification with a person, a celebrity, a relative, a politician or a film character may be important for the individuals "Sen". On the other hand many critical factors such as genetic characteristics, biological factors, development in the 0-6 age period and parent's interest, childhood, the house and close environment in which he/she grew up, and his/her education level are deeply important and contributing to this formation. Also, another variable that is also deeply important is the relation and interaction with digital technologies starting with the Generation Z.

Selfish and individualistic approaches constitute the most important problems of today's world. This is the "Era of Me" that is directly affecting individuals to think themselves separated from nature, society, whole world etc. One of the main reasons of polarization in different fields and interests are related with the perception of "Me" (Şen, 2020a: 197-201).

In the near future, using new digital technologies and applications, the individual will be redefined, all emotional, cognitive, genetic and similar features will become measurable before entering the womb, and the questioning of the meaning of life and existence will radically change for these reasons. The most important risk within the scope of this foresight will be whether this process will be pursued for the collective interests and well-being of all people around the world or for the benefit and interests of the establishment order.

Within the first wave of the COVID-19 pandemic, people in different parts of the world began to need to question life and themselves. COVID-19 was only a global virus that effects people's health and lives. On the other hand, this health risk has caused people all over the world to experience similar feelings, thoughts, fears and processes at the same time. People started to think about the difference between their needs and wants. The consumption culture has been decreased to "Toilet Paper Syndrome" as it can be thought as "Fear of Missing Out- FOMO Syndrome".

As soon as the COVID-19 process is complete and the ongoing health risk is gone, nothing will be the same. The factors and processes of production, the way of doing transactions, consumption styles and ways, structure of products and services, management of perception and experience and all the variables and terms related with management will be changed and transformed according to "The Great Reset". In the long run, the resetting of the systems, societies, institutions and individuals may emerge more meaningful and truthful with "Sen" in the self of every individual.

Conclusion and Discussion

Today, dominant concepts such as globalization and digitalization have great importance in the field of social sciences. According to the short- and medium-term estimates of Covid-19 pandemic crisis, it can be said that recession and economic crises will deepen all over the world.

Remote working and distance education will be part of almost all organizations, and the ability to remotely work and to effectively utilize digital technologies, will be considered as a top qualification by recruiters and organizations. Hence, a rise in the number of millennials in the workplace worldwide might occur and subsequently a fall in the other generations' employment rate, as well as a range in income.

There might be a low spending on experience for a limited period until "fear" stops dominating individuals' life. Meanwhile, fear and emotions might be highly more employed in advertisements and various marketing activities.

Although E-commerce, have been heavily used during the COVID-19 crisis, the traditional "normal shopping" will be dominant again due to the real experience in shopping malls, markets etc. specially in countries that are taking good precautions such as measuring shoppers' temperature before entering stores, additionally due to the inability to utilize or accept technology by several users especially by the older generations.

In the possible second wave of the pandemic, the probability of healthcare workers to quit or go on strike can stand out as an important risk. At the same time, if the second wave of the pandemic occurs, another critical risk can be predicted as an increase in looting, violence and street events.

On the other hand, according to the statistics about welfare, climate change, education, health, racism, polarization and other vital issues for humanity were not managed according to good governance before COVID-19. There is an increasing need for stakeholder management in world governance, where neo-liberal economic policies dominate to today's circumstances. Sustainable growth is one of the important titles for this situation. Digitalization and individual interaction within COVID-19 is an important because it has given some clues about the power distribution and decision-making processes for the global crisis management. Environmental issues, societal problems and lack of good governance criteria's are directly related with the "New World Order" of the established system and this neo-liberal system will not be perceived as sustainable after COVID-19 crisis. The effective and efficient interaction and integration of all global stakeholder systems will be the basis of the change and transformation management in the future. The fact that "relations of production constitute ideology" can determine whether the ideology of the future will develop and be realized through the individual or digital imperialism. Those who will have Big Data, can have the opportunity to translate information and knowledge by processing will have that power. The applications like monitoring systems and social score, performance appraisals are generally in the use of data. At this point of view the producers of information and communication technologies and the parties that has got the data in hand will be the decision-makers and managers of the system. Digital infrastructure and opportunities for the citizens of the world may be an decisive about stakeholder management's good governance practices. Access to digital technology, learning and use should emerge as a fundamental human right, so that the foundations of the digital society and/or the means and needs of being individuals can be laid. Cooperation will stand out, using Big Data and all other digital tools and technologies in the future, a new kind of "digital cooperative system" may form the basis for good governance practices of stakeholder management.

Structures, systems, processes, institutions, organizations, societies are included in all studies in every field, but the individual is not evaluated adequately in the center. It is predictable to change with the COVID-19 crisis. Private, social and professional life roles of individual like; being a parent, friend, manager, employee, consumer, customer etc. will be changed according to the transformation of production and consumption models of "Digital Revolution". Re-definition of the individual may be the starting point of this transformation. Senism is the basis for both the identification of the individual and the re-functioning of all different areas of management. Starting from self-management to the most complex structure's management processes "New Management of The New Normal" may be shaped according to Senism.

Individual's roles in digital world, awareness and perception, self-actualization, digital presence, image, fingerprint and all related variables must be reset according to "The Great Reset". Instead of material improvement of life, well-being may be much more at the center of living styles. As a short- and medium-term result the egoism and self-centered perspective can be dominant for humanity because of the existing economical, political and cultural infrastructures but in the long run, the consciousness about "Sen in me" may make individuals to have a new perception about "The Truth", underlying of the reality.

On the other hand, there is "The Risk of Great Dystopia" within these future scenarios. With all these possibilities and predictions about the systems, organizations and individuals, another risk that needs to be stated is that psychological problems and mental health problems can come forward as the negative impact of both post-COVID-19 trauma and the digital revolution for the individuals. Another source of dystopia that may occur in the world may be anti-democratic, autocratic systems, structures and practices that may arise due to the lack of human focus in applications such as Big Data, Augmented Reality, Robot Technology and Artificial Intelligence. The risk of using new and valuable practices in order to strengthen the establishment and dominate the world can directly increase the possibility of this dystopia.

Thinking and acting proactive, thinking within long term not only for "Short-term Benefits", caring about environmental issues, not doing things for "-As if doing it", caring about "The Others", trying to be "Good Individual" and supporting the "Good Governance" may only be some of the clues of the reset. Fairer, smarter and greener world must be the main purpose for the future. Stakeholder management, good governance and cooperative mutual philosophy can be achieved within the digital world with the wisdom of Senism.

This study summarizes the conceptual structure of the Senism theory as a starting point and basic approach model for the resolution of the change and transformation experienced in a wide framework as many variables can be both a factor and a result. In this context, different variables are proposed in the related fields for future studies in the paper study. In addition to all suggestions, it is suggested that the study should be an example for the studies to be conducted after COVID-19 and allow for comparative studies in terms of the design and interpretation of future studies.

References

Accenture Türkiye Dijitalleşme Endeksi (2016). https://www.accenture.com/t20170202T045842Z__w__/tr-en/_acnmedia/PDF-42/Accenture-HBRRapor-Vodafone.pdfla=en (Access date: 27.06.2020).

Agerfalk, P., Conboy, K., and Myers, M. (2020). Information systems in the age of pandemics: COVID-19 and beyond. European Journal of Information Systems. 29 (3). 1–7.doi: 10.1080/0960085X.2020.1771968.

Ataman, G. (2009). İşletme Yönetimi. 3. Baskı. İstanbul. Türkmen Kitabevi.

Aydeniz, N., Silinir, M., and Karhan, G. (2012). Küreselleşme olgusuna temel yaklaşımlar. Batman Üniversitesi Yaşam Bilimleri Dergisi. 1 (1). 1013-1023.

Bhagwati, J. (2004). In Defense of Globalization. New York. Oxford University Press.

Bhatt, G. D. (2001). Knowledge Management in Organization: Examining the Interaction between Technologies, Techniques, and People. The Journal of Knowledge Management, 5, 68-75.

Buckman, R. (2004). Building A Knowledge-Driven Organization. U.S.A. McGraw-Hill Companies Pbc.

Bragazzi, N. L. (2020). Digital Technologies-Enabled Smart Manufacturing and Industry 4.0 in the Post-COVID-19 Era: Lessons Learnt from a Pandemic.

International Journal of Environmental Research and Public Health. doi: 10.3390/ijerph17134785.

Brynjolfsson, E., Horton, J., Ozimek, A., Rock, D., Sharma, G., and TuYe, H.-Y. (2020). COVID-19 and Remote Work: An Early Look at US Data. doi:10.3386/w27344.

Carroll, N., and Conboy, K. (2020). Normalising the "new normal": Changing tech-driven work practices under pandemic time pressure. International Journal of Information Management. doi: 10.1016/j.ijinfomgt.2020.10218

Dalcher, I., and Shine, J. (2003). Extending the New Technology Acceptance Model to Measure the End User Information Systems Satisfaction in a Mandatory Environment: A Bank's Treasury. Technology Analysis & Strategic Management. 15 (4). 441–455.doi: 10.1080/095373203000136033.

Davison, R. M. (2020). The transformative potential of disruptions: A viewpoint. International Journal of Information Management. doi: https://doi.org/10.1016/j.ijinfomgt.

Dicken, P. (1992). Global Shift: The Internationalization of Economic Activity. Newyork. Guilford Press.

Duygun, A. and Şen, E. (2020). Evaluation of Consumer Purchasing Behaviors in the COVID-19 Pandemic Period in the Context of Maslow's Hierarchy of Needs, Pazarlama Teorisi ve Uygulamaları Dergisi, 6 (1), 45-68.

Ertuna, Ö. (2009). Krizden Alınacak Dersler Yeni Bir Fırsat mı?. MUFAD Journal. 43, 5-43.

Fırat, S. Ü. and Fırat, O. Z. (2017). Sanayi 4.0 devrimi üzerine karşılaştırmalı bir inceleme: kavramlar. Küresel Gelişmeler ve Türkiye. Toprak İşveren Dergisi. 114. 10-23.

Güçlü, N., and Sotirofski, K. (2006). Bilgi yönetimi. Türk Eğitim Bilimleri Dergisi. 4 (4). 351–371.

Hall, G., Laddu, D. R., Phillips, S. A., Lavie, C. J., and Arena, R. (2020). A tale of two pandemics: How will COVID-19 and global trends in physical inactivity and sedentary behavior affect one another?. Progress in Cardiovascular Diseases. doi:10.1016/j.pcad.2020.04.005.

Harrison, R., and Kessels, J. (2004). Human Resource Development In A Knowledge Economy. New York. Palgrave Macmillan Pbc.

Javaid, M., Haleem, A., Vaishya, R., Bahl, S., Suman, R., and Vaish, A. (2020). Industry 4.0 technologies and their applications in fighting COVID-19 pandemic. Diabetes & Metabolic Syndrome: Clinical Research & Reviews. doi:10.1016/j.dsx.2020.04.032

Kalseth, K. and Cummings, S. (2001). Knowledge management: Development strategy or business strategy?. Information Development. 17 (3). 163-172.

Karabıçak, M. (2002). Küreselleşme sürecinde gelişmekte olan ülke ekonomilerinde ortaya çıkan yönelim ve tepkiler. Süleyman Demirel Üniversitesi İktisadi ve İdari Bilimler Fakültesi Dergisi. 7 (1). 113-116.

Keesara, S., Jonas, A., and Schulman, K. (2020). Covid-19 and Health Care's Digital Revolution. The New England Journal of Medicine. doi:10.1056/nejmp2005835.

Koty (2020). China's Social Credit System: COVID-19, Triggers, Some Exemptions, Obligations for Businesses, retrieved from https://www.china-briefing.com/news/chinas-social-creditsystem-covid-19-triggers-some-exemptions-obligations-businesses/, Date of Access: 30.07.2020

Leidner, D. E. (2020). Editorial reflections: Lockdowns, slowdowns, and some in-troductions. Journal of the Association for Information Systems, 21(2). doi: 10.17705/1jais.00600

Mert, G. (2019) Organizasyonlarda Dijital Dönüşüm ve Medya Okuryazarlığı Eğitimi. (Ed. E. Koçoğlu ve Ö. Akman) içinde Medya Okuryazarlığı ve Eğitimi. Ankara, Pegem Akademi.

Mert, G. (2020). Kurumların stratejik yönetim süreçlerinde dijitalleşmenin rolü. Journal Of Social, Humanities and Administrative Sciences, 6(22), 41-58.

Nguyen, C. T., Saputra, Y. M., Van Huynh, N., Nguyen, N. T., Khoa, T. V., Tuan, B. M., Nguyen, D. N., Hoang, D. T., Vu, T. X., Dutkiewicz, E., & Chatzinotas, S. (2020). Enabling and emerging technologies for social distancing: A comprehensive survey. IEEE Access arXiv preprint arXiv:2005.02816.

O'Leary, D. E. (2020). Evolving information systems and technology research issues for COVID-19 and other pandemics. Journal of Organizational Computing and Electronic Commerce. 1–8. https://doi.org/10.1080/10919392.2020.1755790.

Papagiannidis, S., Harris, J., and Morton, D. (2020). WHO led the digital transformation of your company? A reflection of IT related challenges during the pandemic. International Journal of Information Management. doi: 10.1016/j.ijinfomgt.2020.102166.

Richter, A. (2020). Locked-down digital work.International Journal of Information Management. doi: /10.1016/j.ijinfomgt.2020.102157.

Rooney, D. and Mckenna, B. (2010). Wisdom and Management in The Knowledge Economy. London. Routledge Pbc.

Schimmenti A., Billieux J., and Starcevic, V. (2020). The four horsemen of fear: An integrated model of understanding fear experiences during the COVID-19 pandemic. Clinical Neuropsychiatry. 17 (2). 41-45.doi: doi.org/10.36131/ CN20200202.

Schwab, K. and Malleret T. (2020). COVID:19 The Great Reset, World Economic Forum, Forum Publishing, Switzerland.

Şen, E. (2000). Senizm, Gül Yayınları, ISBN: 975-8086-03-0, İstanbul.

Şen, E. (2016). Advertisement, Consumption Culture and Senism, 2nd New Media Conference, April 21, 2016, İstanbul, pp. 117.

Şen, E. (2017a). Kurumsallaşma ve Kurumsal Yönetişim, Beta Yayınları, 2. Baskı, İstanbul.

Şen, E. (2017b). Yeni Ekonomi, Yönetim, Nöro-Yönetim ve Senizm. 2. Uluslararası Ekonomi Yönetimi ve Pazarlama Araştırmaları Kongresi, 24-25 Mart 2017, 250-253.

Şen, E. (2018). Blockchain Teknolojisinin Yönetim ve Birey Üzerine Etkileri. 3. Uluslararası Sosyal Beşeri ve Eğitim Bilimleri Kongresi, 885-886.

Şen, E., Gerni, G. M., Ateşoğlu, H. (2018). Social Score Applications in the Context of Governance Theory: Stakeholder Theory and Blockchain Technology. Critical Debastes in Social Sciences, 154-165. London: Frontpage Publications.

Şen, E. and Batı, G. F. (2020). "COVID-19 Pandemik Krizinin Yönetim ve Ekonomi Politik Üzerine Olası Etkileri", Yönetim, Ekonomi ve Pazarlama Araştırmaları Dergisi, 4(2), 71-84

Şen, E. and Tarabah, N. E. H. (2020). "Knowledge Management and Corporate Governance within COVID-19 Period", Data, Information and Knowledge Management, In: Mert, G., Şen, E. and Yılmaz, O. (eds) ISBN: 978-625-7126-19-9, Nobel Bilimsel Eserler, İstanbul, pp. 541-556.

Şen, E. (2020a). Global Virus of the Digital Village COVID-19 and Senism. Eurasian Journal of Researches in Social and Economics (EJRSE),177-204.

Şen, E. (2020b). New Management and Senism. 5. International EMI Entrepreneurship & Communication Social Sciences Congress, p. 254. June 29-30 2020, Gostivar, N. Macedonia. https://emissc.org/files/E-Book/5.EMI%20Abstract%20BOOK.pdf

Tiwana, A. (2001). The Essential Guide to Knowledge Management E-Business and CRM Applications, Prentice Hall PTR, Upper Saddle River, NJ. s. 37.

Whitelaw, S., Mamas, M. A, Topol, E., and Van Spal, H. G. C. (2020). Applications of digital technology in COVID-19 pandemic planning and response. Lancet Digital Health 2020. doi: /10.1016/.

World Economic Forum (2020a). "The Great Reset", https://www.weforum.org/great-reset/ (Access: 30.07.2020).

World Economic Forum (2020b). "The Great Reset", https://www.youtube.com/watch?v=VHRkkeecg7c&t=1051s (Access: 04.08.2020).

World Health Organization (2020). "WHO Characterizes COVID-19 as a Pandemic", 11 March 2020, https://www.who.int/emergencies/diseases/novel-coronavirus2019/events-as-they-happen, (Access: 30.04.2020).

Yeşil, H. (2010). Küreselleşme ve İşletmelerin Küreselleşme Süreçleri: Karşılaşılan Fırsatlar ve Tehditler. Ekonomik ve Sosyal Araştırmalar Dergisi. 6 (1). 22-72.

CHAPTER 4

Macroeconomic Results of the Effects of Covid-19 Pandemic on the Supply Chain

Erdem Bağcı
{ebagci@bandirma.edu.tr}

Assist. Prof., Bandırma Onyedi Eylül University, Faculty of Economic Administrative Sciences, Balıkesir/Turkey

Abstract

The security of the supply chain significantly affects the macroeconomic performance of countries. because procuring the production factors required for production from transnational regions carries serious risks for production. As a matter of fact, due to the COVID 19 pandemic, when transportation between countries stopped, problems regarding supply started to emerge. In this case, the economic problem in a country has started to turn into a global economic problem. therefore, national and global macroeconomic problems cannot be overcome without ensuring the security of the supply chain. Thus, in this study, the relationship of the supply chain with macroeconomic problems, the importance of the supply chain, the reflections of the COVID 19 pandemic to the supply chain, and the measures to be taken to flexible the supply chain was analyzed. In this context, firstly, the literature has been examined and summarized. Then, reports investigating the effects of the COVID 19 pandemic were analyzed. As a result of the study, it has been determined about the macroeconomic problems that the countries will face if the supply chain is not flexible.

Keywords: Supply chain, pandemic, macroeconomic factors.

Introduction

The COVID-19 pandemic, which has already infected almost 10.005,970 people in 188 countries, resulting in more than 500,000 deaths, has the potential to reach a large proportion of the global population (Johns Hopkins University Center for Systems, 2020). This grave picture of the pandemic is expected to continue. Especially the second wave expectation is increasing day by day. This will lead to deepening of macroeconomic problems. The effect of the COVID-19 outbreak on countries' economies emerges in many dimensions, one of which is the disruption of the supply chain. As a result of commercial globalization, the production structures of countries are articulated. Production processes are also disrupted as transportation and commercial activities between countries decrease due to the pandemic. With the COVID-19 pandemic embracing the entire world, countries began to take measures to keep households in their homes, one after the other, so that their health systems would not collapse. In addition, country borders were closed for free travel. Thus, the global economy began to suffer seriously. Naturally, the supply chain of the sectors that produce depending on the imported input was also negatively affected.

As a result of globalization, production and supply processes are articulated together; it causes negative developments in one country to spread easily to other countries. The phenomenon of globalization stands out with its negative aspects in this process. Thus, it is not enough for a country to be successful in combating the COVID-19 pandemic for its economic recovery. Because it is directly affected by the problems of the other countries that is dependent on in terms of production, export and import. Therefore, economic destruction caused by the COVID-19 pandemic is an issue that needs to be addressed on a global scale. Because the economies of the country are dependent on each other and a country cannot be expected to succeed economically alone in this process.

All countries have set serious obstacles and rules about transportation with the concern that every international transportation vehicle coming from a foreign country carries COVID-19. This resulted in transportation problems by leaving the ferries, planes, ships under Quarantine for a long-time during transportation. Naturally, this process affects the production of goods needed domestically negatively. Along with the negative impact of production, the export of the country and the domestic supply-demand balance have deteriorated. Thus, countries face serious price increases. This will cause countries to face serious inflation globally. Because the required raw materials, or manufactured products cannot be provided due to the deterioration of the supply chain. However, the manufactured products cannot be reached to the destination due to the crashes in transportation. Disruptions in the logistics of goods and raw materials cause an increase in the costs of goods and raw materials. Therefore, disruptions in the supply chain lead to an increase in costs as well as a shortage of goods and services. These developments will create serious inflation in the coming years.

The main purpose of this study is to examine the negative impact of the COVID-19 pandemic on the supply chain and to make predictions on what changes will be expected in the production processes of developing and developed countries. In this context, firstly, the emergence of the COVID-19 pandemic and countries how to react economically to this process are examined. Then, how production processes are affected in the context of developed and developing countries is presented. However, it is emphasized what kind of macroeconomic problems the COVID-19 pandemic causes in countries through the supply chain. In addition, the role of the supply chain is emphasized in terms of macroeconomic effects of COVID-19. As a result, how the COVID-19 pandemic affects the macroeconomic indicators of the countries through the supply chain is also explored and the results of these effects will be emphasized in the coming years.

Countries Manufacturing Output and Supply Chain

The supply chain refers to the process of collecting and supplying raw materials and converting raw materials into final products and services for the customer. The commodities traded in this process may consist of crops, animals, timber, gold or other natural resources. Commodity reaching the consumer can take several steps and these can include locations in several different countries. The finished product goes to one of three locations: a wholesaler, a retailer, or directly to the consumer. The wholesaler or distributor globally combines products from different locations and regions. It then repackages them for marketing and distribution, taking into account customers' wishes. The retailer provides additional services to increase customer satisfaction while providing goods and services to the consumer. This causes the procurement process to be extended and the process to become complex until the product reaches the end customer. For this reason, some manufacturers try to keep the process under control by offering the products directly to the consumer. Production managers decide where to set up the company based on production costs. This encouraged many investments in technology outsourcing for India and China. Businesses try to design every stage of the supply chain to increase their efficiency. As a result, many companies have invested to supply products at lower costs in countries with lower living costs, such as China. As of 2013, Asia reached 26.5% of the global production of products that are part of the supply chain. In addition; China is responsible for half of the global intermediate goods production (Amadeo, 2019). This situation, naturally weakens the supply chain, making it vulnerable to global threats.

To understand the safety and flexibility of the supply chain, it is necessary to examine the world's production structure and production centers. In this context, table-1 that showing the share of manufacturing countries in world manufacturing has been prepared. When table-1 is analyzed, it is seen that China is by far the world leader in manufacturing. Considering that China's share in world manufacturing is 28.37; it is understood that almost 1/3 of the production in the world is produced by China. Thus, the world supply chain passes through China. It should be expected that any economic, political, social, health and similar problems in China will turn the world economy upside down. This clearly states how threatened and rigid the world supply chain is.

Table 1. Manufacturing Output by Countries and Regions (2018)

		Trillion dollars	% of world total
1.	China	4,000	28,37
2.	United States	2,300	16,31

3.		Japan	1,000	7,09
4.		Germany	0,806	5,72
5.		South Korea	0,459	3,26
6.		India	0,412	2,92
7.		Italy	0,314	2,23
8.		France	0,270	1,92
9.		United Kingdom	0,253	1,79
10.		Mexico	0,210	1,49
11.		Indonesia	0,207	1,47
12.		Russia	0,204	1,45
13.		Brazil	0,181	1,28
14.		Canada	0,169	1,20
15.		Spain	0,159	1,13
16.		Turkey	0,147	1,04
17.		Thailand	0,136	0,96
18.		Switzerland	0,129	0,91
19.		Ireland	0,124	0,88
20.		Netherlands	0,102	0,72
21.		Saudi Arabia	0,100	0,71
22.		Poland	0,098	0,70
23.		Australia	0,086	0,61
24.		Malaysia	0,077	0,55
25.		Avustria	0,077	0,55
26.		Sweden	0,074	0,52
27.		Singapore	0,073	0,52
28.		Belgium	0,067	0,48
29.		Argentia	0,066	0,47
30.		Philippines	0,063	0,45
31.		Iran	0,057	0,40
32.		Chech Rebuplic	0,057	0,40
33.		Bangladesh	0,048	0,34
34.		Puerto Rico	0,048	0,34
35.		Romania	0,048	0,34
36.		Denmark	0,046	0,33
37.		Israil	0,044	0,31
38.		Finland	0,042	0,30
39.		Nigeria	0,041	0,29
40.		Egypt	0,041	0,29
41.		Vietnam	0,039	0,28
42.		Colombia	0,037	0,26
43.		UAE	0,037	0,26
44.		Pakistan	0,034	0,24
45.		Chile	0,032	0,23
46.		Venezuela	0,031	0,22
47.		Hungary	0,029	0,21
48.		Portugal	0,029	0,21
49.		Peru	0,029	0,21
50.		Norway	0,026	0,18
51.		Greece	0,021	0,15
52.		Slovakia	0,021	0,15
53.		Ukraine	0,015	0,11
54.		Guatemela	0,014	0,10
55.		Others	0,870	6,17
Total			**14,099**	**100**
Regional		Asia	733,148	52
		Europe	310,178	22
		North Amerika	253,782	18
		Latin Amerika	70,495	5
		Africa	28,198	2
		Oceania	14,099	1

https://howmuch.net/articles/map-worlds-manufacturing-output (24.06.2020)

The United States comes second country in world manufacture. It has a share of 16.3% in the world manufacture of the United States. Thus, 45% of the products manufactured in the world are produced only by two countries (China and the USA). Thus, almost half of the world supply chain is controlled by two countries. If the foreign trade wars between the United States and China, which have been on the agenda recently, continue, the supply chain will continue to be threatened even if the pandemic disappears. Therefore, all parties of the supply chain should review this process and take the necessary steps.

There is a serious accumulation in the Asian region in world manufacturing. Asia has a 52% share in world manufacturing. A potential disaster in the Asian region could naturally paralyze the supply chain. This situation may cause the world to be dragged into a global and economic downturn. At the same time, when we consider the America Region, it is seen that North America has a share of 18% and Latin America has a share of 5%. The share of the American Region in world manufacture is 23% in total. It is seen that Europe has a share of only 22 percent in world manufacturing. When evaluated in general, 97% of world production is concentrated in America, Europe, and the Asia region. To make the supply chain flexible and secure, it is necessary to ensure the distribution of world production worldwide. Therefore, global agreements need to be made for the creation of new manufacturing centers in regions close to demand centers.

Another indicator of the security and flexibility of the supply chain is the development of the share of countries in the import of merchandise. The import development of countries in merchandise can show their role in the supply chain of those countries. In this context, table 2 presents how the imports of merchandise on a regional and country basis changed between 1948 and 2018.

Table 2. World Merchandise Imports By Region And Selected Economy, 1948, 1953, 1963, 1973, 1983, 1993, 2003 and 2018

(Billion dollars and percentage)	1948	1953	1963	1973	1983	1993	2003	2018
World (Value)	62	85	164	594	1883	3805	7694	19394
World (Share)	100,0	100,0	100,0	100,0	100,0	100,0	100,0	100,0
North America	18,5	20,5	16,1	17,2	18,5	21,3	22,4	18,4
United States of America	13,0	13,9	11,4	12,4	14,3	15,9	16,9	13,5
Mexico	1,0	0,9	0,8	0,6	0,7	1,8	2,3	2,5
Canada	4,4	5,5	3,9	4,2	3,4	3,7	3,2	2,4
South and Central America and the Caribbean	10,4	8,3	6,0	4,4	3,9	3,3	2,5	3,3
Brazil	1,8	1,6	0,9	1,2	0,9	0,7	0,7	1,0
Chile	0,4	0,4	0,4	0,2	0,2	0,3	0,3	0,4
Europe	45,3	43,7	52,0	53,3	44,1	44,5	45,0	36,9
Germany (1)	**2,2**	**4,5**	**8,0**	**9,2**	**8,1**	**9,0**	**7,9**	**6,6**
United Kingdom	13,4	11,0	8,5	6,5	5,3	5,5	5,2	3,5
France	5,5	4,9	5,3	6,4	5,6	5,7	5,2	3,5
Netherlands	3,4	3,3	4,4	4,8	3,3	3,3	3,4	3,3
Africa	8,1	7,0	5,2	3,9	4,6	2,6	2,2	3,0

South Africa (2)	2,5	1,5	1,1	0,9	0,8	0,5	0,5	0,6
Middle East	1,7	2,2	2,3	2,7	6,2	3,3	2,8	3,8
Asia	13,9	15,1	14,1	14,9	18,5	23,5	23,5	32,4
China	0,6	1,6	0,9	0,9	1,1	2,7	5,4	11,0
Japan	1,1	2,8	4,1	6,5	6,7	6,4	5,0	3,9
India	2,3	1,4	1,5	0,5	0,7	0,6	0,9	2,6
Australia and New Zealand	2,9	2,3	2,2	1,6	1,4	1,5	1,4	1,4

Note: Between 1973 and 1983 and between 1993 and 2003 import shares were significantly influenced by oil price developments.
(1) Figures refer to the Fed. Rep. of Germany from 1948 through 1983.
(2) Beginning with 1998, figures refer to South Africa only and no longer to the Southern African Customs Union.

https://www.wto.org/english/res_e/statis_e/wts2019_e/wts19_toc_e.htm (22.06.2020).

When table-2 is analyzed, America's share in merchandise import in 1948 increased from 13% to 16.9% in 2003. Then, in 2018, it fell to 13.5%. This shows that the share of the United States in imports decreased after 2003. Germany's import share in merchandise increased from 2% in 1948 to 6.6% in 2018. The import share of Germany increased by up to 9% in 1993 and decreased to 6.6% in 2018. When we look at the Asian region, it is seen that China's share in merchandise imports increased from 0.6% in 1948 to 11% in 2018. Japan's imports of merchandise share, which were 1.1% in 1948, increased to 6.4% in 1993 and then decreased to 3.9% in 2018.

When a regional evaluation is made, while the share of North America Region in world merchandise imports was 18.5% in 1948; its share in merchandise imports increased to 22.4% in 2003. Later, in 2018, the share of the North American Region in world merchandise imports fell to 18.4%. While South America's share in world merchandise imports was 10.4% in 1948, its share in world merchandise imports decreased to 2.5% in 2003. Then, in 2018, the share of South America in world merchandise imports increased to 3%. While the share of Europe in world merchandise imports was 45.3% in 1948, its share in world merchandise imports decreased to 36.9% in 2018. The share of the African Region in world merchandise imports decreased from 8.1% in 1948 to 3% in 2018.

The share of the Asian region in world merchandise imports rose from 13.9 percent in 1948 to 32.4 percent in 2018. When evaluated in general, while the share in world merchandise imports decreased in all regions; the share of world merchandise imports increased in the Asian region. This indicates that the supply chain has completely gone to the control of the Asian region. Asia increases regional commodity imports and provides final goods to meet the needs of other regions. This threatens the flexibility and security of the supply chain.

To better understand the countries and regions where the supply chain is concentrated, table 3 showing the merchandise trade of 50 leading countries in exports and imports was prepared for 2018. When table 3 is analyzed, it is seen that China has a 12.8 percent share in world merchandise exports. At the same time, world merchandise imports are seen to have an 11 percent share. This reveals that China is the leader in world merchandise trade. According to 2018 data, China's share in world merchandise imports increased by 16% and its share in exports increased by 10%. Considering the current merchandise trade of China, the average growth rate of 10% means that in the future, the supply chain will be completely under the control of China.

Table 3. Leading exporters and importers in world merchandise trade, 2018 (Billion dollars and percentage)

Rank	Exporters	Value	Share	Annual percentage change	Rank	Importers	Value	Share	Annual percentage change
1	China	2487	12,8	10	1	United States of America	2614	13,5	9
2	United States of America	1664	8,5	8	2	China	2136	11	16
3	Germany	1561	8,0	8	3	Germany	1286	6,6	11
4	Japan	738	3,8	6	4	Japan	749	3,9	11
5	Netherlands	723	16,1	11	5	United Kingdom	674	3,5	5
6	Korea, Republic of	605	3,1	5	6	France	673	3,5	9
7	France	582	3,0	9	7	Netherlands	646	3,4	12
8	Hong Kong, China	569	2,9	3	8	Hong Kong, China	628	3,3	6
9	Italy	547	2,8	8	9	Korea, Republic of	535	2,8	12
10	United Kingdom	486	2,5	10	10	India	511	2,7	14
11	Belgium	467	2,4	8	11	Italy	501	2,6	11
12	Mexico	451	2,3	10	12	Mexico	477	2,5	10
13	Canada	450	2,3	7	13	Canada (1)	469	2,5	6
14	Russian Federation	444	2,3	26	14	Belgium	450	2,4	10
15	Singapore	413	2,1	11	15	Spain	388	2,1	10
16	United Arab Emirates (1)	346	1,8	10	16	Singapore	371	2	13
17	Spain	345	1,8	8	17	Chinese Taipei	286	1,5	10
18	Chinese Taipei	336	1,7	6	18	Switzerland	279	1,5	4
19	India	326	1,7	9	19	Poland	267	1,4	14
20	Switzerland	311	1,6	4	20	United Arab Emirates	253	1,4	-6
21	Saudi Arabia (1)	299	1,5	35	21	Thailand	250	1,4	13
22	Poland	261	1,3	11	22	Russian Federation (2)	249	1,4	5
23	Australia	257	1,3	11	23	Vietnam (1)	244	1,3	15
24	Thailand	252	1,3	7	24	Australia (1)	236	1,3	3
25	Malaysia	247	1,3	14	25	Turkey	223	1,2	-5
26	Vietnam (1)	246	1,3	15	26	Malaysia	217	1,2	12
27	Brazil	240	1,2	10	27	Austria	193	1,1	10
28	Czech Republic	202	1,0	11	28	Brazil (1)	189	1	20
29	Austria	185	0,9	10	29	Indonesia	189	1	20
30	Indonesia	180	0,9	7	30	Czech Republic	184	1	13
31	Turkey	168	0,9	7	31	Sweden	170	1	10
32	Sweden	166	0,9	8	32	Saudi Arabia, (1)	135	0,8	0
33	Ireland	165	0,8	20	33	Hungary	121	0,7	13
34	Hungary	126	0,6	11	34	Philippines	115	0,7	13
35	Norway	123	0,6	18	35	South Africa(1)	114	0,7	12
36	Denmark	109	0,6	6	36	Ireland	106	0,6	19
37	Iran (1)	108	0,6	16	37	Denmark	102	0,6	10
38	Slovak Republic	94	0,5	12	38	Romania	98	0,6	14
39	South Africa	94	0,5	6	39	Slovak Republic	94	0,6	13

40	Iraq (1)	89	0,5	41	40	Portugal	89	0,5	13
41	Qatar (1)	86	0,4	28	41	Israel (1)	88	0,5	22
42	Romania	80	0,4	13	42	Norway	88	0,5	6
43	Finland	76	0,4	12	43	Finland	78	0,5	11
44	Chile	75	0,4	9	44	Chile	74	0,5	14
45	Kuwait, (1)	72	0,4	30	45	Egypt	72	0,5	17
46	Portugal	68	0,4	10	46	Argentina	65	0,4	-2
47	Philippines	67	0,3	-2	47	Greece	65	0,4	15
48	Argentina	62	0,3	5	48	Bangladesh (1)	62	0,3	16
49	Kazakhstan	61	0,3	26	49	Pakistan	60	0,3	5
50	Nigeria	61	0,3	36	50	Ukraine	57	0,3	15
	Total of above	18167	93,3	-		Total of above	18217	91,7	-
	World	**19475**	**100,0**	**10**		**World**	**19867**	**100,0**	**10**

(1) Secretariat estimates
(2) Imports are valued f.o.b.

https://www.wto.org/english/res_e/statis_e/wts2019_e/wts19_toc_e.htm (22.06.2020).

It is seen that the United States, which ranks two in the world goods exports, imports 8.5% of world merchandise exports, and 13.5% of world merchandise imports. Table-3 shows that China is a leader in world merchandise exports and the United States is a leader in world merchandise exports. While the rate of increase in the world merchandise export share of the United States is 8%; The rate of increase in import share is 9%.

Germany is the third country in world merchandise exports and imports. Germany has an 8% share of world merchandise exports and a 6.6 percent share of world merchandise imports. It is seen that Japan is in fourth place in world merchandise trade. Japan ranks fourth in both world merchandise exports and World merchandise imports. Japan's share in world merchandise exports is 3.9%, while its share in world merchandise exports is 3.8%. In this case, it is seen that Japan is in a Neutral position in world trade. The rate of increase in the share of Germany and Japan in world merchandise imports is higher than the rate of increase in world merchandise exports.

Data in table-3, show to what extent the world merchandise trade is concentrated in certain countries and regions. Thus, it clearly shows how fragile the supply chain is. In world merchandise trade, the clustering of production in certain regions and the monopolization of procurement opportunities pose a great risk. To manage this risk, it is important for macroeconomics to create and diversify supply opportunities in different regions and countries with direct investments.

The Effects Of The Covid-19 Pandemic On The Supply Chain

Supply chain is a system established by companies so that they can easily access the materials needed. With the emergence of unexpected events such as COVID-19 pandemics, this chain can be severely damaged. Because the supply chain consists of an international network. Globally, all countries make an effort to close everyone's homes to protect their citizens from pandemics. This situation naturally causes many economic activities to stop. Thus, the economies of all countries are negatively affected by this process. It is clear that economic and social costs will increase as this situation continues. In particular, vulnerabilities in the global supply chain have begun to emerge slowly in many sectors (Lee and Wright, 2020).

The COVID-19 pandemic has shown how important it is to establish mechanisms for adaptation, crisis management, and proactive response to risks that may arise in an environment of uncertainty. It is observed that companies that have a strong supply chain and create a flexible structure in the supply chain have recovered rapidly. Many companies around the world manufacture by relying on intermediate goods, raw materials and supply opportunities in China, southeast Asia and the neighboring countries with low cost production opportunities. In recent years, these companies have begun to rethink the supply chain they have established with these countries, against future uncertainties. Because it is seen that the risks that emerge in a global sense regarding the trade wars, nationalism and protectionism actions that occurred before the pandemic have started to affect the supply chain. However, it is seen that the risks related to the supply chain have not been eliminated yet. With the emergence of the general impact of the COVID-19 pandemic on international trade, the logistics and procurement process has been severely affected. For this reason, it has been observed that companies are unable to fulfill their obligations towards their customers and face operational failures. This showed that the reliability and flexibility of the supply chain should be taken more seriously (Hedwall, 2020.)

The effects of the COVID-19 pandemic on the supply chain can be summarized as follows (KPMG, 2020);

- Commercial promotional and communication organizations have been canceled.
- International travel restrictions have been applied.
- Many countries have imposed curfews.
- Stores and Restaurants were closed.
- There are difficulties and delays in the supply of raw materials.
- Production has come to a halt.
- Restrictions apply in logistics activities.
- Shipments are delayed and logistics costs increased.
- Additional customs tariffs apply.
- There are difficulties in international payments.
- There are problems in foreign trade.
- Global economic problems are deepening.
- Demand in the market is changing and falling.

The common feature of countries whose supply chain is most affected by the COVID-19 pandemic is their high level of foreign dependency. Therefore, these countries will begin to review their foreign dependency levels.

Effects of Demand and Supply Shock on Supply Chain

When the COVID-19 pandemic influenced China, it was discussed how the effects of the supply shock, which will occur as a result of the disruption of the production of products produced in China, will reflect on the developed and developing markets. In this process, the companies have been discussing which goods and how they can produce from their domestic markets in order to solve the problems they encounter in the supply of goods and services due to the products and raw materials they cannot obtain from China. In this context, necessary measures must be taken to make the supply chain flexible (Seifert, 2020a). It is possible for companies whose supply chain is under global threat to flexible the supply chain by taking measures according to five pillars. These are vulnerability, Management Culture, Procurement, Operations and Demand & Visibility. The clustering of companies producing the supply materials of goods and services produced worldwide creates a serious problem for the supply chain. This makes the supply chain vulnerable. For this reason, the raw materials and materials needed for the supply chain to be flexible should not be obtained only from the companies clustered in a certain region. Corporate management's approaches to flexibly supplying the supply chain are also very important. As a matter of fact, management can perceive the flexibility of the supply chain as workload and cost. In this case, efforts to flexible the supply chain remain limited. Another reason for disruptions in the supply chain is the vulnerability of suppliers. Therefore, suppliers should also be reviewed to flexible the supply chain. Whether the supplier has managed adequate risk management should be controlled. Another factor that needs to be emphasized regarding the flexibility of the procurement process is the operational phase. In this process, it is necessary to calculate inventory turnover rates and times. It is also important to calculate the supply distances to make operational processes more effective (Seifert, 2020a).

The macroeconomic effects of pandemic arise with the contraction in demand. The contraction in demand directly affects the sales level of companies. The decline in the sales and revenues of firms causes two main problems. First, it results in debt payment problems due to the drop in sales and revenue. This situation increases the debt burden of companies and causes bankruptcies. Second, the supply chain deteriorates due to the drop-in sales and revenue (ULISA12, 2020). Because when new orders are not received and uncertainty occurs, new investments are postponed, and naturally investments decrease. Input usage decreases due to the decrease in investments in the sector. The decrease in the labor force and capital demand causes a contraction in factor markets. This process results in increased unemployment and reduced employment. This situation causes the contraction in production and the deterioration in the supply chain in the market to deepen. As a result of all this, there is a decrease in the income of economic units. The fall in revenues narrows the demand again and leads to the formation of a vicious circle (Ozili and Arun, 2020).

In extraordinary periods, serious changes occur in the behavior of consumers. With the spread of the COVID-19 pandemic, consumers seem to be making maximum demands on some products. This is explained by the bullwhip effect previously suggested by Jay Forrester. This situation naturally causes a shock in demand. The shock in demand creates pressure on the supply chain and triggers the disruption of the supply chain. Expected fluctuations in product prices, expected fluctuations in demand, lack of information, increase in order batching and free return policies. Some measures can be taken to eliminate the bullwhip effect caused by extraordinary periods of demand shocks and reduce the impact on the supply chain. These are improved communication and better forecasts, eliminate delays, reduce size of orders and good customer service (Wins, 2020).

Expected Changes In The Supply Chain After COVID-19 Pandemic

Thanks to the pandemic, the supply chain was found to have a fragile and weak structure. The pandemic has unprecedentedly affected global trade and investments. Multinational companies had to go to a narrowing of the serious problems they faced. Economic agencies had to struggle seriously to supply basic necessity products. Because they faced serious difficulties due to the weakness of the supply chain. Serious lessons need to be drawn from this process. Each country should be expected to develop new policies related to the supply chain (Lin and Lanng, 2020).

It is possible to strengthen the supply chain by making use of digitalization and smart systems. Because, traditional supply chain management has many problems such as uncertainty, high cost, complexity and vulnerability. Smarter systems are required to overcome these problems of the traditional supply chain. For example, the internet of things (IoT) will be requested to be used more quickly in the management of the supply chain. In a study, it was determined that using the internet of things (IoT) technologies in supply chain management, it will automatically record the process of defining products, products will be easily followed globally, transparency will be achieved, time and cost savings will be achieved and customer satisfaction will increase. This will naturally ensure the flexibility and security of the supply chain (Abdel-Basset et al., 2018: 615-616). With the effect of the pandemic, it is expected that digitization and the use of smart systems will take place faster in the supply chain management process. In this case, it is predicted that companies and sectors that adapt rapidly to the digitization process will provide competitive advantage.

The future risks expected to have a negative impact on the supply chain are: trade wars, global politics and national policies. In the future, investing in technology and ensuring reliability, sustainability and flexibility in the supply chain will play an important role in ensuring competitiveness. The reliability of the supply chain for the past 10 years before the pandemic was already under discussion. The tension between the USA and China, especially since 2019, was already threatening the security of the supply chain. Because it has become an important production center and has assumed the role of the factory of the world. In this case, the tension between China and the USA naturally threatens the global supply chain in the world. As a matter of fact, some firms were observed to move from China to other countries after the tension. Some of these companies have shifted their investments to Mexico and Vietnam. Thus, while these two countries increased their markets in consumer goods and technology, media and telecommunications (TMT) sectors to 12% and 9% until 2019; China has lost its investments in these sectors. However, these countries are not likely to be a substitute for China. Because China accounts for 60% of global consumer goods exports and 41% of global TMT exports. In order for countries outside of China to benefit from supply chain investments; they will have to make huge investments to increase their production capacity and provide an attractive environment for land, labor and logistics (Hedwall, 2020).

Efforts To Protect The Supply Chain From The COVID-19 Pandemic

Developing countries play an important role in reducing the economically destructive effects of COVID-19. Especially, G20 countries should rapidly implement trade policies that can protect lives around the world by improving access to affordable medical supplies. A joint effort should be made to restrict policies that put this access at risk. Foreign trade can also play a key role in macroeconomic recovery. Since COVID-19 harms industries worldwide, G20 countries must work together to keep their supply chain running. It is also necessary to organize an international meeting and to make important decisions to help rebuild the world economy and prevent global conflicts that may occur in the future. At the top of these decisions is to exclude the health system on a global scale from a commercial purpose and to take trade measures to support health systems and protect the right to life. In this context, lower tariffs should be applied for Drugs, medical devices and other medical materials and even the tariffs should be removed completely. Besides, tariffs on Medicines and medical equipment are relatively low, but disinfectants and other personal protective products required to combat pandemics still face high tariffs and non-tariff barriers in many countries. Companies and countries acting jointly to combat the COVID-19 pandemic have created a common ground for action to keep the supply chain alive and secure. Thus, efforts should be made to eliminate export bans with a structure to be created under the umbrella of the World Trade Organization. Especially, the export and import of food, medicines and similar compulsory necessity products should be provided without tariff. In the field of health, social studies that are independent of profit are required. For example, the intellectual property rights of research in the field of health need to be reconsidered. The COVID-19 pandemic should provide an environment that promotes more global trade cooperation, not protectionism in the world economy. Thus, the COVID-19 pandemic should be expected to increase global cooperation. Global Trade rules are needed to promote investment and trade. With the reform to be made in the World Trade Organization; Countries' joint initiative and efforts are required to remove obstacles to world trade and to ensure international cooperation (González, 2020).

Today, businesses are focused on the needs of their customers and are working hard to keep the supply chain intact. However, this situation is not sustainable. Because they behave constantly in reactive mode. However, it is possible to be more prepared for the future by planning. For this, companies have to analyze the weak points of the current supply chain. Instead of reacting firms to negative situations in the future; it is possible to make more proactive decisions by evaluating future possibilities. Thus, it is possible for them to be more prepared for unmissable negativities. Although no company can fully predict the future, it is possible to create a smart global supply chain by using smart systems. In this context, companies can leverage artificial intelligence (AI) and other technologies. The secret of companies 'success in the market depends on securing global companies' supply chain. Today the supply chain has become incredibly complex (Lee and Wright, 2020).

Blockchain technological innovation has an important function in the formation of a sustainable supply chain. However, there are factors that negatively affect the adoption of blockchain technology in the supply chain. These factors; technological capability, organizational strength, and environmental compliance. Technological ability and organizational power factors are internal factors. The environmental component includes an externally sized and broad category that negatively affects the organization in the supply chain. Technological barriers express basic problems that arise with blockchain technology such as security, accessibility, and immaturity of the technology, and these barriers will not be difficult to eliminate. Organizational obstacles, on the other hand, represent policies and business culture stemming from management. Elimination of these obstacles is possible with the ability to persuade. Environmental factors, on the other hand, can be said to have created an environment in which large masses can be convinced for redesign under the influence of the pandemic (Kouhizadeh et al., 2020:5).

Many companies are installing vertical integration to control the supply chain and protect against threats. This strategy gives them more control over the production process and costs. For example, Apple's application, which maintains high design standards through vertical integration from design to retail, is very successful. This gives the company enough competitive advantage to be virtually monopolized when it comes to high-tech, innovative computers, smartphones and music players (Amadeo, 2019).

Analysis of Relationship Between the Supply Chain and Macroeconomic Factors

The main macroeconomic factors consist of economic growth rate, inflation rate, unemployment rate, and industrial production indicators. These factors have a direct link with the supply chain. Indeed, the supply chain consists of the link to economic activities. If a deterioration in economic activities occurs, the supply chain is also deteriorating. Deterioration in the supply chain is directly reflected in macroeconomic factors. For example, as a result of the deterioration in the supply chain, the increase in the prices of goods and services and additional costs will lead directly to the rise in inflation rates. On the other hand, achieving efficiency in managing the supply chain will reduce supply costs and naturally pressure on the prices of goods and services to decrease. In this case, the security and flexibility of the supply chain have an important role in the fight against the inflation problem of national economies. In a study analyzing the relationship between the performance of a global supply chain (or supply network) consisting of factories, procurement centers, and distribution centers and macroeconomic factors such as oil prices, labor costs, exchange rates, and trade barriers; It is stated that the relationship between macroeconomic factors and the supply chain is directly related to the local demand and the right balance in labor intensity in production (Fioravanti et al., 2009).

The disruption in the supply chain will cause damage to production in economies that are dependent on imports. This will result in a decrease in production, an increase in unemployment, an economic contraction, and an increase in poverty. In particular, the fact that China has dominant power in the global supply chain and is the determinant of the supply chain, the risks caused by the elimination of the flexibility of the supply chain have started to be discussed before the pandemic. It is known that countries such as Vietnam and Mexico, which have the potential of being a procurement center being close to the USA, due to the dependence of the USA economy on the production of china, are on the agenda to be new procurement center for the USA. It is understood that Mexico has made efforts to be supplier the USA and offers advantages for direct investments. The slow decline of China's low-cost appeal, especially as a result of wages that started to increase in China, indicates that yawning in the supply chain will begin (Siavelis and Christopher, 2015).

The supply chain is threatened by natural disasters. The impact on local productivity can last decades after an incident. If a disaster is bad enough, it can slow global growth. For example, in 2011, since Japan damaged the ports caused by the earthquake, Japan negatively affected the supply of 20% of the semiconductor equipment and material supply in the world. Indeed, since Wings, landing gear and other important airline parts were produced in Japan, Boeing's 787 productions were damaged. The US gross domestic product slowed in 2011 due to the suspension of the Japanese auto parts factory (Amadeo, 2019).

Overall, factors such as unemployment rate, inflation rate, economic growth rate, and industrial production indicators, all known as macroeconomic factors, are directly linked to the manufacturing, trade, and services sectors. When there is a contraction in the production, trade, and services sectors; the rate of economic growth also slows down, unemployment rates increase, and inflation rates rise if the increasing demand is not met due to lack of production. In this case, the supply chain deteriorates and becomes vulnerable to external shocks, it does not have a flexible structure; production causes negative effects on trade and services sector. In this context, the problem of the supply chain is not only the national problem of a country's economy; it is a global problem that must be solved for the global economy. Therefore, countries need to act jointly and take measures and develop policies to ensure the structure and security of the supply chain.

Conclusion

In the early days of the COVID-19 pandemic, the effects of the pandemic on the economy were expected to be in a deep V shape and then the economy would recover rapidly. However, it has been observed that a serious economic recovery has not started yet, even though 6 months have passed since the start of the pandemic. Indeed, if no vaccine is available, the pandemic is expected to continue in waves.

It seems that the general impact of the pandemic and the measures taken against the pandemic on the economy will continue. This shows that companies cannot fulfill their obligations in terms of logistics and supply. Therefore, it is clear that serious measures should be taken.

There will be a balance between securing the supply chain and controlling supply costs. To be more precise, securing the supply chain becomes more important than procurement costs. Companies need to use their communication channels effectively while creating the bridge duty between their customers and sellers in order to secure the supply chain.

Innovation can be used to establish the necessary control mechanisms and operational risk management to ensure the reliability of the supply chain. The elements that make up the supply chain need to be diversified. It is necessary to establish different channels with alternative suppliers instead of supplying only from certain and limited companies. At the same time, foreign trade arrangements for import and export should be made by governments. It is possible to create different supply chains in different suppliers and different regions in different countries and to create a flexible structure against external influences.

Thanks to the pandemic, companies that trade on a global scale will have to analyze the supply chain in more detail. Thus, companies will direct the products they supply to different countries for the security of the supply chain. This will bring restructuring in the supply chain. With this restructuring process, developing countries will be able to attract new investments. This process should be expected to bring the redistribution of resources and the change in production structure in the world economy. Thus, countries that are prepared in terms of legal, democracy and freedoms and build a strong structure in terms of trained workforce will receive a significant share of the distribution of these investments. Thus, countries that are already making the necessary preparations will provide advantages in terms of macroeconomic issues such as employment, economic growth, income distribution, balance of payments deficit. Companies that take the necessary lessons from the pandemic process and succeed in getting strong from this process will no doubt gain in the future. At the same time, countries that make the necessary preparations and have strong companies in this process will also have a more stable structure in terms of economy in the future.

In this context, it is recommended that all countries review their own supply chains and invest in a way that will diversify their supply structures and make their supply chains flexible and strong. For example, in meeting Europe's supply needs; Turkey, according to the Asian countries, it is clear that providing more benefits. Europe, a part of its investments in Asia, scroll to the neighboring countries such as Turkey will provide substantial benefits to the European supply chain. Safety should be taken into consideration before costs in the supply chain. In this context, it should adopt the principle of safe supply instead of cheap supply.

References

Abdel-Bassct, M., Manogaran, G. and Mohamed, M. (2018). Internet of Things (IoT) and its impact on supply chain: A frame work for building smart, secure and efficient systems. Future Generation Computer Systems. Volume 86. September 2018. Pages 614-628.

Amadeo, K. (2019). How the Supply Chain Affects the U.S. Economy. https://www.thebalance.com/what-is-the-supply-chain-3305677 (Last accessed on 29 June 2020).

CSSE. (2020). Johns Hopkins University Center for Systems Science Engineering Dashboard. https://gisanddata.maps.arcgis.com/apps/opsdashboard/index.html#/bda759474 0fd40299423467b48e9ecf6 (Last accessed on 20 June 2020).

Fioravanti, R., Menezes, Mozart. and Goentzel, Jarrod. (2009). Supply Chain Sensitivity to Macro Factors. https://www.pomsmeetings.org/ConfPapers/011/011-0890.pdf (Last accessed on 12 June 2020).

González, A. (2020). This is Why Keeping Global Supply Chains Moving is Key To Overcoming COVID-19. https://www.weforum.org/agenda/2020/04/g20-trade-international-health-supplies-coronavirus-covid19-pandemic (Last accessed on 22 June 2020).

Hedwall, M. (2020). The ongoing impact of COVID-19 on global supply chains. https://www.weforum.org/agenda/2020/06/ongoing-impact-covid-19-global-supply-chains/ (Last accessed on 10 June 2020).

Kouhizadeh, M., Saberi, S. and Sarkis, J. (2020). Blockchain technology and the sustainable supply chain: Theoretically exploring adoption barriers, International Journal of Production Economics. Volume 231. 107831.

KPMG. (2020). Covid-19'un Tedarik Zinciri Üzerindeki Etkilerini Yönetmek İçin Olası Stratejik Hamleler. https://home.kpmg/tr/tr/home/gorusler/2020/03/kovid-19-tedarik-zincirine-etkilerini-yonetmek.html (Last accessed on 15 June 2020).

Lee, J. and Wright, J. (2020). COVID-19 and shattered supply chains. https://www.ibm.com/downloads/cas/OVZ3GZRG (Last accessed on 22 June 2020).

Lin, J. and Lanng, C. (2020) Here's how global supply chains will change after COVID-19. https://www.weforum.org/agenda/2020/05/this-is-what-global-supply-chains-will-look-like-after-covid-19/ (Last accessed on 20 June 2020).

Ozili, P. and Arun, T. (2020). Spillover of COVID-19: Impact on the Global Economy Available at SSRN: https://ssrn.com/abstract=3562570. (Last accessed on 20 June 2020).

Seifert, R.W. (2020a). Digesting the shocks: how supply chains are adapting to the COVID-19 lockdowns. https://www.imd.org/research-knowledge/articles/supply-chains-adapting-to-covid-19/ (Last accessed on 22 June 2020).

Seifert, R. W. (2020b). The five pillars of supply chain resilience, https://www.imd.org/research-knowledge/articles/the-five-pillars-of-supply-chain-resilience/(Date of access: 20.06.2020).

Siavelis, R. and Christopher, C.G. (2015). Three global macroeconomic trends to watch. https://www.supplychainquarterly.com/articles/993-three-global-macroeconomic-trends-to-watch (Last accessed on 28 June 2020).

ULİSA12. (2020). Kovid-19 (Koronavirüs) Salgınının Ekonomik Etkileri. https://aybu.edu.tr/yulisa/contents/files/ULI%CC%87SA12_Kovid_19_Ekonomik_Etkiler.pdf (Last accessed on 13 June 2020).

Wins, M. (2020). Understanding the bullwhip effect in Supply Chains, https://www.supplychain-academy.net/understanding-the-bullwhip-effect-in-supply-chains/(Last accessed on 23 June 2020).

CHAPTER 5

The Prevention Paradox of the COVID-19 Crisis in Germany. Science Communication in Times of Uncertainties.

Lutz Peschke
{lutz.peschke@bilkent.edu.tr}

Bilkent University, Department of Communication and Design, Ankara/Turkey

Abstract

During the COVID-19 pandemic, Germany did not face an overload of the healthcare system because of early testings and analyses and strictly executed measures including a three months lasting lockdown measures. But the resulting economic problems led to a prevention paradox. Instead of satisfaction because of better situations compared with countries like the U.S., Brazil and Iran, the protest of citizens against still existing measures increased. This paper analysed the medial function "Spotter of uncertain knowledge" and "Live Performer", which were identified as new roles of scientists in public appearances during the COVID-19 crisis, and its impact on the prevention paradox. It could be found that the transparent communication of uncertain knowledge created trust in science, while certain live performances of research activities generated risk of misinterpretation. Reliable scientific processes were often misused by certain newspapers and social media to draw an image about unprofessional scientists where personal conflicts were foregrounded.

Keywords: COVID-19 pandemic, SARS-CoV-2, prevention paradox, science communication.

Introduction

The SARS-CoV-2 which was firstly discovered at the end of December 2019 in Wuhan/China became the biggest global health challenge of the millennium. The problem of the novel coronavirus is that many people are infected and do not realize their disease directly but became super-spreader of the virus unconsciously. For instance, Böhmer et al., (2020) described that the first patient in Germany was infected by a Chinese employee (patient 0) from the Chinese branch of a German company based in greater Munich. She travelled from Shanghai to Munich on January 19, 2020, to execute a workshop and attend several meetings in the company. During the travel and after the arrival in Munich airport, patient 0 felt unusual chest and back aches. The patient reported fatigue during her whole stay in Germany and attributed the symptom to jetlag. Back in Shanghai on January 22, patient 0 felt feverish, was tested positive for SARS-CoV-2 on January 26 and was hospitalized the next day. Meanwhile, she had transmitted SARS-CoV-2 to many people during her stay in Germany and while travelling. In the following weeks, mass events became hotspots of contagions in Europe. On February 11, 40,000 football fans from Bergamo watched the Champions League football game of their club Atalanta vs. Valencia in Milan's San Siro stadium and celebrated the victory afterwards in pubs and bars. One week later, there were 6,728 confirmed SARS-CoV-2 cases in the province of Bergamo (The Guardian, 2020). On February 15, a couple celebrated carnival in Heinsberg/Germany. While dancing, singing, and drinking on the so-called 'Kappensitzung', a special carnival session, and in the following street carnival, they were in contact with an undefined number of people (Felbermayr et al., 2020). As a consequence, Heinsberg became the epicentre of the COVID-19 pandemic in Germany. It was the first time that a transmission chain in Germany could not be traced back. On March 6, the German Robert Koch Institute (2020) declared Heinsberg an international risk area. In March, authorities in Germany and the Nordic countries identified Ischgl in Austria as a major SARS-CoV-2 hotspot. Ischgl in Tyrol is a popular ski resort, well-known because of its après-ski parties in different bars. Several hundred people form many countries were infected between February and March (Felbermayr et al., 2020; Karnitschnig, 2020).

In 2002/2003 approximately 8,000 people worldwide were infected with SARS-1. In June 2020, the total number of people infected with SARS-CoV-2 was more than 8 million people worldwide. As a consequence, the world is facing an infection rate which is three orders of magnitudes higher. In a period of several weeks, the daily life of scientists, economists, politicians and the public were focused on the pandemic. Medical practitioners and scientists had to establish an efficient emergency care, to understand the impact of the virus on human bodies and the dynamics of the pandemic. Economists had to understand the impact of lockdowns and curfews on the economy. The politics had to decide on drastic measures like lockdowns and curfews considering the newest results of medical research, ethical and legal standards and regulations and economic impacts. Besides, they had to provide financial support to establish efficient networks for scientific collaborations and testing. The health system had to ensure a minimum of medical supplies, like emergency beds, protective masks, gloves and medicine. Additionally, medical researchers in academia and economy started the research and development of vaccines.

But beside the high differences between SARS-1 and SARS-CoV-2 regarding the infection rate, the mediatization of the global communication changed as well in the 20 years between the two pandemics. In the beginning ot this century, during the SARS-1 pandemic, there were no social media with user generated news, no smartphones with potential of user generated live broadcasts and accordingly the network activities between people were almost reduced to web pages and e-mail communication. Today, scientists are confronted with a new kind of visibility. During the period between March and May 2020 the media-based public followed the newest development about the pandemic as a live spectacle on television and in the social media networks. The informationalism as a technological paradigm of the network society described by Castells (2004) was exaggerated by the network media themselves but also by the speed of the pandemic developments. Within three months, daily developments of active cases changed significantly. Besides, political measures and scientific statements were announced and discussed nearly every day. Last but not least, the spectators of the "live event" COVID-19 pandemic were involved actively by the threat of infections and the measures decided by the politics. All topics together were assimilated with the network media activities where the knowledge production of scientists, politics and the media-based public were discussed and negotiated publicly.

From the perspective of the healthcare system, the first wave of the COVID-19 pandemic had been overcome quite successfully between March and May in Germany, compared with the situation in other countries like the U.S., Brazil or Iran. The intensive care units in hospitals were not overloaded at no time and the fatality rate was relatively low. But many people have faced big economic problems since then. As a result, a part of the public is impatient and in doubt whether the measures of the politics mainly based on recommendations of the scientists were appropriate. The role of the virologists expected by the society was to supply the public with unbiased information. 85% of the respondents of a servey within the scope of the COVID-19 pandemic stated, that they need to hear more from scientists and less from politicians (Edelman Trust Barometer, 2020). Compassion like described by Cingi and Eroğlu (2019) are obviously not wanted. Scientists and politics regard their recommendations and measures as success while a part of the society blames them retrospectively as overdone panic-mongering. This chapter will shed light on the impact of public communication of scientific discourses on this prevention paradox. After the summary of the chronology of the COVID-19 pandemic in Germany, the phenomenon of the prevention paradox will be discussed in the context of selected scientific statements and publications aiming to better understand the impact of public scientific discourses on the dissatisfaction which are normally executed in peer events without participation of the public.

Chronology of COVID-19 pandemic in Germany between March and May 2020

The detection of pandemic developments in Germany was based on nation-wide tests which were proceeded by hospitals and health organisations. Figure 1 shows the number of weekly proceeded SARS-CoV-2 test between March and

May 2020 in Germany and Turkey. It reveals that the numbers of proceeded tests in Germany were much higher than fo instance in Turkey.

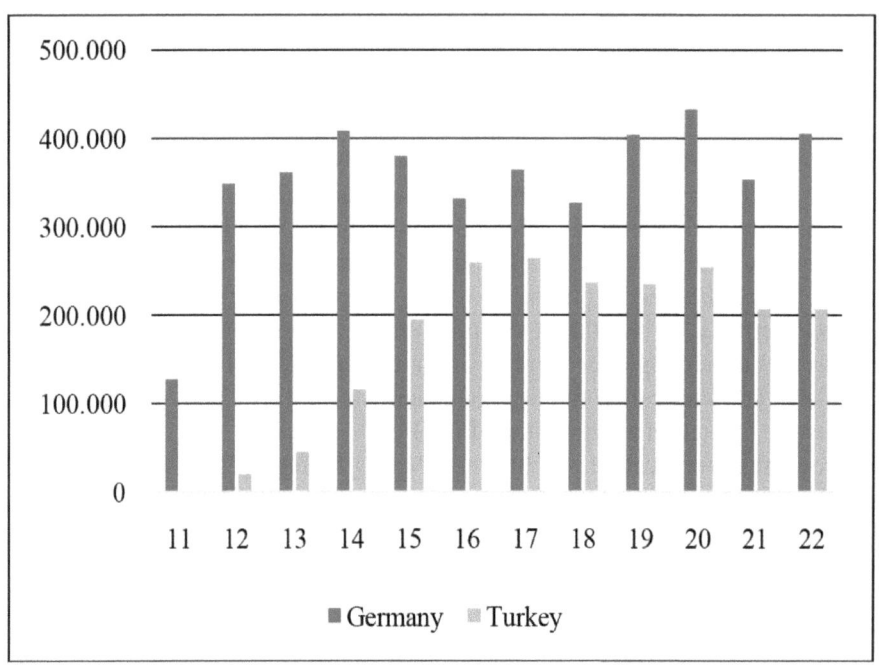

Fig. 1. Numbers of SARS-CoV-2 tests in Germany and Turkey between March and May 2020 (calendar week 11-22)
(https://www.rki.de/DE/Content/InfAZ/N/Neuartiges_Coronavirus/Risikogebiete.html; https://covid19.saglik.gov.tr/ ; https://en.wikipedia.org/wiki/COVID-19_pandemic_in_Germany#6%E2%80%9312_April).

Chronology of measures in Germany

The number of active cases of COVID-19 infected people started to increase exponential in the first week of March and reached its maximum on April 6, 2020 with 72,865 active cases in Germany. Active cases consider only COVID-19 infected people which were tested positive and exclude cases of the people which were recovered and people who died before. After April 6, the number of active cases started decreasing to 9,689 on May 31, 2020 (see Figure 2).

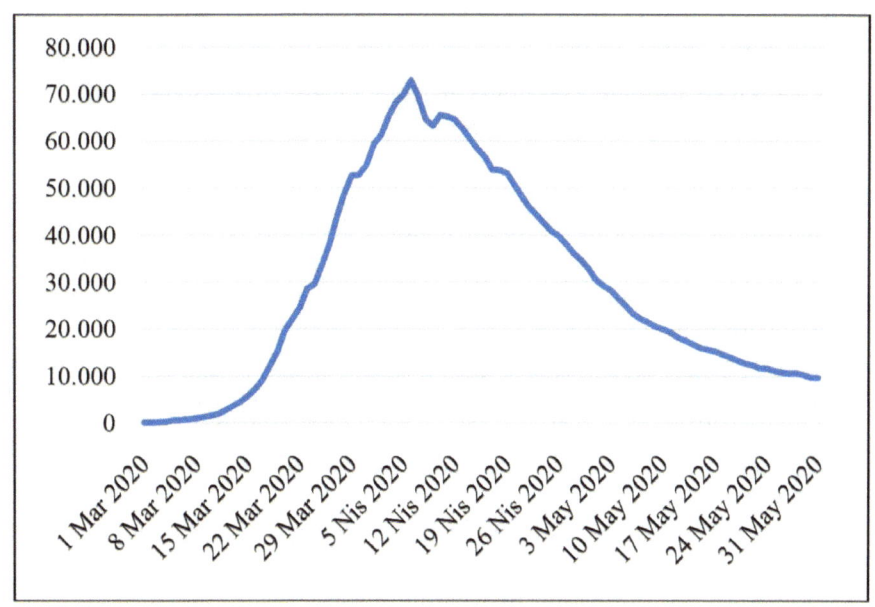

Fig. 2. Number of active cases in Germany between 1 March and 31 May (https://www.worldometers.info/coronavirus/).

During this period, the following measure were taken by the government and different institutions:

- Between March 4 and May 17, the Robert Koch Institute published a daily situation report on its web portal with actual statistics, information about assessments and measures by the Germany government.
- On March 6, after the 25th matchday, the 1st German Soccer League (Bundesliga) interrupted its season until May 16.
- On March 9, all kind of huge events were forbidden in Germany.
- On March 16, schools and kindergartens stopped their physical activities. Schools started with online classes. Additionally, hotels, restaurants, bars and fitness centres had to close their businesses. At the same day, the Federal State Bavaria declared the state of emergency.
- On 17 March, the Robert Koch Institute changed the health threat risk for COVID-19 in Germany to "high".
- On 22 March, lockdowns were imposed in six German states. Other states banned physical contact with more than one person outside of a household.
- On 23 March, the Robert Koch Institute changed the health threat risk for COVID-19 in Germany to "very high".

- On Mach 26, the Federal Ministry of Education and Research allocated 150 million Euro for a national network of academic medical research into COVID-19. The coordinator became Charité-Universitätsmedizin Berlin.
- On March 31, Jena in Thuringia implements mandatory mask-wearing in public spaces.
- On April 2, the Robert Koch Institute included people without symptoms in mask-wearing recommendation. The previous recommendation targeted only people with symptoms. A general obligation to wear masks in public was discussed but not supported by the federal government and most regional governments.
- On April 15, Chancellor Angela Merkel stated after a video conference with the Minister Presidents of the 16 Federal states, that Germany achieved a "fragile intermediate success" regarding the SARS-CoV-2 infection rate. The social life remained restricted. But Several measures of successively relaxing the lockdown were decided.
- On April 20, shops with retrial space with less than 800 square metres were allowed to reopen their business to the public.
- On April 27, obligation of wearing masks was executed in all Federal States.
- On 30 April, museums, monuments, botanical gardens and zoos, as well as religious services were allowed to open under defined physical distancing conditions.
- On May 6, all shops were allowed to reopen. Schools and kindergartens started the successively opening of physical classes. Chancellor Merkel authorized the local governments for relaxing and immediately reimposing measures according to their local and regional situations.
- On May 16, the German 1st Soccer League continued their matchdays as the first Soccer League worldwide but without the participation of audience.

In several media discourses, March 9 (prohibition of huge events with more than 1,000 participants), March 16 (lockdown of schools and kindergartens, shutdown of hotels, bars, restaurants, fitness centres) and March 23 (curfews and ban of physical contacts, lockdown of little shops, Robert Koch Institute changed the health threat risk for COVID-19 in Germany to "very high") are regarded as three milestones in the COVID-19 crisis in Germany (cf. Klein, 2020).

Chronology of scientific results and statements in Germany

The political decision of the imposition of measure described above, were accompanied and partially motivated and recommended by scientific results and statements.

On March 21, the German National Academy of Science Leopoldina published the first Ad-hoc-Statement. Leopoldina was founded 1652 as German Academy of Natural Scientists and was appointed to the National Academy of

Science in 2008. The two main tasks are the representation of German science in foreign states as well as the consultancy of politics and public. In the first ad-hoc statement the academy confirmed that a "Germany-wide temporary shutdown (of approx. 3 weeks) with consistent physical distancing seems advisable at this time" to control the COVID-19 pandemic which were urgently necessary at that time to correspond to the threats. The measures consist of the triad "(1) containment of the epidemic, (2) protection of vulnerable population groups, and (3) capacity increase in the public healthcare system and in the public supply of critical goods and services". The development of drugs and vaccines had to be pursued with the highest priority (Leopoldina, 2020a).

On April 2, Abele-Brehm et al. (2020) published a monograph with recommendations how to organize the combat of corona pandemic in a sustainable way. The authors worked out recommendations of measures to ensure a good health supply for the people on the one hand and to enable that the measure can be kept up during the required time range. Therefore, they recommended a stepwise transition to a risk-oriented strategy, which combines a relaxation of restraints in the economic and social environment with a continuously efficient health protection. The monograph recommends explicitly a suitable communication strategy with the society considering that a differentiated step-by-step plan is highly complex and the feeling of threat among the people is tangible and real. Therefore, a communication is required which is objective, consistent, persuasive and in accordance with Germany's system of values.

One day later, on April 3, Leopoldina published the 2nd Ad-hoc-Statement (Leopoldina, 2020b). The academy states that especially three measures are very important. Firstly, mouth and nose protection reduces the transmission of the virus. But to reach this goal, the nationwide availability of protective masks is required. Self-made mouth and nose protection as well as scarves should be used to bridge the shortage of masks. Secondly, Leopoldina strongly recommends a short-term use of mobile phone data supporting to identify infected people and their contact with other infected people. Three days before, on April 1 the association PEPP-PT introduced their protocol as basis for technologically suitable app solutions. Germany, France, and other countries started developing apps based on a protocol called Pan-European Privacy Preserving Proximity Tracing (PEPP-PT, 2020). It relies on short-range Bluetooth signals to gauge the proximity between two devices without logging their exact locations and without centralized data storage based on cloud solutions, which helps sidestep some privacy concerns. The proximity tracing approach is based on the concept that the app creates a temporary ID which does not enable the identification of the user. Rather, if two smartphones with the running app approach each other, they exchange their IDs encrypted (PEPP-PT, 2020). Third, the high testing capacity of over 350,000 tests/week should be further increased. Leopoldina agrees with Abele-Brehm et al. (2020) that the high willingness of Germany's population to implement the recommended measures can be enhanced by transparent and regular communication activities.

On April 9, the virologists Streeck from University Hospital Bonn and the Minister President of North Rhine-Westphalia Laschet present first results of the so-called Heinsberg Study. The final results were published at May 4 (Streeck et al., 2020). They have investigated the infection fatality rate (IFR) in Gangelt, a village of the district Heinsberg. IFR is the indicator of ratio of deaths in comparison to those infected. With the help of the IFR and the number of deaths, the total number of infections in similar demographic areas like Gangelt. The comparison of the number of officially reported infections revealed that the number is five times higher than the number of people which were officially SARS-CoV-2 positive tested. Accordingly, a total of 1.8 million infections could be assumed which means that the unreported cases were approximately 10 times higher than the cases which were officially reported at that time (ibid.).

Due to the announcement that Chancellor Merkel will meet the Federal State Minister Presidents to discuss further measures and step-by-step relaxations, Helmholtz Association of German Research Centres published a position paper on April 13 with a systemic epidemiological and immunologic point of view on the COVID-19 crisis (Wiestler et al., 2020). It is agreed upon the assumption that the slowdown of the virus distribution can be ascribed to the imposed lockdown measures of the Government. The Helmholtz society consider the temporal progress of the Reproduction number R(t) evident (Figure 3).

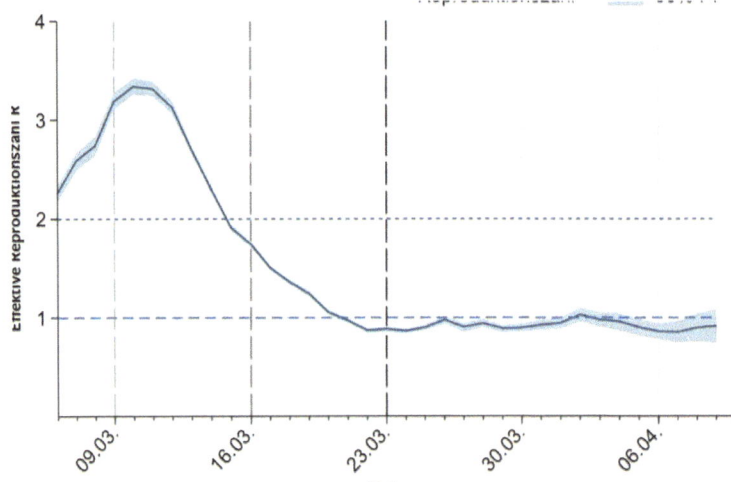

Fig. 3. Temporal progress of the effective reproduction number (Robert Koch Institute, 2020).

The authors describe three scenarios. (1) $Rt > 1$ would stress the healthcare system. (2) $Rt = 1$ could be achieved with step-by-step relaxations of measures but it requires contact restrictions most probably and the workload of the healthcare system will remain very high for many years. (3) $Rt < 1$ can be permanently achieved with continuous contact restriction. With stricter early measures the ideal Rt can be reached. The third is the recommended scenario from the epidemiological perspective.

On the same day, April 13, Leopoldina published its 3rd Ad-hoc-Statement (Leopoldina, 2020c). Beside the already existing agreement that reliable data are urgently needed and the recommendation of the development of a contact tracing app, the academy described the need of mitigating psychological and social impacts which includes especial at-risks groups like children in difficult familial situations or victims of domestic violence. Additionally, it considers that the measures of governments aiming to protect life and health entail restrictions on other legal interests. Therefore, political decisions have to recognise the multidimensionality of the problem and should take into account these perspectives of those at different risks as well. Leopoldina recommends strongly to gradually reopen the educational sector and to start with children of primary and lower secondary level schools, since younger children are more dependent on in-person care, guidance and support. Furthermore, the National Academy of Science gave recommendations for the insurance of stability through economic and financial policy and the chance to set the course for sustainability and not to neglect and weaken measures which were already supported by broad scientific evidence as well as a political and public consensus.

On April 29, Dorsten presented the first version of a study which showed the results of analysis of viral loads in patients of different age categories. It revealed that the viral load in very young people do not differ significantly from the viral load of adults. Based on the results of the study, Drosten warned not to reopen schools and kindergartens unlimited in the current situation, since it cannot be excluded that children are as infectious as adults (Jones et al., 2020). The presented study was modified and published as preprint version on June 3, 2020.

On May 13, the Helmholtz Center for Infection Research (HZI) and the ifo Institute – Leibniz Institute for Economic Research at the University of Munich published a common paper with systemic calculations about the impact of different measures and relaxations on economy and healthcare. The collaborative work could show that the situation of April 20 can be regarded as status quo with the lowest negative impact on economy and healthcare. Only little relaxation of shutdown measures can be tolerated. Strong relaxation does not arise conflicts between economy and healthcare. The costs would increase in both systems. Therefore, stronger relaxations are not recommendable for both, the economy neither the healthcare (Dorn et al., 2020).

On May 27, Leopoldina presented the 4th Ad-hoc-Statement focused on patient-oriented medical and care services which should be provided for all patients during a pandemic. The concept considers short, medium and long-term activities. This statement additionally presents concepts of measures aiming to lead to a more robust and adaptive healthcare system (Leopoldina, 2020d).

The Prevention Paradox in Germany

German virologists, economists, and social scientists as well as politicians regard the relatively fast recovery from the pandemic as a big success based on the efficient collaboration between science, politicians and public. As shown in Figure 3, the Rt value decreased under 1 before the curfew was decided on March 23. As mentioned above, the Helmholtz Association of German Research Centres published a paper about the importance of a Rt value less than 1 on April 13. At that time Rt were ever since less or more stable. For the media-based public, it was not easy to understand why the lockdown measures were very strict although the Rt value promised an unproblematic situation of the pandemic. As long as the news showed horrible films about the pandemic situation in Italy, the public understood the need for the measures. But the more coverages dealt with the economic problems of Germany in the context of the pandemic the more impatient the public became.

The term "prevention paradox" in the context of epidemiology was firstly defined by Rose as "a measure that brings large benefits to the community offers little to each participating individual" (Rose, 1981). To understand the dissatisfaction of a part of the public and allegation against the scientists and politics as a prevention paradox assumes that the measures and recommendations of them were appropriate but not appreciated. Hereafter, the communication activities and the appearance of scientists should be analysed.

The visibility of scientists

Public scientists during the COVID-19 pandemic

Public understanding of science processes are preconditions for the knowledge circulation in the between the systems academia/education and media-based society. They occur with help of different media functions. On the one hand, media generate interest and relevance which keeps the public in the process of knowledge acquisition and avoids the early abruption (Peschke, 2019). On the other hand, media support popularisation of science and decreases the complexity of scientific knowledge (Becerir and Peschke, 2019). Furthermore, media initiate peer-learning processes where peer groups of the public negotiate scientific knowledge with help of self-organised and spontaneous discursive events (Folkvord et al., 2019). The COVID-19 crisis generated a media setting of a research field which was passed in fast motion. Between March and May 2020, Germany faced pandemic developments shaped by social, economic and scientific uncertainties. During the pandemic crisis, previously unknown virologists became public heroes overnight. Peschke (2020) analysed the appearance of scientists in the four most popular talk shows of the public TV channels ARD and ZDF. Between March and May 2020, the main topics of all talk shows were related with the pandemic crisis. According to the topics, this time range could be divided in four periods.

The first period (March 1-15) dealt mainly with the uncertainty of the pandemic. The talk guests discussed mainly the uncertain knowledge about SARS-CoV-2 ("Zwischen Hysterie und begründeter Angst: Wie gefährlich ist das Coronavirus?" (Between hysteria and reasonable fear: how dangerous is the coronavirus), title of the talk show "Hart aber Fair", March 2, 2020) and guessworks about measures and economic impacts ("Erhöhte Ansteckungsgefahr: Gesundheit schützen, Jobs riskieren?" (Increased contagiousness: protecting health, risking jobs?), title of the talk show "maybrit illner", March 12, 2020). The second period (March 16-22, 2020) discussed mainly the consciousness of the pandemic ("Deutschland im Ausnahmezustand: Gewinnen wir den Kampf gegen Corona?" (Germany in emergency situation: Can we win the fight against corona?), title of the talk show "Anne Will", March 22, 2020). The scientists were asked which measure are recommended and about the state of knowledge about the novel coronavirus. In the third period (March 23-April 15, 2020) the pandemic was understood as a real threat. Measure decided and executed were evaluated ("Kampf gegen Corona: Genug Geld, genug Kraft, genug Zeit?" (Fight against corona: Enough money, enough power, enough time?) "maybrit illner", March 26, 2020) and the consequences for the economy were discussed ("Das Virus befällt die Wirtschaft: Wie viel bleibt von unserem Wohlstand?" (The virus infests the economy: how much wealth will be left for us?) "Hart aber fair", March 30, 2020). During the fourth period (April 16-29, 2020) plans of relaxation were discussed, since the number active cases continuously dropped at that time ("Vorsichtig aus der Krise : Wie hart trifft uns die Normalität?" (Carefully get out of the crisis: how hard will the normality affect us?), "Anne Will", April 19, 2020; "Freiheit in kleinen Schritten: Wie schädlich wird die Quarantäne?" (Freedom by little and little: how harmful is the quarantine?) "Hart aber fair, April 20, 2020). The fifth period (April 20-May 6, 2020) dealt mainly with the relaxation measures, especially whether the relaxation measures are suitable or too early decided ("Deutschland macht auf: Mutig oder riskant?" (Germany opens: courageous or risky?), "maybrit illner", April 23, 2020; "Infektionswelle: Lockert Deutschland Maßnahmen zu forsch?" (infection wave: Does Germany relax too early?) "Anne Will", April 26, 2020; "Raus aus dem Stillstand: Hat die Regierung den richtigen Plan? (Get out of standstill: Does the government have a good strategy?) "Anne Will", May 3, 2020). During the sixth period (after May 6, 2020), the talk shows dedicate their discussion mainly the uncertainties of the new normality, the protests against still existing measures like wearing masks, the prohibition of huge events and the economic crisis ("Pandemie und Protest – kann der Virus das Land spalten?" (Pandemic and protest – can a virus split a country?), "maybrit illner", May 14, 2020; "Milliarden gegen die Krise – wird das Geld richtig investiert?" (Billions against the crisis – is the money good invested?), "Anne Will", May 25, 2020; "Kinder und Eltern zuletzt - scheitern Schulen am Virus?" (Kids and parents last of all – do the schools fail because of the virus?), "Hart aber fair", May 25, 2020).

Conventionally, scientists appear in talk shows as enlighteners, evaluators, consultants and visionaries. They explain scientific facts, evaluate political and social measures, consult politicians as well as the society and give prognosis about future developments closely related with the knowledge and state-of the art of the present time. But during the pandemic crisis between March and May 2020, two new medial functions of scientists could be identified. The virologist appeared in this context mainly as *Life Performer* and *Spotters* of uncertain knowledge. They talked about ongoing studies and research projects in an early stage, often criticised by peers and the public and negotiated uncertain knowledge with the insisting hosts which defend and represent the impatient public. It could be found that public perception of scientists as Spotters of uncertain knowledge and Life Performers is unfamiliar for both, the media-based public and the scientific community. The negotiation of uncertainties and performance of scientific work in the public provided a new perspective of public communication of science, since the media-based and culture-based public has become part of the fight against SARS-CoV-2 as spectators and actors (Peschke, 2020).

Virologists versus Economists and Ethics?

At the first glance, during the COVID-19 crisis healthcare and economic interests clash. Lockdown or curfew measures are planned and executed to control the contagiousness of SARS-CoV-2 aiming to avoid an overload of intensive care beds etc. But the shutdown of companies generates pressure on companies which cannot compensate their workload with home office work. Many companies and private services suffer from the measures during the pandemic. At the same time, the society faces mental health problems and violence in families like depressions, suicides as well as abuses of children and women. Accordingly, the discussions of the experts during the first two periods were shaped by questions of priorities in the context of the infection rates. A fast increase of the infection rate leads to a high level of endemic infection in a short time. The advantage is that many people will have anti-bodies after a short period and a normal life could be possible. Supporters of this herd immunity strategy prefer this strategy but neglect the risk of an overload of the healthcare system. German virologists agreed that this strategy is very risky. Many people would die because of shortages in health care. Therefore, they recommended measures to flatten the curve of active cases. But a flattened curve enlarges the period of the pandemic which is fatal for the economy and the societal life. Accordingly, economists and ethical thinkers warned at the beginning of a complete and extensive lockdown, since freedom of people's activities is one of the personality rights which is guaranteed in the constitutions of the countries as fundamental rights. But under emergency situations because of public health and public interest these rights can also be limited (Güneş Peschke, 2014). Virologists like Schmidt-Chanasit stated during the second period that an extensive lockdown is not necessary at that moment but there should be measures such as the police preventing formation of groups in the public ("Markus Lanz", March 18, 2020). During the third period, the attitudes of virologists, economists and ethical thinkers converged. A lockdown was regarded as necessary, since they agreed that SARS-CoV-2 pandemic has strong impact on health, economy and social life in similar ways which cannot be negotiated in a separate and competing discourse. Rather, the discourses were proceeded in a collaborative way where the knowledge and activities of SARS-CoV-2 were understood as an emancipated knowledge producer in the natural environment of societies. The knowledge circulation around the systems academia, economy, media-based and culture-based public as well as politics were extended by a fifth entity of the SARS-CoV-2 as part of the natural environment of societies. The discourses after the third period were proceeded in the understanding that SARS-CoV-2 has its own dynamics which have to be included in all innovation processes and knowledge productions. This understanding is comparable with the extension of the Quadruple Helix model to a Quintuple Helix innovation model of Carayannis et al. (2012) which describes conditions for sustainable developments in the context of the five systems (1) education, (2)economy, (3) natural environments of societies, (4) media-based and (5) culture-based public and politics. The adaptation of this model as described by Peschke (2020) reveals that the combat of the COVID-19 pandemic needs the understanding of the fight against this crisis as a sustainable innovation process. Accordingly, the Helmholtz Center for Infection Research (HZI) and the ifo Institute – Leibniz Institute for Economic Research at the University of Munich (ifo) could show that the situation of measures on April 20 can be regarded as status quo with the lowest negative impact on economy and healthcare while stronger relaxations are not recommendable for both, the economy neither the healthcare (Dorn et al., 2020). The systems immunologist Meyer-Hermann scrutinized in the fourth period whether the goals of health care and economy are possibly the same ("Anne Will", April 19, 2020). He presented these results the study mentioned above during the sixth period ("Markus Lanz", May 20, 2020).

Example for live-performed scientific studies I: Heinsberg study by Streeck

Henrik Streeck is a professor in virology und the director of the Institute for Virology und HIV research at the Faculty of Medicine of Bonn University. Among the most frequently mentioned virologists in nationwide and regional press at that time range, Streeck ranks on 2nd place (Dambek and Tack, 2020). He participated three times the talk show "Markus Lanz", two times "maybrit illner" and once "Hart aber fair". As mentioned above, Streeck and the Minister President of North Rhine-Westphalia Laschet presented first results of the so-called Heinsberg study on April 9, 2020. He already has explained in the "maybrit illner" talk show on April 5 that he wanted to create scientific facts, since the public do not need opinions but need scientific facts to better understand certain measures ("maybrit illner", April 5, 2020). He hoped at that time to better understand the numbers of undetected COVID-19 cases in Germany with help of this study. The final results were published on May 4 (Streeck et al., 2020). They investigated the infection fatality rate (IFR) in Gangelt, a village of the district Heinsberg. IFR is the indicator of ratio of deaths in comparison to those infected. With help on the IFR and the number of deaths, the total number of infections in similar demographic areas like Gangelt. In comparison with the number of officially reported infections revealed that the number is five times higher than the number of people which were officially SARS-CoV-2 positive tested. Accordingly, a total of 1.8 million infections could be assumed which means that the unreported cases were approximately 10 times higher than the cases which were officially reported at that time (Streeck et al., 2020). Streeck mentioned once more the uncertainty that no expert knows which is the right way ("Hart aber fair", March 23, 2020).

The Heinsberg study itself but especially the way it was communicated to the public was discussed on Twitter in a very polarized way. The Heinsberg study was scientifically criticized mainly because of statistical deficiencies (i.a. Neher, 2020). But most of the criticisms were focused on the way how the study was communicated to the public. Drosten criticized in a press briefing that the summary of the data was not presented as a manuscript before firstly presented to the public and politics in April 2020 (Kreutzfeld, 2020). Alex M. Adams (@AlexMAdams2) complained

"Not peer reviewed, shady contacts to economy and politics, jumping to conclusions. #Germany you can do better" (Adams, 2020).

Guido Warlimont (@warligu) judged

""...a research team seeding misinformation..." Very outspoken comment by @c_drosten on @hendrikstreeck 's research and the #Heinsbergstudie [...]. A research communication disaster..." (Warlimont, 2020).

But also the newspapers and TV news covered the Heinsberg study in different ways. For instance, the newspaper "taz" tweeted and framed Drosten's criticism of Streeck's Heinsberg study as a dispute of researchers:

"Der eine hat tolle News aus der Forschung im besonders vom #Coronavirus betroffenen Kreis #Heinsberg. Der andere zerreißt diese Neuigkeiten in der Luft." (one [virologist] had great news of the research especially about the coronavirus in Heinsberg. The other shoot the news down in flames), (taz, 2020).

Woopen, medicine ethics and member of the board of experts of the Minister President of North Rhine-Westphalia was against the early publication of the first results. She stated that the public discourse of the experts is not a dispute between virologists. The data of Heinsberg study did not present any useful results at that time when it was presented in April. She complained about the intervention of politics in scientific processes. According to her, Laschet wanted to announce first results before the conference of the Minister Presidents with Chancellor Merkel on April 14, 2020. One of the reasons for Laschet's rush was the fight for the interpretational sovereignty, since Laschet and the Minister President of Bavaria Söder try to get into a good position in the upcoming run for the candidacy for the chancellorship as successor of Merkel in 2021. But the public became uncertain because of the peer criticism among scientists as a result of the political interventions in scientific processes ("Markus Lanz", April 14, 2020).

Example for live-performed scientific studies II: Charité study about the viral load in children by Dorsten.

Christian Drosten is a virology professor at Charité University Hospital Berlin. He is one of the discoverers of SARS-CoV. He became well-known in the public because of his NDR radio podcast "Coronavirus Update". According to Dambek and Tack (2020), he is the most frequently mentioned virologists at that time range. On 20 April, Drosten is acknowledged with the "Special Award for Outstanding Science Communication in the COVID-19 Pandemic" of the German Research Foundation (DFG) and the Stifterverband (Deutsche Forschungsgemeinschaft, 2020). He has participated the talk show "maybrit illner" three times. On April 29, Dorsten presented the first version of a study which showed the results of analysis of viral loads in patients of different age categories. It revealed that the viral load in very young people does not differ significantly from the viral load of adults. Based on the results of the study, Drosten warned not to reopen schools and kindergartens unlimited in the current situation, since it cannot be excluded that children are as infectious as adults (Jones et al., 2020). The presented study was modified and published as preprint version on June 3, 2020. Already on April 16, he stated in "maybrit illner" that we do not know how children get infected. Therefore, it is not clear what the impact of reopening of schools is. It is not clear whether kindergartens are super spreader like in the case of influenza. It is also not clear, why infections in household happens directly ("maybrit illner", April 16, 2020).

Dorsten's study presented the discussion of whether and how schools and kindergartens should reopen again. Similar to Streeck's Heinsberg study, the main criticism of the scientific community was targeted at the time of presentation which was regarded as too early. In both cases, the virologists were compelled by political pressure or needs. Within the scope of Dorsten's study about the viral load of children new aspects of peer criticism can be identified. Held (2020) concludes that "[t]he present study cannot be seen as conclusive. The original analysis by Jones et al. (2020) suffers from small sample sizes among children and adolescents. A reanalysis of summary data with a test for trend suggests that there is moderate, but not overwhelming evidence for increasing viral load with increasing age. A reanalysis of the original data on individual level could bring more insights into the relationship between viral load and age." Stoye (2020) states that the study is "carefully and competently executed, especially considering the extreme time pressure. [But] there are obvious limitations to quickfire reanalysis without raw data, and everything I have to say is accordingly tentative. [...] There are many good arguments against a quick reopening of schools, but the Charité study does not add to them."

These and some other scientific statements and feedbacks were collected by the German newspaper "Bild". The newspaper with the highest numbers of readers in Germany asked Drosten for a statement regarding four scientific quotes according to his study within one hour [sic!]. Dorsten commented this doubtful procedure of "Bild" with the tweet "I have better things to do" (Drosten, 2020). Tschermak (2020) and Lobo (2020) described very detailed the way how "Bild" frames scientific discourses as dispute and the adjustment of scientific opinions on newest scientific results as unprofessionalism. Beside "Bild", there were a plenty of German newspapers which covered the COVID-19 pandemic with serious contributions of science journalist and scientific guest authors.

As mentioned, scientific criticism and reviews of papers by peers is one of the daily businesses of researchers. Conventionally, these reviews and discourses are proceeded during conferences or in correspondences which are only accessible by the public. The shift of scientific discourses to the public is quite exceptional. Since the public interest of scientific opinions during the COVID-19 pandemic was very high, especially during the curfew and shutdown of services and business, certain scientific topics are negotiated publicly. Especially, peer criticism uttered through guest articles in newspapers caused conflicts. In the context of Dorsten's study about the viral load in children, the virologist Kekulé wrote an article in "Der Tagesspiegel" where he stated that a reanalysis of the gathered data cannot rescue Drosten's paper (Kekulé, 2002).

Kekulé's appearance in German talk shows during the pandemic differed from the appearance from other virologists because of his populistic statements. For instance, in the first medial period of the pandemic, he commented measures discussed by politicians and scientists:

"Es ist jetzt nichts wo man hysterisch werden muss, sondern die Maßnahmen, die wir ergreifen, müssen mit Augenmaß sein und müssen vernünftig klingen. Wenn natürlich die Regierung immer wieder sagt, hustet euch in die Ellenbeuge, wascht euch die Hände und gebt euch keine Hand mehr, [...] ehrlich gesagt das erinnert mich [an] diese Filme, wo man früher [...] darauf hingewiesen [hat], [...] wenn ein Atomkrieg ausbricht, soll man unter den Tisch kriechen und Aktentasche über den Kopf halten. [...] Es ist ein bisschen hilfloser Versuch" (It is nothing why we should become hysteric, but our measures should be planned carfully and should sound convincing. But when the Government repeat again and again, you should cough in the crook of your arms, wash your hands and don't shake hands [...] honestly, it reminds me on films of the past with instructions that in case of an atom bomb attack, you should creep under the table and put your brief case on your head. A it is a bit a helpless attent" ("Markus Lanz", March 11,2020).

He qualified his statement some minutes later but not before receiving the kudos of the audience.

Kekulé's public criticism started a harsh discussion on twitter where Dorsten intervened regularly.

He stated

"Kekulé macht Stimmung. Seine Darstellung ist tendenziös. Er kennt unsere Daten nicht und zitiert falsch. Kekulé selbst könnte man nicht kritisieren, dazu müsste er erstmal etwas publizieren." (Kekulé proceeds cheap propaganda. His statements are baised. He does not know our data and cites wring. It is not possible to criticize Kekulé, because he does not publish anything.) (Drosten, 2020).

He replied a criticism of Benjamin Werthmann (Werthmann, 2020) ("Wenn jetzt die Wissenschaftler öffentlich aufeinander einprügeln, gewinnt am Ende die Bild." – If scientists swing at each other publicly, finally "Bild" will win.) as followed:

"So sieht es aus. Kekulé ist zum Glück bisher der Einzige, der sich so verhält. In unserer Community spielt er keine Rolle." (Indeed. Luckily, Kekulé is the only one at the moment, who act like this. Now, he is immaterial in our community.) (Drosten, 2020).

Kekulé tried to objectify the dispute with interviews in German radio channels (Deutschlandfunk, 2020). But the social media network reacted mainly with partially hash comments supporting Drosten's attitudes.

Discussion

The majority of German citizens were satisfied about the measures recommended by scientists and decided by the politician. Approximately half of the citizens regard the measures as efficient. But Germany experiences a third wave of polarization, after the debates of refugee and climate politics. Around 20% of the German society evaluated the measures as too strict. Many of protesters on the street protest in different context, often with populistic backgrounds. The pattern of protesters is unclear, but the tenor of the protest is that mask obligations, curfews and prohibition of huge events were overblown claiming that there was no emergency situation at any time. To counter this prevention paradox clear and reliable scientific statements are required. A survey executed in Germany and nine other countries on March 6-10 revealed that 74% were worried that there are a lot of fake news and false information being spread about the virus. 45% stated, it has been difficult for them to find reliable and trustworthy information about the virus and its effects, and 85% of the respondents said, they need to hear more from scientists and less from politicians (Edelman Trust Barometer, 2020). Additionally, the use of a mobile engagement platform can have a significant impact on health outcomes (Cingi et al., 2015). As mentioned above, Peschke (2020) identified two new medial functions of scientists during the COVID-19 crisis, Spotter of uncertain knowledge and Live-Performer. As Spotter of uncertain knowledge virologists, economists and ethical thinkers acted mostly in a very commendable way. With help of talk show appearances, podcasts and social media contributions, they informed the public about SARS-CoV-2, COVID-19 and the economic and societal consequences. The exceptional situation was the high degree of uncertainty of knowledge. The novel coronavirus was discovered in December 2019. Two and a half months later, Robert Koch Institute evaluated the health threat risk for COVID-19 in Germany as "high". Measures had to be recommended and executed in a situation of high uncertainties regarding the knowledge about SARS-CoV-2. The success of science communication had its origin in the precise information of the scientists about what they know and what they do not know. The clear communication of uncertain knowledge combined with the public revision or adjustment of knowledge which they understood retrospectively as wrong or incomplete in the context of new scientific results created trust among the majority of the public. But as Live-Performer, most of the leading virologists revealed weak points influenced by coverage of traditional media and in the context of the Quintuple Helix collaboration. It can be demonstrated with the examples of Streeck's Heinsberg study and Drosten's Charité study, detailed described above. Medical scientific results which are regarded as very important for the community are conventionally uploaded on a preprint server before the peer review process of the papers. The data base of both studies was confirmed as reliable by the scientific community, but the preprint version of the papers had weaknesses according to the peer feedback. These are very typical situations during scientific research processes, so far. The special situation of knowledge production within the scope of both studies was the live performance in the public. Due to the COVID-19 pandemic with the high societal impact, all scientific activities were observed by the media-based public very carefully. While in contexts other than pandemic crisis scientific papers are almost noticed and appreciated by scientific peers, all kind of scientific results were negotiated by the media-based public, an unusual situation for scientists. As a consequence, scientific criticism, for instance Dorsten's critisicm of the Heinsberg study and Kekulé's criticism of the Charité study became a live event, covered by many newspapers and the social media community with different interests other than describing the scientific procedure. The criticism itself and the involved performers became the main actors of the live event.

Besides, media coverage which describe uncertainties in the knowledge production and the negotiation of scientific results among peers as unprofessionalism, contributes to a decrease of public trust in science. Instead, it connotes a lack of scientific credibility, provokes the drift of citizens towards medial parallel universes with conspiracy theories and fake news and stabilize the prevention paradox.

Conclusion

The central aspect of this paper is the impact of science communication on the prevention paradox in Germany. Comparing with other countries all over the world, the first wave of COVID-19 crisis in Germany did not create an emergency state, as assumed by scientists. One of the reasons was the early start of diagnostics in Germany and the execution of consequent measures combined with a high discipline of the citizens. But the absence of an overload of the healthcare system and the economic problems because of the three months lasting lockdown measures led to a prevention paradox. Instead of the public's satisfaction because of Germany's better situation than countries like the U.S., Brazil and Iran, the protest of citizens against the still existing measures increased. This paper analysed the communication activities of virologists, economists and ethical thinkers in the context of the pandemic crisis and their impact on the prevention paradox. It could be shown that the medial function "Spotter of uncertain knowledge" countered the prevention paradox. The clear communication of limited knowledge and dynamic knowledge about SARS-CoV-2 and COVID-19 supported the public understanding of the pandemic and increased the trust in scientific knowledge. The demand of the majority on more scientific information rather than political debates were fulfilled in a transparent way. But the cases of Heinsberg study and Charité study revealed that the live performing scientists within the scope of scientific research contain the risk of misinterpretation of the public. Reliable scientific processes were often misused by certain newspapers and social media to draw an image about unprofessional scientists where personal conflicts were foregrounded. This paper was focused on selected aspects about the impact of communication activities on media coverage and social media feedback as indicator for satisfaction and dissatisfaction of the society during the pandemic crisis. It should encourage further research about science communication research in the context of protest movements.

References

Abele-Brehm, A., Dreier, H., Fuest, C., Grimm, V., Kräusslich, H.-G., Krause, G., Leonhard, M., Lohse, A. W., Lohse, M. J., Mansky, T., Peichl, A., Schmid, R. M., Wess, G., and Woopen, C. (2020). *Die Bekämpfung der Coronavirus-Pandemie tragfähig gestalten. Empfehlungen für eine flexible, risikoadaptierte Strategie.* ([To organize the combat of corona pandemic in a sustainable way. Recommendation of a flexible, risk adapted strategy]. Munich: ifo Institute – Leibniz Institute for Economic Research at the University of Munich. Retrieved from https://www.ifo.de/en/publikationen/2020/monograph-authorship/die-bekampfung-der-coronavirus-pandemie-tragfahig-gestalten. (Last access on 22 June 2020).

Adams, A. M. (@AlexMAdams2, 2020, May 4) I have never before seen such a catastrophic handling of preliminary scientific data like with the #Heinsbergstudie. Not peer reviewed, shady contacts to economy and politics, jumping to conclusions. #Germany you can do better. [Tweet]. Retrieved https://twitter.com/AlexMAdams2/status/1257293892434776065 (Last access 26 July 2020).

Becerir, M. C., and Peschke, L. (2019). How Science Communication Delivers Meaningful Frameworks About Industry 4.0 to the Public Sphere. In N. M. Durukbaşa, & M. G. Gençyılmaz (Eds.) *Proceedings of the International Symposium for Production Research 2019,* p. 292. Cham: Springer Nature Switzerland

Böhmer, M. M., Buchholz, U., and Corman, V. M. (2020). Investigation of a COVID-19 outbreak in Germany resulting from a single travel-associated primary case: a case series. *Lancet Infect Dis 2020.* URL: https://doi.org/10.1016/S1473-3099(20)30314-5.

Carayannis, E. G., Barth, T. D. and Campbell, D. F. J. (2012). The Quintuple Helix innovation model: global warming as a challenge and driver for innovation. *Journal of Innovation and Entrepreneurship 1*(2). http://www.innovation-entrepreneurship.com/content/1/1/2.

Castells, M. (2004). Informationalism, networks, and the network society: A threoretical blueprint. In M Castells (Ed.): *The Network Society. A cross-cultural perspective* (pp. 3-45). Cheltenham: Edward Elgar.

Cingi C., Yorgancioglu A, Cingi C. C., Oguzulgen, M. D., Muluk, N. B., Ulusoy, S., Orhon, N., Yumru, C., Gokdağ, D., Karakaya, G., Çelebi, Ş., Çobanoğlu, H. B., Unlu, H. and Aksoy, M. A. (2015). 'The "physician on call patient engagement trial" (POPET):measuring the impact of amobile patient engagement application on health outcomes and quality of life in allergic rhinitis and asthma patients'. *Int Forum Allergy Rhinol.* 5:487–497.

Cingi C. C., Eroglu E. (2019). 'Compassion Fatigue in Health Care Personnel' *Osmangazi Journal of Medicine* *41*(1): 58 -71. Doi:10.20515/otd.449810

Dambek, H., and Tack, A. (2020). 'Medienpräsenz von Virologen. Drosten ist die Nummer eins - aber nicht überall'.[Media presents of virologists. Drosten is number one – but not everywhere]. Retrieved from https://www.spiegel.de/gesundheit/corona-virus-christian-drosten-ist-nummer-eins-bei-medienpraesenz-von-virologen-a-e3d97148-06db-4b9d-bb5d-511543f7cf43 (Last access on 12 July 2020).

Deutschlandfunk. (2020, May 29). Virologe Kekulé zu Drosten-Studie. "Auf der Auswertungsseite sind ein paar Fragezeichen dran". Talk of Alexander Kekulé with Christoph Heinemann. Retrieved from https://www.deutschlandfunk.de/virologe-kekule-zu-drosten-studie-auf-der-auswertungsseite.694.de.html?dram:article_id=477623.

Deutsche Forschungsgemeinschaft. (2020). Special one-time prize for exceptional communication during the Covid-19 pandemic. https://www.dfg.de/en/funded_projects/prizewinners/special_prize_covid19/index.html (Last access on 22 June 2020).

Dorn, F., Khailaie, S., Stöckli, M., Binder, S., Lange, B., Peichl, A., Vanella, P., Wollmershäuser, T., Fuest, C., and Meyer-Hermann, M. (2020). Das gemeinsame Interesse von Gesundheit und Wirtschaft: Eine Szenarienrechnung zur Eindämmung der Corona- Pandemie [The common interst of heathcare and economy: A scenarios calculation to control the corona pandemic]. *ifo Schnelldienst Digital* *1*(6). Retrieved from https://www.ifo.de/en/publikationen/2020/article-journal/das-gemeinsame-interesse-von-gesundheit-und-wirtschaft (Last access on 12 July 2020).

Drosten, C. (2020, May 28). Kekulé macht Stimmung. Seine Darstellung ist tendenziös. Er kennt unsere Daten nicht und zitiert falsch. Kekulé selbst könnte man nicht kritisieren, dazu müsste er erstmal etwas publizieren. https://twitter.com/c_drosten/status/1265858395564847104 (Last access 26 July 2020).

Drosten, C. (2020, May 28). So sieht es aus. Kekulé ist zum Glück bisher der Einzige, der sich so verhält. In unserer Community spielt er keine Rolle. Retrieved from https://twitter.com/c_drosten/status/1265863344042455040 (Last access 26 July 2020).

Drosten, C. (2020, May 25). Interessant: die #Bild plant eine tendenziöse Berichterstattung über unsere Vorpublikation zu Viruslasten und bemüht dabei Zitatfetzen von Wissenschaftlern ohne Zusammenhang. Ich soll innerhalb von einer Stunde Stellung nehmen. Ich habe Besseres zu tun. [Tweet]. https://twitter.com/c_drosten/status/1264934434756755456 (Last access 26 July 2020).

Edelman Trust Barometer. (2020). Special Report: Trust and the Coronavirus. Retrieved from https://www.edelman.com/sites/g/files/aatuss191/files/2020-03/2020%20Edelman%20Trust%20Barometer%20Coronavirus%20Special%20Report_0.pdf (Last access 26 July 2020).

Felbermayr, G., Hinz, J., and Chowdhry, S. (2020). Après-ski: The Spread of Coronavirus from Ischgl through Germany'. Covid Economics Vetted and Real-Time PapersIssue 22. Retrieved from https://cepr.org/sites/default/files/news/CovidEconomics22.pdf. (Last access on 14 June 2020).

Folkvord, F., Peschke, L., Baş, G., Vitiello, S, and Spunda, N. (2019). Peer Learning Methodology for Sustainable Energy Usage. In NM Durukbaşa, & MG Gençyılmaz (Eds.) *Proceedings of the International Symposium for Production Research 2019,* p. 64. Cham: Springer Nature Switzerland.

Güneş Peschke, S. (2014). *The Protection of Personality Rights (Roma Hukukundan Günümüze Kişilik Haklarının Korunması).* Yetkin, Ankara.

Held, L. (2020). A discussion and reanalysis of the results reported in Jones et al. (2020). Retrieved from https://osf.io/bkuar/ (Last access 26 July 2020).

Jones, T. C., Mühlemann, B., Veith, T., Biele, G., Zuchowski, M., Hoffmann, J., Stein, A., Edelmann, A., Corman, V. M., and Drosten, C. (2020). An analysis of SARS-CoV-2 viral load by patient age. Preprint-Server medrxiv.org. Retrieved from https://www.medrxiv.org/content/10.1101/2020.06.08.20125484v1 (Last access on 22 June 2020).

Karnitschnig, M. (2020). The Austrian ski town that spread coronavirus across the Continent. *Politico.* Retrieved from https://www.politico.eu/article/the-austrian-ski-town-that-spread-coronavirus-across-the-continent. (Last access on 13 June 2020).

Kekulé, A. (2020, May 28). Drosten-Studie zur Ansteckung von Kindern. "Die Statistik neu zu berechnen, kann die aktuelle Arbeit nicht retten". Der Tagesspiegel. https://www.tagesspiegel.de/wissen/drosten-studie-zur-ansteckung-von-kindern-die-statistik-neu-zu-berechnen-kann-die-aktuelle-arbeit-nicht-retten/25866488.html (Last access 26 July 2020).

Kekulé, A. (2020, May 29). Hier noch ein Versuch einer Versachlichung der Debatte über die #Covid-19 Studie von @C_Drosten. Es geht schließlich um den wissenschaftlichen Inhalt und nicht darum, wer Recht behält. Retrieved from https://twitter.com/AlexanderKekule/status/1266343307560583168 (Last access 26 July 2020).

Klein, O. (2020). Debatte über Reproduktionszahl - Warum der Corona-Lockdown nicht sinnlos war. [Debate about the reproduction number – why the corona lockdown was not meaningless]. Retrieved from https://www.zdf.de/nachrichten/politik/coronavirus-reproduktionszahl-diskussion-100.html. (Last access on 20 June 2020).

Kreutzfeld, M. (@MKreutzfeld, April 10, 2020). Hier nochmal das entscheidende @c_drosten-Zitat aus dem Pressegespräch: "Es ist ja normalerweise eben auch so, dass wissenschaftliche Daten erstmal zumindest in Form von einem wissenschaftlichen Manuskript geschrieben werden. [1/2] [Tweet]. Retrieved from https://twitter.com/MKreutzfeldt/status/1248600553166376961 (Last access 26 July 2020).

Leopoldina. (2020a). Coronavirus Pandemic in Germany: Challenges and Options for Intervention'. 1st Ad-hoc-Statement, 21 March 2020. Retrieved from https://www.leopoldina.org/uploads/tx_leopublication/2020_03_24_Leopoldina_ad_hoc_statement_coronavirus_en_final_02.pdf (Last access on 22 June 2020).

Leopoldina. (2020b). 2nd Ad-hoc-Statement: Coronavirus Pandemic–Measures Relevant to Health. https://www.leopoldina.org/uploads/tx_leopublication/2020_04_08_2ad_hoc_statement_coronavirus_en_final_01.pdf (Last access on 22 June 2020).

Leopoldina. (2020c). 'Coronavirus Pandemic –Sustainable Ways to Overcome the Crisis'. 3rd Ad-hoc-Statement, 13 April 2020. Retrieved from https://www.leopoldina.org/uploads/tx_leopublication/2020_04_13_Leopoldina_Coronavirus_statement_3_en.pdf (Last access on 22 June 2020).

Leopoldina. (2020d). Coronavirus Pandemic: Medical Care and Patient-Oriented Research in an Adaptive Healthcare System. 4th Ad-hoc-Statement, 27 May 2020. Retrieved from https://www.leopoldina.org/uploads/tx_leopublication/2020_4ad_hoc_statement_covid-19_en.pdf (Last access on 22 June 2020).

Lobo, S. (2020, May 27). "Bild"-Chef Reichelt gegen Virologe Drosten Bloß nicht vernünftig. Retrieved from https://www.spiegel.de/netzwelt/bild-zeitung-gegen-christian-drosten-bloss-nicht-vernuenftig-a-1d69020c-870d-435b-a348-5ee447a975f4 (Last access 26 July 2020).

Neher, R. (@richardneher2020, May 4). The preprint on #SARSCoV2 seropositivity in Gangelt, Germany was released. Despite its title, it provides limited information on the infection fatality rate, but it might give some useful bounds on seropositivity (around 15%). [Tweet]. Retrieved from https://twitter.com/richardneher/status/1257288261288054787 (Last access 26 July 2020).

PEPP-PT. (2020). Pan-European Privacy-Preserving Proximity Tracing. https://www.pepp-pt.org/ (Last access on 22 June 2020).

Peschke, L. (2019): *Infografiken. Visualität und Wissensaneignung in der mediatisierten Welt*, p.44. Wiesbaden: Springer VS.

Peschke, L. (2020). Let's talk about science. The appearance of scientists in talk shows during the COVID-10 pandemic in Germany and Turkey. (submitted).

Robert Koch Institute. (2020). Informationen zum Aussetzen der Ausweisung der internationalen Risikogebiete / besonders betroffenen Gebiete in Deutschland. Retrieved from https://www.rki.de/DE/Content/InfAZ/N/Neuartiges_Coronavirus/Risikogebiete.html. (Last access on 30 March 2020).

Robert Koch Institute. (2020). Erfassung der SARS-CoV-2-Testzahlen in Deutschland. (Acquisition of SARS.CoV-2 test numbers in Germany). *Epidemiologisches Bulletin 25*.

Rose, G. (1981). Strategy of prevention: lessons from cardiovascular disease. *British Medical Journal, 282*, 1847-51.

Stoye, J. (2020). A Critical Assessmentof Some Recent Work on COVID-19. Retrieved from https://arxiv.org/pdf/2005.10237.pdf (Last access 26 July 2020).

Streeck, H., Schulte, B., Kümmerer, B.M., Richter, E., Höller, T., Fuhrmann, C., Bartok, E., Dolscheid, R., Berger, M., Wessendorf, L., Eschbach-Bludau, M., Kellings, A., Schwaiger, A., Coenen, M., Hoffmann, P., Stoffel-Wagner, B., Nöthen, M. M., Eis-Hübinger, A.-M., Exner, M., Schmithausen, R. M., Schmid, M., and Hartmann, G. (2020). Infection fatality rate of SARS-CoV-2 infection in a German community with a super-spreading event. Preprint-Server medrxiv.org. Retrieved from https://www.medrxiv.org/content/10.1101/2020.05.04.20090076v2 (Last access on 22 June 2020).

taz. (@tazgezwitscher, April 9, 2020). Der eine hat tolle News aus der Forschung im besonders vom #Coronavirus betroffenen Kreis #Heinsberg. Der andere zerreißt diese Neuigkeiten in der Luft. #COVID — 19. Retrieved from https://twitter.com/tazgezwitscher/status/1248326084460007424 (Last access 26 July 2020).

The Guardian.com (2020). Bergamo mayor says football match escalated infections in Italian province. Retrieved from https://www.theguardian.com/world/2020/mar/24/bergamo-mayor-says-football-match-escalated-coronavirus-infections-italian-province. (Last access on 13. June 2020).

Tschermak, M. (2020, May 5). Wie die „Bild"-Redaktion mit schmutzigen Tricks versucht, Christian Drosten zu zerlegen. Retrieved from https://bildblog.de/121365/wie-die-bild-redaktion-mit-schmutzigen-tricks-versucht-christian-drosten-zu-zerlegen/ (Last access 26 July 2020).

Turkish Ministry of Health (2020). Türkiye'deki Güncel Durum (Current Situation in Turkey) Retrieved from https://covid19.saglik.gov.tr/ (Last access on 20 June 2020).

Warlimont, G. (@warligu, 2020, May 5) „...a research team seeding misinformation..." Very outspoken comment by @c_drosten on @hendrikstreeck 's research and the #Heinsbergstudie @glob_solutions panel discussion (min. 10). A research communication disaster... [Tweet]. Retrieved from https://twitter.com/warligu/status/1257693117245001728 (Last access 26 July 2020).

Werthmann, B. (2020, May 28). Wenn jetzt die Wissenschaftler öffentlich aufeinander einprügeln, gewinnt am Ende die Bild. Retrieved from https://twitter.com/benwerthmann81/status/1265859432682000384 (Last access 26 July 2020).

Wiestler, O. D., Marquardt, D., Heinz, D., and Meyer-Hermann, M. (2020). 'Systemic epidemiological analysis of the COVID-19 epidemic'. Opinion of the Helmholtz Initiative. Retrieved from https://www.helmholtz.de/en/current-topics/coronavirus/statement-of-the-helmholtz-initiative-systemic-epidemiological-analysis-of-the-covid-19-epidemic/ (Last access on 22 June 2020).

Wikipedia. (2020). COVID-19 pandemic in Germany. Retrieved from https://en.wikipedia.org/wiki/COVID-19_pandemic_in_Germany#6%E2%80%9312_April (Last access on 20 June 2020).

Worldometers.info. Retrieved from https://www.worldometers.info/coronavirus/ (Last access on 14 June 2020).

CHAPTER 6

Hybrid-Covid Process Management: The New Economy and Sustainable Network Organization Approach - A New Model Design

Murat Adil Salepçioğlu[1], Turgay Ceyhan[2]
{muratsalepcioglu@aydin.edu.tr ; turgayceyhann@gmail.com}

[1] Assist. Prof., Istanbul Aydin University, Faculty of Economics and Administrative Sciences, Department of Business Administration, Istanbul/Turkey

[2] Assist. Prof., Burdur Mehmet Akif Ersoy University, Bucak Faculty of Business, Department of Economics and Finance, Burdur/Turkey

Abstract

From the traditional management-organization theories to the modern management-organization theories and from these theories to the port-modern management-organization approaches, the changes in the management processes in general lead to a transformation in the organization models in line with the economic trends it is. Changes in these management processes and organizational models arise from the need for businesses to adapt to economic developments faster, more dynamically and more effectively. In order to ensure their sustainability against possible risks, organizations trying to adapt to these conditions in the face of changing conditions are trying to implement new strategies by choosing a variety of methods and at the same time applying mixed models against these factors.

It brings together organizational models suitable for digitalization, which emerged with the concept of New Economy, which is also referred to as digital economy or information economy as of the 21st century, and which is the most important trend of the new economy, in order to develop more dynamic business models in line with the requirements of this new economy. . Especially with Covid-19, the increasing power of digitalization in the pandemic period has increased even in everyday life and the management-organization structures of the enterprises have entered a rapid transformation process in order to adapt to this and ensure their sustainability. As a result of both the new economy and the pandemic process, it can be envisaged that the years 2020-2035 will be a phase in which hybrid organizational models will be developed, with a kind of mixed or more used expression, and then more permanent new types of management approaches and organizational models will emerge.

In this study, an analysis and approach of how hybrid structures envisaged in the near and medium term can be presented. A sustainable network-type organization approach and a new model design were evaluated by reviewing the traditional, current and post-modern approaches, examining the effects of the new economy on management processes and organizational models.

Keywords: Digital & New Economy, Matrix & Network Organizations, Virtual Companies, Hybrid Organization, Covid-19.

Introduction

Contemporary and current Post-Modern practices refer to managerial and organizational practices that further develop hybrid opinions and concepts created by blending particularly Modern Management-Organization Theories with Traditional or Pro-Modern Management Organization Theories and turn them into more in-depth practices.

In other words, Post-Modern opinions arise from the new developments and practices in the structural analyses and job designs set forth in Management and Organization Theories. This change and transformation occur due to both business processes and organization structures.

Post-Modern approaches that are basically taken into consideration with the "Environmental Adaptation Approach" of organizations and in connection with their capabilities for change and the effects of their realized changes, are set forth either regarding the activities of enterprises or as based on the relations of enterprises with their employees.

Our study aims to particularly to shed light on new organization models that can emerge in a more medium-term projection of the future, by attempting to examine how, in the context of the transformative impact of the process that emerged with Covid-19, organizations could head towards a hybrid organization in the near future in accordance with their capacity for adaptation therewith.

The most important factor here is to study the developments by examining certain organization models set forth as post-modern, by examining certain post-modern managerial practices in order to analyze what kinds of results can be given in practice by the new approaches that could arise from economic change and from their impacts on organizational change.

An analysis will later be conducted based particularly on the concepts of "old economy-new economy" mentioned in the literature, about the direction that post-modern management and organization approaches will evolve. Based on the claim that each economic development creates a system suitable for itself, the opinion will be asserted that the "New Economy" will replace the concept of "industrialization" based on mass production with "virtualization" based on technology.

It is observed that the process of digitalization, together with globalization and increasing competition as well as technology, is starting to create an organizational structure that us fully independent of traditional management-organization processes particularly in governance.

Enterprises are now shifting from resource optimization more towards organization optimization. And this is a fundamental opinion that emerges with the "Population Ecology" approach. Therefore, it is based on the hypothesis that the environmental conditions of enterprises at the time of their incorporation impact the organization population for the rest of their lifecycle (Koçel, 2014: 427) And this can be interpreted as, that particularly this period which emerged with the Covid pandemic will impact the organizational structures of the present-day enterprises in the future as well. It should be admitted that changes such as online working, remote access and the new working conditions referred to as the new normal that emerged with the pandemic, deeply impacted organization structures.

This process will obviously not remain limited with the pandemic. New conditions exist from the new normal to the new global. At this point, it can be foreseen that based on the assumption that the adaptation and population processes in organizations will also impact post-modern approaches, the change that emerges in these structures will further evolve towards hybrid organizations, which refer to the joint use of multiple organization structures or the organization of operation functions in a different direction or structure (Berberoğlu, 2004: 104). And this allows us to consider a new organization model that is affected by the process of economic change, with a more dynamic management structure.

In order to consider such a new model, we need to analyze the paradigms of the new economy in addition to examining the important parameters. In fact, we can pose the following question: Will today's dominant trend from management complication to organizational simplicity, be able to transform into a management strategy where network organizations will be more dominant in the context of sustainability in the near future?

It could be said that as much as the transformative impact of information technologies on organizations, this digital transformation also accelerated developments such as business strategies, quality-oriented human management, efficiency increase, economic sustainability and not only vertical but also horizontal simplification. The new economy or the digital economy can also be referred to as the deepening of globalization. However, it could also be said that the corona pandemic gave a large impetus to these rapid developments.

Changes in the field of Management and Organization depend on socio-economic changes and changes in the economy in general, in other words, they depend on the effects of the variables in the environment in which the organizations exist. The most fundamental basis of these factors is the transformative power of enterprise structures for adapting to economic developments. The fact that the new global economy is built on knowledge-based economy makes it important to transform knowledge into an organization that requires it to be available as quick as possible. As much as adapting to economic fluctuations caused by sudden unexpected developments such as the pandemics, organizations must have innovative management processes and knowledge-based organizations in order to be sustainable, in other words, to not be eliminated by natural selection in a sense. Then, the manner of how these knowledge-based organizations should be becomes important.

Outlook on Post-Modern Management Organization Approaches

Post-Modern Management and Organization Approaches include Post-Modern contemporary and current approaches focused on operation activities directly concerning all the enterprises, such as Total Quality Management, Lean Management, Matrix Organization, Personnel Empowerment, Network Organization, Corporate Governance, Strategic Cooperation, the New Economy, Virtual Organization, Innovative Organization or Hybrid Organization Structures, and the literature also includes contemporary and current approaches that focus on the relation between the organization and the employees of that organization, such as Organizational Citizenship, Organizational Loyalty, Organizational Vigor, Organizational Deviation, Organizational Alienation, Organizational Cynicism or Organizational Climate.

As we asserted, based on the fact that both the New Economy and Network Organizations had an impact on the emergence of Hybrid Management Processes during the Covid process, we should foresee that it would be more useful to consider certain issues that constitute the basis of such approaches.

In this respect, in addition to having to take into consideration Matrix, Network and Virtual Organizations that we can define as Non-Traditionalizing Management Organization Models, we will first need to analyze the efficiency-based Total Quality Management approach, the Personnel Empowerment approach that we may consider as a catalyst for empowering project-team works and particularly the New Economy approach that we will consider as an environmental factor for organizations.

Post-Traditional Management and Organization Approaches

We can say that we use the expression Post-Traditional Management and Organization Approaches instead of Post-Modern Management and Organization Approaches other than those contributed to the literature by Traditional and Modern Management and Organization Theories. In this context, if we use the definition of Tradition for Classical and Neo-Classical Management and Organization Theories, we can depict Traditional and Modern Management and Organization Theories together as Traditionalizing Theories.

The contributions of Classical Management and Organization Theories can be described as hierarchical, functional and bureaucratic managerial processes and organization types. The most significant factor contributed to these theories by the neo-classical theories can be stated as Human Resources. It can be said that Modern Management and Organization Theories cover new opinions that contain the Strategic Management approach in the context of Systems and Contingency. What is described with the Non-Traditionalizing Management and Organization Models is expressed as models for certain practices that deepen the Classical, Neo-Classical and Modern Management and Organization Theories, containing new and contemporary concepts and practices and included in the Post-Modern Management and Organization Approaches in the literature

Organization Models are not hierarchical, functional and bureaucratic although included among Post-Modern Management and Organization practices and approaches, that are based on strategic human management rather than human resources and that also overlap with the "Environmental Adaptation" and "Population Ecology" Approaches more, can be examined as Non-Traditionalizing or Post-Traditional Models.

Matrix, Network and Virtual Organizations are the leading ones among these models. However, as we mentioned above, Total Quality management had an impact of strengthening both "Personnel Empowerment" and "Matrix Organizations".

However, there is a growing importance of the most important impact of socio-economic transformation, which emerges in the context of the changes and developments expressed with the concept of the "New Economy" as an "Environmental Factor". It can be claimed that enterprise organizations will start to transform more into the form of "Hybrid Organizations" with the impact on business life of the global change and digitalization, which is perceived to have deepened particularly with Covid-19 (the Corona Pandemic). As mentioned above, we can assert that such hybrid organizations should be knowledge-based, in order words, be network organizations in order to transmit information in the fastest manner.

We can the necessary clues by examining the mentioned concepts, approaches and practices more closely in order to express an opinion on whether that is the case. For this, we can elaborate on "Total Quality Management, Personnel Empowerment and Strategic Partnerships". The mentioned approaches will be examined below with the assumption that they have a significance that impacts the post-modern management and organization concepts, practices and approaches set forth after them.

The Concept of Total Quality Management

As expressed above, the Concept of Total Quality Management and the emergence of TQM as a Management Approach can be considered as a technique that results in significant changes in practices and that can renew itself.

It could be said that, putting forth an understanding based more on horizontal organization rather than vertical organization in decision-making processes particularly from a managerial perspective, Total Quality Management is based on the approach of empowerment in practice and had the impact of developing a structure that reduces levels in hierarchy by relatively eliminating the distinction of "decision-maker - performer".

In this respect, the significance of TQM should be assessed in terms of it leaving a lasting impact directly on the business processes of the enterprise among Post-Modern Management and Organization Approaches. This is because, on one hand, it strengthened the "personnel empowerment" approach through delegation in business processes, and on the other hand, it strengthened teamwork, in other words "project organizations" in business modes through quality chambers in particular. The next stage of project organizations is "Matrix Organizations" in the literature.

According to Edward Deming's quality approach, Post-Modern Management can be achieved not with strict quality control methods in goods or services but through improvement and continuous development of production and service processes. Quality will thus become part of the product. This approach laid the foundations of Total Quality management. The Deming Cycle (the PDCA Cycle: Plan, Do, Control, Act) includes the four known basic activities.

In the broadest sense, Total Quality Management can be defined as a philosophy of management that foresees the fulfillment of predetermined customer requirements and expectations through continuous improvement of business processes. This style of management can also be defined as a process directed by the customer in providing service to internal and external customers through a philosophy, management and instruments focused on quality.

Total Quality Management primarily requires implementing continuous development principles to increase efficiency, profitability and quality. The thought that "Consumers are buying our product as it is anyway. Why produce a better one?" is incorrect. Not falling behind in the competition for quality, efficiency and cost is very important in global competition. The conditions of competition in the business world get more difficult as consumers' expectation increase for high quality and low cost.

The purpose of any produced product or provided service should be to ensure higher customer satisfaction. The mindset that supports the concept of continuous development is established accordingly. Employees that manage to have a holistic view of business processes and have a better understanding of their profession obtain more successful results. Employees with different education and experience also have different performances. Corporate quality culture and teamwork contribute to employees working with a common faith and achieving common goals.

Career management, performance evaluation and promotion systems in companies should motivate employees. Lack of motivation has a negative impact on the efficiency of employees and on their contributions. A successful teamwork is not possible under such conditions. It is also very important to encourage R&D and innovation works.

The competitiveness and quality of a product is determined in the production process of that product. In other words, a product should be ensured to have high quality while it is produced. If one employee produces and another employee checks the produced products and separates the flawed ones, it is not possible to achieve quality and efficiency through such method. In such cases, there should be as many checking employees as there are producing employees. This reduces efficiency and increases cost.

Lack of professional training and knowledge, the sense of being content with what is at hand, lack of prevalence of the consciousness of continuous development and failure to pay attention to search for the better are significant problems among employees. Raising quality consciousness among consumers is very important. The expectations of consumers play a significant part in raising the level of quality.

This approach based on continuous improvement, quality based on increase in efficiency and participation of employees at every level in order to fully and timely respond to customer expectations in line with process management, emerged as an important philosophy that also impacted later approaches. Today, Total Quality management, which is an effective practice with the excellence approach, has transformed in to a management model used by organizations as an indispensable infrastructure in a way.

The Concept of Personnel Empowerment

Total Quality Management can be considered more as a management factor focused on emphasizing employee participation. This post-modern approach, which can be expressed as Personnel empowerment or Employee empowerment, is based on an approach that allows employees (workers) to use initiative under knowledge, capability and defined responsibilities and participate in decision-making processes.

In order to fully implement personnel empowerment, in addition to being included in the decision-making process, it is also important to have a strong bond between employees' own objectives and the strategic objectives of the organization. And this constitutes the basis of another approach that increases enterprise performance. This is the approach known as Balanced Scorecard, which is a performance indicator that increases the power of organizations against global competition. The resulting performance scorecard of the enterprise will also be an input for implementing new strategies. The Personnel Empowerment approach refers to an indispensable condition in a way as the basis of these stages.

Uncertainties such as global change and the pandemic and fluctuations in consumer trends, accelerate decision-making processes and bring forth personal leaderships based on business processes.

Another result of delegation based on the limits of responsibility obtained with empowerment, has been an acceleration in reducing hierarchical structure and triggering a more horizontal and lean management.

Also, the concept of Personnel Empowerment supports a modern understanding based on Human Resources Management (HRM) rather than Personnel Management. On the other hand, socio-economic changes are carrying this HRM approach towards the stages of Strategic HR and even Human Management. The literature survey shows that "socio-economic processes crystallize the significance of Strategic Human Resources Management which rose to prominence with globalization" (Çanakçıoğlu and Salepçioğlu, 2019: 8-11).

In this context, Personnel Empowerment also allows Matrix Organizations to get empowered in a sense, by considering strategic Human Management not as hierarchical but as horizontal organization, based on the notion that the worker doing the work should know that work process better. As it will be discussed in subsequent chapters, Matrix Organizations have a somewhat hybrid structure that conforms to both vertical and horizontal types of organization. Therefore, the Personnel Empowerment approach empowers both horizontal organization design and a leaner understanding. And this constitutes a competitive advantage that increases enterprise performance through increase in efficiency.

Strategic Partnerships Approach

Strategic Partnerships can, in a sense, be considered as one of the main parameters in the establishment of "Network Organizations". Establishing Strategic Cooperation could also be considered as a course of action that could be referred to as a kind of solidarity between organizations in the face of global competition. Cooperation between organizations to reinforce their power in their weaknesses in order to increase their competitiveness against the uncertainties and changes of the external environment, is significant in terms of networking.

The reasons for establishing strategic cooperation are as follows:

➢ Enter a new market or regional or international markets or grow in existing products or markets: According to the diversification strategy, which is a basic growth strategy, enterprises enter new product markets and particularly international markets with enterprises experienced in this regard. Such cooperation allows the parties to benefit from each other's knowledge and experience and mitigate their risks in new products and markets. Cooperation is also made for developing existing products and markets.

➢ Preserving existing position in the industry or market: Attempt is made to increase internal efficiency by joining forces between enterprises on various topics against both potential competitors that could enter the market or the potential behaviors of other enterprises in the market.

➢ Strengthening by joining assets and abilities: Enterprises join their existing assets and abilities by cooperating to preserve their advantages over their competitors.

➢ Increasing enterprise value (share value): The share value of two or more enterprises on the capital market can increase as a result of cooperation. Enterprises cooperate to obtain such capital gain.

➢ Preventing uncertainties: If there are high uncertainties in products and markets, it becomes possible for enterprises to cooperate to understand the environment and share information.

➢ Preventing competition or protection against competition: The purpose of cooperation is to increase efficiency is to fill the idle capacities of assets and abilities in order to reduce expenses and mean costs, and thereby make savings.

➢ Sharing new processes, technologies and know-how: Mostly enterprises in different and various product markets and which do not compete directly, cooperate to create synergy by sharing their processes, technologies and know-how.

➢ Enterprises sometimes cooperate to catch up to their competitors. This is usually seen as cooperation made by enterprises to support their basic abilities which are not in leader position.

Strategic partnerships are based on an approach that overlaps with the concept of "Strategic Management". Strategic Management is defined as the science and art of creating, implementing and assessing decisions that cover all the functions of the enterprise in order to ensure that the organization achieves its objectives. And the "Corporate Management" approach as an instrument of strategic management, can be expressed as a responsible and accountable understanding of management and as considering this process as reporting processes. Corporate management can be viewed as a management technique that seeks answers to the question of who will determine and arrange the items of the organizational brain and body, such as the mission, vision, strategy, structure, culture and leadership mode of an organization. For the concept of corporate management, the aforementioned transparency, accountability, responsibility and equitability have been accepted as the universal principles of corporate management throughout the world.

Transition from Traditionalism to Post-Modernity with the Organizational Network and Virtuality Approach

Network organizations that emerged as a form of organization required by globalization, are closely related to the development of technology and have the nature of changing the structure of the organization (Özdemir, 2010: 261).

Developing information and communication networks in particular are developing the relations of companies based on organizational cooperation in an extraordinary manner. Companies are able to provide better and more effective service to consumers and meet customer demands more quickly with organizational networks. Networks facilitate the production and business processes of companies and ensure that products are offered at low costs in domestic and foreign markets. Also, companies establish business relations with suppliers through technological networks and thus increase their competitiveness.

In the organizational sense, the information age that started with technological developments unfolded new operation modes referred to as virtual organization. These organizations are different from traditional organizations in the process of fulfilling management functions such as planning, organizing, directing, coordination and supervising. Therefore, the management processes of these enterprises undergo a significant change with virtualization.

Through virtualization, traditional organizations' coordination structure based on a certain hierarchy were replaced by coordinations based on trust, harmony and cooperation. In this context, whereas traditional organizations were more individual-oriented, authority-based and had a static structure; virtual organizations are team-oriented, knowledge-based and have a dynamic structure. Virtual companies can inspect their own performance and the performance of their partner organizations using the auto-control method and implement more flexible rules and procedures. In the virtual organization structure where horizontal and vertical relations become important, workers sometimes work independent of time and space and communication is realized at a much higher level with respect to the past (Çakmak, 2016: 37-55).

Use of other information technologies besides computers allows organizations to perform effective activities. Innovations and developments in software and the strong technological infrastructure that is created, increases the success and efficiency of organizations in business processes. Adopting an innovative management approach and following technological changes and adapting them to the enterprise are important in terms of employee motivation and the sustainability of the organization (Çakmak, 2016: 37-55).

Outlook on Organizational Models Based on Theoretical Approaches

As much as the importance of managerial processes, the most important approach that allows us to take into consideration organizational designs as an important input is Total Quality Management as we discussed above.

The Systems and Contingency Approaches in particular, included in the Modern Management and Organization Theories, had influence in the emergence of the concept of Total Quality, which is based on the principles of continuous improvement and efficiency in order to respond to customer expectations against competition, by stating that organization structures will exhibit a system open to environmental factors and dependent on conditions. However, with the adaptation and population approaches, Total Quality Management turned into a "human resources, continuous development, employee participation and customer oriented" management approach and is an important approach and practice as a post-modern practice based on "process management".

As again mentioned above, as one important impact of the concept of Total Quality, Personnel Empowerment approach, which can be expressed as Quality-Oriented Human Management, also requires a new system design by emphasizing a new business and organization design.

On the other hand, it can also be seen that Strategic Partnerships emerge as sourcing cooperation used by enterprises to increase their competitiveness and sustainability in global markets. Strategic factors that are important in terms of Outsourcing on one hand and both Resource Dependency and Organizational Economics on the other hand, set forth such strategic cooperation.

The fact that organization structures cooperate to optimize the resources they need for sustainability in accordance with open-system approach and rationalize their operating casts to organize their resources in the most economic manner, constitute the basic parameters of Strategic Partnerships.

It can therefore be foreseen that Total Quality, Personnel Empowerment and Strategic Partnerships have a great impact in establishing knowledge-based network organizations, in other words, hybrid organizations. In accordance with this foresight, it can be asserted that enterprises need to also have new organizational models if they realize total quality, personnel empowerment and strategic cooperation that will be deemed necessary, in their corporate strategies.

Matrix organizations, network organizations and virtual organizations are the most prominent concepts are the leading concepts among such models. We can refer to such organizations as network organizations in general. Although network organizations are understood in general in the literature, it is obvious that the modern structure that we can also refer to as new economy, internet economy or digital economy, is an information economy. Generating and sharing information and managing this process can be referred to as information network organization models. Therefore, in this study we will refer to the concept of network organization models to identify all three models.

This is because, this network structure includes matrix organizations for generating information in organizations, network organizations for sharing information between organizations and virtual organizations for managing information.

All these network structures have been transformed into hybrid models that shape the organizational structures of the future with the information economy, digital economy or the "new economy" approach as more commonly used. We will analyze these concepts in order to clearly explain this transformation.

In this context, in terms of division of labor, specialization and effectiveness, the transformation of project-team organizations into matrix organizations occurs together with the transition to network organizations. With the impact of efficiency, effectiveness and also competition strategies, these developments are observed to have a course more suitable to socio-economic changes, the trends of the new economy and the more dynamic, rapid and innovative conditions generated by information economy.

Transition to Network Organizations

The main difference is the decentralization of management. It is a series of organizations or commercial centers coordinated from a single control point. Network organization structure is characterized by high diversity, the reason being the diversity of the external conditions in which such organizations operate. The participants of network structures are companies-suppliers and goods manufacturers, trade and finance enterprises and service companies. Companies are distinguished according to the merger method and the principle of distribution of power and resources where such types of network organizations are distinguished such as vertical or horizontal.

However, in this study, matrix organizations are also examined and recommended to be evaluated as an internal network structure of the enterprise - organization, in other words as network organizations that accelerate information flow.

Matrix Organizations

A matrix about the flow of power is established in this organization. In functional departments power flows vertically from senior managers to junior managers and flows horizontally between the management levels of project departments and functional departments. This bidirectional power constitutes a matrix. This organization is therefore referred to as a binding matrix organization.

Project managers work as project coordinators by moving in the functional departments of the organization. Engineers, specialists, technicians and similar employees working in functional departments can be borrowed for a project. However, they mainly report to their own departments.

In matrix organizations, specialization occurs in the functional field on one hand and in the field of the project, product or region on the other hand. Specialization and merger take place in two directions in this type. — Standardization: Performed by issuing certain principles in roles and methods and predetermining how to behave in each encountered situation. Standardization is achieved most strongly in the matrix structure, however, methods that lead to standardization such as budgeting and programmed information flow can be used here as well. The degree of complexity in an organization can be determined with the amount and time of the roles performed and methods used. The degree of complexity is low in simple enterprises and highest in the matrix organization.

It shows the willingness and degree of enabling change. Developing the ability to respond rapidly to environmental impacts, creating departments that can continuously deal with changes, increasing the capacity to reduce environmental impacts through internal measures being open to implementing innovations can be listed among the efforts to ensure flexibility. Based on this definition, the matrix model is the most flexible form of organization structure.

Costs: The matrix structure is the most expensive system in terms of cost ratios. Establishing a region-based organization structure is less expensive than matrix organization.

Field of Use: The matrix organization structure has a field of use that will achieve success and enable flexibility in enterprises that aim to rapidly grow in the international sphere, have many products and require close supervision of the works due to the nature of the field of business.

Network Organizations

The main feature of these types of structures is that the tasks and activities required to be performed to produce goods or render services and the resources required for this are distributed over various enterprises rather than being collected within a single enterprise. It is observed that this is a form of "joint venture" in a sense or a result of "outsourcing" practices in a sense, due to "vertical separation" In addition, it would be more appropriate to approach such structures with an interdisciplinary organizational logic (Koçel, 2014: 453-461).

In this respect, network organization structures reinforce and provide competitive advantage to enterprises by joining the "main ability" of each enterprise. Enterprises that execute these functions with a market mechanism constitute network organization structures by bringing together their main abilities as mentioned below;

Internal Network Organizations: Enterprises attempt to develop internal entrepreneurship and flexibility with an internal network organization in order to gain competitive advantages on the markets. Although resources remain within the same enterprise in this network organization structure, functions are conducted by enterprises that have the ability to act independent of one another. Internal enterprises that act independent of one another are coordinated by the central enterprise.

Balanced Network Organizations: This organization structure is a form of outsourcing. Enterprises focus on their core topics and try to outsource other functions in order to achieve flexibility and sourcing effectiveness. The supply chain established with this method results in the emergence of balanced network organizations. Enterprises that get together in a network for long-term strategic purposes and which are fully independent of one another, consist of external suppliers and the principal company.

Dynamic Network Organizations: Unlike internal and balanced network organization, this network structure mostly has a prevalent mode of outsourcing. In this structure, enterprises get together to realize certain projects through provisional agreements. Dynamic network organizations therefore have a shorter and more provisional relation with respect to other network structures.

Virtual Organizations

The term virtual is used to identify a network that consists of independent companies that get together usually provisionally to produce a product or to render or provide a service.

However, the needs that arose during the pandemic showed that such organizations will be more permanent. Virtual organizations are usually associated with terms such as virtual office, virtual teams and virtual leadership. The final objective of a virtual organization is to provide innovative and high-quality products or services by responding to customer demands.

In this sense, the term virtual has its roots in the IT industry. When a computer seems to have higher storage capacity than it actually does, this is called virtual memory. Likewise, when an organization collects resources from various companies, it is observed to have more abilities than a virtual organization.

The partners of virtual organizations share the risks, costs and results in a global market. The common features of these organizations can be listed as having interrelated relations within boundaries interwoven by information networks and having purposes motivated by common success.

Transition to Hybrid Organizations in Post-Modern Approaches and the Effects of the New Economy

Network organizations that emerged as a form of organization required by globalization, are closely related to the development of technology and have the nature of changing the structure of the organization (Özdemir, 2010: 261). Developing information and communication networks in particular are developing the relations of companies based on organizational cooperation in an extraordinary manner. Companies are able to provide better and more effective service to consumers and meet customer demands more quickly with organizational networks. Networks facilitate the production and business processes of companies and ensure that products are offered at low costs in domestic and foreign markets. Also, companies establish business relations with suppliers through technological networks and thus increase their competitiveness.

In the organizational sense, the information age that started with technological developments unfolded new operation modes referred to as virtual organization. These organizations are different from traditional organizations in the process of fulfilling management functions such as planning, organizing, directing, coordination and supervising. Therefore, the management processes of these enterprises undergo a significant change with virtualization.

Through virtualization, traditional organizations' coordination structure based on a certain hierarchy were replaced by coordinations based on trust, harmony and cooperation. In this context, whereas traditional organizations were more individual-oriented, authority-based and had a static structure; virtual organizations are team-oriented, knowledge-based and have a dynamic structure. Virtual companies can inspect their own performance and the performance of their partner organizations using the auto-control method and implement more flexible rules and procedures. In the virtual organization structure where horizontal and vertical relations become important, workers sometimes work independent of time and space and communication is realized at a much higher level with respect to the past (Çakmak, 2016: 37-55).

Use of other information technologies besides computers allows organizations to perform effective activities. Innovations and developments in software and the strong technological infrastructure that is created, increases the success and efficiency of organizations in business processes. Adopting an innovative management approach and following technological changes and adapting them to the enterprise are important in terms of employee motivation and the sustainability of the organization (Çakmak, 2016: 37-55).

The New Economy or the Information Economy

We had stated that it would be more correct to examine and consider the aforementioned Organization models as the consequences of economic globalization in particular and as transformations created in organizations by changes occurring in the environment in parallel with economic developments. In this context, we can state that each industrial revolution creates its own processes and management organization approaches.

For example, we can state that mass production model developed with electricity and the digital production model developed with the internet. As structures changes occurred also in organizations after electricity, transformations are continuing to take place in organizations also after the internet.

The digitalization impacts of technological motion and the new economy are also further driving the hybridizing hybrid organization model, and as will be discussed later, hybrid models of different dimensions can also be foreseen with the increase of complexity due to pandemics such as the Covid-19. And it is obvious that such Hybrid models can be structures more focused on digital economics.

In this respect, it is very important to consider the matter from this aspect. Therefore, we need to deepen the analysis at this point in our study.

Accordingly, the technological advances to be introduced by Industry 4.0 in particular, have been examined under nine topics. These advances can be briefly outlined as follows (Boston Consulting Group, 2015):

➤ Big Data and its Analysis: Big datasets obtained from various sources integrated with production and management systems can be processed and analyzed.

➤ Autonomous Robots: Robots will be able to operate autonomously, flexibly and in cooperation.

➤ Simulation: Machines, products and humans will be simulated prior to physical production to ensure that production processes are more effective within artificial reality and thereby, quality is increased. Fatih Mehmet Öcal – Kıvanç Altıntaş OPUS

➤ Merging Horizontal and Vertical System Integration: Today, supplier and customer relations are detached from each other in many companies. Companies, departments and activities will become more interwoven when system integration is ensured.

➤ Internet of Things - IoT: It is an electronic communication environment where machines can directly communicate with each other on industrial platforms.

➤ Cyber Security: Systems that will resolve security problems that can emerge due to the increasing virtual interconnection of companies and processes.

➤ Cloud System: The transfer of industrial data exchange, monitoring and inspection processes to the cloud environment.

➤ Additive Manufacturing: Traditional manufacturing techniques consist of three stages. These are cutting, drilling and shaping processes. In the additive manufacturing system, the product is created in a short period of time by adding thin layers over each other using 3D printing technology.

➤ Augmented Reality-AR: Although these systems are currently in initial stage, companies will use augmented reality a lot to develop decision-making and business processes. In the virtual world, operators will be able to interact with their machines, change their parameters and receive operational data/maintenance instructions by pressing a button.

At this point, starting to consider the concept of the "New Economy" in this context will allow us to present our recommendations on what kind of hybrid organization model can be created by all the aforementioned factors.

The New Economy - From Industrialization to Virtualization
Definition and Scope of the New Economy

The concept of new economy in the broadest sense refers to the economic activity industry located at the center of creating and implementing electronic information technologies (Zagler, 2002: 338). The definition of new economy by Nordhaus is built on computer hardware, software and communication devices. The new economy covers information creation, development and distribution processes. Three main sectors are included in this process. These are the hardware that processes information, the communication system that collects distributes the information and finally, the software, which ensures that the whole system is managed by humans (Nordhaus, 2000: 1). According to Salvatore, new economy refers to the rapid development and spread in the use of information and communication technologies based on computers, software and communication systems (Salvatore, 2003: 534).

The phenomenon of new economy is a reality today that impacts and shapes the world with many concepts such as the internet, e-commerce, m-commerce, wireless communication, company mergers, risk capital, dotcoms, adhocratic organization structures and operation ecosystems (Öz, 2019: 98). New economy is actually the economy that constitutes the economic basis of globalization. Economic activities are performed based on information in this economic structure. Innovation, creativity and high competition steer the economy globally. Information and communication technologies are the most important elements of new economy. These technologies allow individuals, public organizations and companies to communicate more actively, thereby reducing operating costs and increasing efficiency (Kevük, 2006: 322).

Features of the New Economy

The features of the new economy can be basically listed as follows:

Information: The new economy is based on information due to information technologies. In the information economy, information is generated by brain workers and information consumers, i.e. individuals. Companies and industries will be able to achieve success as they make new inventions and innovations, develop new products, provide new services and increase information intensity in the goods they produce and services they render (Aktan and Vural, 2004a: 94).

Digitization: Telecommunication, satellites, cable lines and wireless communication facilitate the means for transportation, energy and communication today. The transition from copper cables to fiber-optic cables offers a faster, more efficient and stronger structure (Margherio, 1999: 9-10).

Globalization: The new economy is global. The disintegration of the bipolar world created a new, dynamic and variable global environment where economic walls have disappeared to a great extent. The information on the internet and in digital environment have a key role, individual companies have independently become part of e single economy rather than operating in a national, regional or local area (Barışık and Yirmibeşcik, 2006: 42).

Network Economy: The new economy is one that integrates with communication networks. The replacement of analog lines with digital communication lines and the transition from the classical main system to a web-based system have resulted in significant transformations in business life. The process of information being subject to commerce accelerated with information networks and the digitalization of information (Aktan and Vural, 2004a: 4).

Virtualization: The transformation of information from analog to digital allows for physical assets to become virtual. In time, this virtualization started to change corporate processes, structures and relations, and therefore, economic activities (Barışık and Yirmibeşcik, 2006: 41).

Innovation: If a new and successful product is developed and released to the market, the new objective of the company should be to produce and set forth a more advanced version (Barışık and Yirmibeşcik, 2006: 41). And the profitability and competitiveness of the company is shaped accordingly anyway.

Flexible Organization Structure: The Taylorist organization structure has been replaced by flexible organization structures. Such organizations reduce the waste of resources and integrate a creative way of thinking that takes into consideration the changing conditions in every step of the manufacturing process to increase the efficiency of capital and labor (Aktan and Vural, 2004a: 101).

The Concepts and Approaches of Old Economy and New Economy and an Environmental Factor

Old, complex and hierarchical structures have been replaced by a new system that shares and absorbs information. The old economy's production factors of labor and capital are being replaced by information and creativity. The individual is more participating and competitive and continuously renews himself/herself. The widespread and effective use of local and global information is being supported in all sectors and entrepreneurship is encouraged (Kaya, 2005: 16-21; Ata, 2009: 33).

Although the agricultural, industrial and service sectors of the industrial society maintain their significance, the information sector has also been added among them. All boundaries are disappearing because the markets are dynamic and competition is globalized and consumers can purchase goods and services instantly (Aktan and Vural, 2016: 5). As a result of the developments in electronic communication technology; information can be accessed much quicker in most of the world, societies can establish broad relations with each other with comfort and new cooperation can be made in the economic, social, cultural and political fields (Bayraç, 2003: 43).

In the industrial society, production is performed with steam engines, electrical motors and internal combustion engines, whereas in the network society, development and production are organized based on information networks, information connections, IT systems and symbol transmissions (Meder, 2001: 74). The understanding of mass production focused on standard goods and services has ended and the flexible production that takes into consideration the changing demands of consumers and uses IT technologies in production. In the new economy, information flows from social organizations from the individuals of the society (Bayraç, 2003: 46; Erçakar and Çolakoğlu, 2019: 252).

Companies now do not act alone in their production and sales decisions, but in the framework of cooperation and partnerships. In this system, the model of flexible economy based on market instruments has risen to prominence rather than the state-centered control economy. Information technologies have increased the means to educate the masses rapidly and to transform them into qualified individuals. Persons able to use information technologies can access the information they seek in any field and achieve a new power in the face of companies providing goods and services. This forces companies to completely act in a customer-oriented manner (Talas and Kaya, 2014: 31). In the system created by the industrial revolution, the leadership role in technology and negotiation power on the market depended on producers, whereas in the new economy the market power balance has shifted towards enterprises and distributors that provide service to consumers (Bayraç, 2003: 56).

Basic Dynamics of the New Economy - From Industrial Technology to Digital Transformation

Network-based information economy has simplified the relations between individuals, institution and enterprises to a great extent. The new economic model is actually a result of a modern economic system and requirement. The new industry is based on extraordinary technologies and information that change permanently. In this context, the basic dynamics of the new industrial society are intellectual technologies, digital transformation and information workers.

Computers, mobile phones, tablets and wearable technological products (spectacles, clothes etc.) are important instruments of technological transformation. These instruments allow accessing systems, tools and other persons and sharing data. Consumers can particularly access product information, compare various products and do shopping through smartphones and tablets. They can also share their opinions about products on the internet and social media through these instruments. Likewise, company managers and employees can access corporate data and analysis software through these instruments to exchange opinions with their colleagues and stakeholders on corporate social cooperation platforms (Banger, 2016).

Additionally, software and hardware systems, satellite technologies, micro-electronic technologies, flexible automation technologies and digital technology, fiber-optic technology, laser technology, smart terminal, teleprocessing, videotex, teleconference, fax, CD-ROM and video disks are information technologies that increasingly developed in the 21st century. On the other hand, advanced material technologies, biotechnology and genetic engineering, energy technologies, nuclear energy, aviation and aviation technologies are classified as generic technologies under new fundamental technologies. Technological advances preceding generic technologies impacted the production of only a certain product or industry, whereas these technologies have a wide range of implementation in the economy and provide economic efficiency in a broader area (Houghton and Sheehan, 2000: 2).

Many developments took place during the last thirty years such as the emergence of the mass market, the development of personal computers, the maturing of digital design tools and computerized manufacturing. It would be a useful approach to position digital economy at the center of these changes that have been ongoing for a long time. The increase in outsourcing and offshoring, the trend from the manufacturing sector to the services sector in the 2000s and fluidity in the global economy that emerged with multi-national companies, have started an information technology transformation in recent times (Sturgeon, 2017: 2). In this context, digital economy covers a series of economic, social and cultural activity conducted online regarding the use of information and communication technology. Digital economy cases information and communication technologies to be used at high levels, information to be turned into a market value and be processed economically and facilitates business and manufacturing processes (Dikkaya and Aytekin, 2019: 1286).

In the network or information society, development and production are organized based on information networks, information connections, information systems and symbol transmissions. This on the other hand eliminates the time and space limits of communication and thus creates a highly competitive environment. Therefore, a market system is created to which entry is very easy and a high price competition takes place (Meder, 2001: 74; Aslan, 2007: 306).

The internet and its applications, which is one of the most important network technologies, is used frequently in commercial transactions. The frequent use of the internet in economic and commercial activities has created interned-based commercial enterprises such as e-commerce and e-business and caused companies to operate at the international level by eliminating national boundaries. Companies' traditional and usually local understanding of commerce is now being replaced by a global understanding of commerce. The restructuring or transformation based on information and communication technologies, required by such reasoning, has become mandatory for companies. The production, advertisement, sale and distribution of goods and services can be easily performed through communication networks (Yılmaz, 2013: 249).

The information age and technologies have created new professions and qualifications. This change essentially refers to a radical transformation from the industrial worker to the information worker (Gelgeç and Hatırlı, 2018: 100). The trend towards information employees took place in parallel with technological progress. Therefore, advance technological capital expenses increase the demand for trained labor force (Işık, 2019: 7).

The information worker force is distinguished from the industrial worker in certain respects. The information worker is more independent, more productive and has ceased to be an extension of the machine. He/she is typically a skilled and specialized worker. These workers are younger and better trained. The new workers resemble independent artisan workers rather than interchangeable assembly line workers. Also, they create their production style and lifestyle based on change, uncertainty and flexible organization (Salur, 2012: 42).

Information workers who contribute to information exchange and trade, continue their activities in topics such as planning, research, development, analysis, arrangement, accumulation, systematization, distribution and marketing (Işık, 2019: 7-8). Although many processes are performed as dependent on technologies in information-intensive enterprises and economies, the basic factor to be considered here is information workers who ensure that the system is operated. Brain workers are pioneers for ensuring that the system operates well. These workers play a significant role in the rise and development of the network economy (Kevük, 2006: 325).

Restructuring in the New Economy

The new economic system has started to show its impacts more prominently in countries that have an important position in the global economy. Today, technologically advanced countries, in other words, countries with a strong information-based economy also have international competitive advantage. The fact that knowledge, creativity and skills have gained importance is changing the competition style of companies and the sources of comparative advantages among countries. The increase in the importance of information-centered economies is, on one hand, having important impacts on the requirement for growth, manufacturing organization, employment and qualified labor force, and on the other hand, requires new policies and practices concerning competition and the industry (Coates and Warwick, 1999: 11).

New Production Organizations and Modes of Organization

The Fordist mode of production mostly used in the 20th century and which conformed to Keynesian polices started to lose its significance as of the 1970s. Profits and efficiency dropped significantly with the 1973 oil crisis. This was also a crisis of the industrial society. Therefore, the crises of Fordism initiated a new structuring process in production. The developments in information technologies that took place thereafter had a deep impact on the process of social, political and economic transformation (Sapancalı, 2001: 122; Bozkurt, 2014: 126).

Technological developments and particularly the use of micro-electronic technology in production made mass production ineffective. Thus, the flexible production systems known as Post-Fordism emerged. Flexibility in manufacturing technologies have also brought high efficiency in production, time and cost saving and competitive advantage (Aktan and Vural, 2004a: 108).

Computer technology has accelerated the developments in flexible and programmable manufacturing technologies including micro-electronics and telecommunication, computer-aided design and manufacturing, digital-controlled machinery, flexible manufacturing systems, micromarketing and in-house networks. These new technologies play a significant role in the emergence of new manufacturing systems. Companies are trying to adapt their installation and business organizations to the new conditions (Kelleci, 2003: 8-9).

Network economies that emerged as a result of the applications in modern computer and communication technologies is determining the structure and operating style of organizations. Companies are integrating with each other through various communication networks (Özgüler, 2002: 7; Bayraç, 2003: 51). The competition in global markets that is increasing through information technologies is causing companies to prefer more flexible and horizontal modes of organization. Also, company structures based on highly qualified labor, technology and flexible business organizations (lean production, works requiring high performance etc.) are standing out. By the virtue of information technologies, they establish network relations with consumers and suppliers, react quickly to changes and thus gain an important competitive advantage (Kelleci, 2003: 8). Establishing networks helps companies increase their competitiveness. Due to the rise in costs, the increase in complexity and the expansion of the scope of technology, companies operate by establishing alliances based on technology and cooperation with other institutions and companies (Aktan and Vural, 2004b: 18).

Qualified Labor - Artificial Intelligence and Flexible Production Structure

The use and production of information technologies is increasing the demand for qualified labor and thus increasing human capital investments (Aslan, 2007: 304). The unqualified or semi-qualified blue-collar workers in the industrial society were conducting production depending on the pace of the machinery; whereas today, the personal knowledge and skills of the new workers has become important. The technological changes and innovations taking place in the new economy are acting to the advantage of the qualified labor force (Aktan and Vural, 2004b: 21; Bozkurt, 2014: 187).

In addition to the quality of labor, the production systems have also undergone structural changes. In Taylorism, where each task was planned and standardized to the smallest detail, the workers going between machines was causing a waste of time and low efficiency. The Fordist production organization was put into force to prevent this and workers were re-positioned around machines. Attempt was thus made to increase efficiency with the line system that minimized the waste of time (Buyruk, 2018: 608-609). Taylorist manufacturers achieved efficiency in production through economies of scale;

the manufacturers in flexible organization structures increase efficiency in the production of goods and services by utilizing economies of scope and the human capabilities of their employees, without conceding economies of scale (Aktan and Vural, 2004b: 21). Production in the post-Fordist production method is conducted in differentiated market segments and with flexible specialization. In this method, the different demands and preferences of consumers are taken into consideration (Gale et al., 2002: 50).

In today's international competition, demand is decreasing for cheap labor with traditional methods and for production of natural resources, which is being replaced by new industries based on information. Traditional production in markets is being replaced by flexible production, flexible automation, and inexpensive and high-quality robotic technologies that can change according to the needs of the market. Flexible production mechanisms allow manufacturers to quickly adapt to market conditions and competitors to overcome the bottlenecks encountered on the market (Bayraç, 2003: 46).

The conditions of competition are getting increasingly more difficult and severe in the new economic order, where the mode and organization of production changes with technological developments (Sapancalı, 2001: 122). Information and communication technologies that find a broad range of applications in the economy are spreading economic efficiency to a wide area. For example, robots that emerged with the entry into service of very effective and fast control and which started being utilized in automated production and the industry, increased efficiency higher than before (Bayraç, 2003: 49). Wide use of the internet and the development of robotic means of production signals a decrease in the use of human labor and an increase in automation (Buyruk, 2018: 606).

Artificial intelligence technologies constitute the most advanced and most important stage of flexible production today. Public, corporate and commercial modes of organization are equipped with smart systems surrounded with artificial neural networks, thinking with digitized data, storing enterprise information in databases and communicating internally and with other organizations. The invention of machines that can perform arithmetic and logical operations enables transferring the function of the human brain to machines in the production process (Baştan, 2003: 188-189). Smart human behavior is combined with machine capabilities or in order to exceed such capabilities, the required behavior is taught to the machine. Many systematic tools and machines are become operable autonomously without human intervention. Effective results are thus obtained by analyzing high volumes of data that technically exceeds human capacity (Önder, 2019: 4).

Post-Industrial Jobs

The information devolution and technologies are creating new jobs and professions. In the new economic system, jobs are becoming independent of physical space due to technologies such as the internet. Technological developments and therefore the change in the production model have created new information workers that work on their own, as part-time, on a project/contract basis, as flexible, remotely and upon call. These types of jobs save time, reduce transportation costs, provide higher autonomy and control power to workers over their works (Kelleci, 2003: 28-29; Aksoy, 2012: 402).

The increase in the need for white-collar workers in the post-industrial age has led to the creation of working environments that provide assurance to people during and after their working life, offer the means for development and support professional experience. As one of the most important catalysts of this period, information technologies have created new professions in certain technical fields. The number of jobs requiring high knowledge and skills have increased particularly as a result of the fast spread of information technologies. Engineers, software developers, system analysts and computer programmers are some of such profession groups (Aksoy, 2012: 401-402). Having high qualification, formal education and theoretical-analytical knowledge and being able to use and apply this knowledge is very important in the jobs of the new age. Frankly, the work structure of the new economy includes high amounts of information transfer (Salur, 2012: 77).

Towards Virtual Companies

Although virtual companies, which actually have a deeper meaning than virtual organizations, are based on virtual organizations in essence, they can be used to define new kinds of enterprise models that have a broader meaning.

The new economy includes digital concepts, topics and elements. The fact that information is digital-centered has created a virtual economy based on digital networks. The strong circulation networks of the economy have transferred corporations and economic relations into the virtual world (Gelgeç and Hatırlı, 2018: 101).

The extraordinarily fast development of the internet was very effective in the spread of virtual workplaces. Therefore, the internet has a very strategic importance in all kinds of virtual jobs. Information technologies such as e-mail, www, phones and computers in particular are integral parts of the virtual workplace. In other words, technological infrastructure is indispensable for a virtual company. Both labor and customers use information and technology a lot in the virtual environment. Particularly the internet has facilitated and lowered the cost of virtual working on a global level (Bozkurt, 2014: 157).

New technologies integrate markets and change the nature of economic activities. Virtual organizations, communities and markets have started to emerge with the increase in the use of information technologies. People, companies and organizations are getting together on a virtual platform through the internet and markets is being established. Electronic business/commerce has also started to get even more important during this process (Kelleci, 2003: 9).

People in various parts of the world can do their job in virtual workplaces, on the same project and at different time zones. These companies can respond to demand faster than traditional enterprises (Bozkurt, 2014: 157). Transferring business processes into the virtual environment ensures that information spreads quickly and thereby increases and globalizes competition.

Impacts of Digitalization on the New Economy

In the 21st century when the digital economy is growing, research and innovations are advancing rapidly, information and qualified labor force are becoming more important than ever, communication systems are gaining broad capacity and flexibility and prices and costs are being pulled down. Global competition has changed the market understanding of companies and created an effective market system where buyers and sellers can easily find each other, directly interact and move with only minor costs (Barışık and Yirmibeşcik, 2006: 40).

Conversion of information into a productions factor leads to the production of new goods and services and the emergence of different production processes. Therefore, information is the fundamental element of the innovation process. Digitalization is accelerating this process. However, the cost of copying and market release of goods produced based on digital production is very low. Therefore, marginal and mean costs gradually decrease with the amount of production in the manufacture of digital goods (Gelgeç and Hatırlı, 2018: 103).

The network economy allows companies to operate between countries for production and commerce purposes. Strong local networks also require a global network structuring. The countries in this network structuring directly benefit from technological activities and opportunities (Afşar, 2015: 224).

Transnational economic integrations, deregulation and developments in the internet and wireless communication technologies have fundamentally altered the structure of financial and commercial services. The internet and similar technologies create new distribution channels for manufactured goods on one hand and contribute to the development of important financial innovations on the other hand (Saatçioğlu, 2005: 152). Digital technology ensures that the goods and services produced in domestic and foreign companies are distributed, marketed, sold ad delivered quickly in the electronic environment (Barışık and Yirmibeşcik, 2006: 44). E-commerce and communication networks reduce commercial costs and make it possible to set prices in a better manner (Claessens et al., 2002: 1-2).

Developing information technologies and the internet have changed the environment in which economic activities are conducted throughout the world. The way that workers work, employer-worker relations, competitors and customers, marketing, production and management environments are changing and being highly affected by these new technologies. The technology and information revolution that is being experienced is bringing forth a new economic model. This new economic model is a large modal ranging from banking, healthcare, education, online commerce and customer requests to the advertisement sector. Enterprises that manage to use information technologies effectively, turn them into e-commerce and adapt to the requirements of the network economy gain competitive advantage on international markets (Akata et al., 2015: 3-4).

Post-Covid-19 Transformation in the New Economy

Computerization, miniaturization, digitalization, satellite network, fiber-optic and internet technologies, which are important elements of globalization, will further broaden, deepen and accelerate the process of changing the world, the society and daily life. Enterprises are compelled to develop new mindsets for the production processes. Keeping pace with global and dynamic competition requires companies to adopt and implement modern methods such as production in computer environment, computer-aided engineering, design and manufacturing. Hence, competitiveness in the shrinking world economy is based on producing new technologies and the ability to rapidly convert these technologies into production (Bayraç, 2003: 47-49).

Network effects are increasing very rapidly today. Issues such as office work, business practices, project-based works, decision mechanisms and risk management can be realized through the internet. We will need to get accustomed to and manage new methods of working that we did not experience until now (Kalkınma Bakanlığı, 2018: 6).

A transition is taking place towards a period of smart production as a result of developments in the fields of artificial intelligence, three-dimensional printers, robotic systems, internet of things, cloud computing, virtual reality, augmented reality, machine learning, deep learning, additive manufacturing, cybersecurity, simulation models, modeling and horizontal/vertical software integrations. In this period, objects can communicate with each other, robots are used more actively and artificial intelligence and virtual reality applications are spreading. The new structure that emerged with all these and the internet technology is having a deep impact on production, the economy and the working process (Ministry of Development, 2018: 5; Buyruk, 2018: 606).

In this period, other objects are able to communicate through the internet of things and new automation systems, new data exchange and new production technologies are being implemented. Objects can perform many tasks and operations using chips and sensors in various areas from infrastructure to smart factories. Production can be performed in factories with no workers and products and manufacturing machinery can communicate via radio frequencies (Buyruk, 2018: 606-607).

Past digital electronic communication systems can shape the future. However, in order for this potential to be effective, technological development must be utilized together with a human resources organization that has the suitable skills. The integration of digital electronic communication systems and artificial intelligence applications with a qualified labor force will yield the required results in establishing smart organizations. The new mode of organization should be established based on the cooperation and coordination of qualified software and hardware specialists, system analysts and designers, system administrations and well-trained operators. Organizations must employ qualified labor that can adapt to such technological change (Baştan, 2003: 199-201).

Economic Sustainability Approach

The relation between sustainability and corporate governance is established through various concepts. The 'stakeholder theory, corporate governance principles and the concept of ethics' will be discussed in this study as some of these concepts, to explain the relation between corporate governance and sustainability. Corporate governance achieves a theoretical framework with the stakeholder theory. The environmental, economic and social aspects and priorities of companies that focus on corporate sustainability fully change. The relation of corporate governance with sustainability is supported by the stakeholder theory. According to the stakeholder theory, a corporation is responsible towards its customers, suppliers, employers, the society and other stakeholders as much as towards its shareholders. Considering this responsibility in a universal context, we can reach the conclusion that corporations are also responsible towards future generations. In this sense, enterprises that aim for sustainable growth should adopt a universal system of thought and set their strategies also in consideration of the interests of future generations.

Environmental performance and financial performance are not in conflict and support each other. The financial performance of an enterprise that pays regard to social and environmental interests increases in the long term, an enterprise with a good financial performance benefits the society and the environment and, in this sense, there is a mutually supportive cycle between social performance, environmental performance and economics performance. Therefore, each environmental, social and economic sustainability of an organization is separately important. Economic sustainability must have a strategic significance for organizations in this framework as well.

And this requires a sustainable and dynamic managerial approach that can adapt to economic change. And this has made it more important for organizations to be more sustainable for adapting to economic transformation in the new economy with the Covid-19 and to take into consideration the changing sustainability criteria. The new economy and digitalization induce these structures to be more network-type under the mentioned criteria.

Conclusion and Evaluation
Process and Network-Oriented Dynamic Design: Hybrid-Covid Model Sustainable Organization Approach

Network organizations are flexible and can change continuously. Network connections contribute to companies in sustaining their existence, gaining competitive advantage and opening to global markets. Two important changes are taking place in companies, from centralization to de-centralization and from hierarchy to networking. In the new management and organization model, mutual solidarity between companies and units is essential and it is desired to achieve organizational purposes collectively. Network organizations compete on offering the best service and solution to internal and external customers through strategic cooperation (Özdemir, 2010: 261).

Many companies are strategically entering into a series of agreements with other domestic and foreign organizations for the purpose of reducing costs, obtaining new technologies, rapidly responding to customer demands, entering new markets and increasing their flexibilities in general. Businesses and markets can no longer be restrained to geographical borders and are turning into a complex and global network. The complexity of the international business environment causes companies to make cooperative agreements with suppliers, customers, competitors and allies. Companies constitute a network of complex business relations with these agreements. These organizational relations eventually become an integral part of globalization. Mergers, joint ventures, cooperative free agreements and short- and long-term agreements between companies characterize today's business world. Modern organizational network models consist of horizontal integrations that include mergers between large companies (Özdemir, 2010: 264).

The technological and digital revolution has caused a deep change and transformation in the business world. As a requirement of digital transformation, companies are entirely changing and transforming their organizations from automation to robotization, from artificial intelligence to freelance working. Corporate models based on continuous learning and innovation are being established (Dalkılıç, 2017). Next-generation technologies are very significant in terms of occupational safety, business stability and increase in efficiency. A flexibility model based on corporate mobility strategy is of key importance on the course of employing remote labor and becoming a more agile organization (CIO, 2020).

In addition to telecommuting, companies are able to offer the opportunity to work from collective centers and satellite offices that spread over wide areas, are closed to residential points and offer shared workspaces. The home office is being replaced by flexible and hybrid environments. Online tools and utilities are facilitating business processes. Our daily work and our form of contacting customers is changing. Rather than interacting face-to-face with customers, it is possible to talk to and hold meetings with them more through teleconference.

The mainstream channel for advertisement and marketing works is shifting from television and printed publications to digital. Accordingly, companies are also considering to shift their organizations and all meetings and activities to digital. Scaling down central office spaces and the transfer of organizations to digital will reduce waste on one hand and enable establishing more sustainable structures on the other hand (Mikro Yazılım, 2020).

The New Economy and the Economic Change discussed in detail above and the management-organization approaches we considered before, are bringing forth a hybrid structure as we tried to expressed.

However, the real problem is that digital technologies, virtual organizations and in fact, virtual offices that we began to feel much more rapidly and to a greater extent in business life with the effects of Covid-19, have started to become some of the main parameters of the information economy.

Produced goods and services are offered to the market over virtual networks. Through virtual organizations, consumers can get information about the price, quality and nature of the products more easily and customer demands can be responded more quickly and effectively. Information networks strengthen the organizational relationships of companies and facilitate their domination in domestic and international markets.

The fluidity of global economy and the fact that service sectors become more important than the production sector lead to institutional transformations in terms of technology. Innovations based on knowledge and post-modern technologies have an extremely increasing impact on productivity and profitability of companies. Information, creativity and entrepreneurship gain importance by network-based flexible organizational structures and digitalization, and all these factors increase the chances of success for the organization.

On the other hand, both network organizations and virtual organizations and even virtual companies cannot manage this change and cannot complete organizational transformations with a hierarchical organization, without developing a matrix structure.

In this context, developing and realizing matrix structures in organizations may, in addition to being structures that are more integrated with speed- or customer-oriented activities in production processes, provide the opportunity for stronger sustainability. And this may provide the means for the organization to have a more hybrid structure in terms of innovative efficiency during uncertainties such as the pandemic.

In this context, matrix structures emerge as a significant correlation in horizontal organizations that are replacing vertical organizations. The three important organizational relations in matrix structures can be considered as the relation of managers inside functional units, the relation between managers and specialists involved in the work and project within specialized departments and last, the relation between the project manager (responsible) and team members in that project (Koçel, 2014, p. 387-388). However, particularly when approaches are put forward about adaptation and the environmental adaptation and change in organizations, lean management and organization models have developed where matrix structures ceased to merely be project based but turned into the operation mechanism of the organization. And this gives us process renewal (change engineering) initiated with lean management in business processes concerning the whole enterprise, and matrix organizations as part of total quality management, which has become the most essential point of organizations as a more lasting arrangement.

Matrix structures are a management model that emerged with the approach of contingency condition dependency in modern management organization theories and also associated with strategic management. However, today, many organization structures are encountered that left project organizations and adopted the matrix model as a requirement of restructuring.

Besides the dynamic effects offered by the matrix structure to organizations, it is known that there are certain criticisms that it fails to solve certain problems. For example, there are criticisms that it is open to confusion and disorder and causes employee performance valuation problems and conflicts. However, if solutions are developed to these and similar problems of matrix structures, they could be considered to provide the opportunity to do business more dynamically and with higher efficiency within the socio-economic DNA that we examined in detail as the new economy or the information economy.

In this context, it could be assessed that, taking into consideration the approach of organizations regarding adaptation to the environment and change, matrix structures will be able adapt and provide the necessary response to these changes by considering this with an adaptation approach in general. And this will also provide us significant inputs for heading towards a model that can absolutely be associated with the approaches of population ecology and natural selection as in nature.

And this is based on a process-driven approach that can be considered together with the new approaches in organizations, such as transition from quality control to total quality that is standing out particularly in post-modern management organization approaches, organization restructurings and network organizations, problems encountered in process renewals, benchmarking between enterprises, strategic human resources and personnel empowerment, and even delayering - zero hierarchy through virtuality and virtual organizations.

In addition to requiring a process-driven change based on information, the new economy requires the organizational model we will design to comply with a process management that maximizes information flow.

We can assert that such matrix structures will generate a hybrid solution that will ensure information flow and allow for process-driven management. Enterprise structures, network organizations and/or virtual organizations all need organizations with the capacity process information and give the fastest response to economic developments. Besides, in the light of the topics examined above, matrix organizations as the social-DNA of these structures are standing out as a type of molecular dynamics of enterprises.

And this constitutes the most important building blocks, which we can define as Hybrid-Covid, that will take us to a more dynamic and process-driven organization model that is more responsive to the changes and developments in the new economy. In a sense, this structure seems to have evolved into a hybrid model in terms of Lean Quality Analysis (Salepçioğlu, 2000) with leanization (matrix organizations), quality-oriented strategic collaborations (network organizations) and new economic trends (virtual organizations) in the context of globalization.

In conclusion, the Hybrid-Covid model organizations can be described as an interwoven hybrid process management and an interwoven network structure that transfer enterprise structures first to matrix dynamics, then to network connections and finally to virtual companies through virtualization. And in this form, as a management-organization strategy they can be considered as a Sustainable Network Organization Model.

References

Afşar, B. (2015). Yeni Ekonomi Üzerine Bir İnceleme. Süleyman Demirel Üniversitesi İktisadi ve İdari Bilimler Fakültesi Dergisi. 20 (4). 221-239.

Akata, K. G., Dikdak, S., and Kırbaş, İ. (2015, Aralık). Yeni Ekonomide Bilgi Dönüşümlerinin Teknoloji Açısından Toplum ve İşletmeler Üzerindeki Etkileri. 20. Türkiye'de İnternet Konferansı. İstanbul Üniversitesi. İstanbul.

Aksoy, B. (2012). Bilgi Teknolojileri ve Yeni Çalışma İlişkileri. Ege Akademik Bakış. 12 (3). 401-414.

Aktan, C. C., and Vural, İ. Y. (2004a). Yeni Ekonomi ve Yeni Rekabet. Türkiye İşveren Sendikaları Konfederasyonu. Rekabet Dizisi: 1. Yayın No: 253. 1-160.

Aktan, C. C., and Vural, İ. Y. (2004b). Yeni Ekonomi. Mercek Dergisi. 9 (36). 1-24.

Aktan, C. C., and Vural, İ. Y. (2016). Bilgi Toplumu, Yeni Temel Teknolojiler ve Yeni Ekonomi. Yeni Türkiye. 1 (88). Bilim ve Teknoloji Özel Sayısı. 1-37.

Aslan, Ö. (2007). Yeni Ekonomi: Özellikleri ve Endüstrileri. Sosyal Siyaset Konferansları Dergisi. 52. 299-318.

Ata, A. Y. (2009). Yeni Ekonomik Düzenin Kavramsal Çerçevesi ve Ekonomilere Sunduğu Fırsatlar: Adana Ekonomisi Üzerine Bir İnceleme. Çukurova Üniversitesi Sosyal Bilimler Enstitüsü Dergisi. 18 (1). 27-48.

Banger, G. (2016). Yeni Teknolojiler, Yeni İş Gücü. https://bizobiz.net/yeni-teknolojiler-yeni-is-gucu/.

Barışık, S., and Yirmibeşcik, O. (2006). Türkiye'de Yeni Ekonominin Oluşum Sürecini Hızlandırmaya Yönelik Uyum Çabaları. Uluslararası Yönetim İktisat ve İşletme Dergisi. 2 (4). 39-62.

Baştan, S. (2003). Yapay Zeka, Yeni İletişim Teknolojileri ve Örgütsel Değişim: Akıllı Örgüte Doğru. Yönetim ve Ekonomi: Celal Bayar Üniversitesi İktisadi ve İdari Bilimler Fakültesi Dergisi. 10 (1). 187-203.

Bayraç, H. N. (2003). Yeni Ekonomi'nin Toplumsal, Ekonomik ve Teknolojik Boyutları. Osmangazi Üniversitesi Sosyal Bilimler Dergisi. 4 (1). 41-62.

Berberoğlu, G. (2004). Örgütleme. Koparal, C. (Ed.). Yönetim Organizasyon. (p.104-114) içinde. Eskişehir: Anadolu Üniversitesi Yayını No: 1457.

Boston Consulting Group. (2015). Industry 4.0: The Future of Productivity and Growth in Manufacturing Industries. Access address: https://www.bcg.com/publications/2015/engineered_products_project_business_industry_4_future_productivity_growth_manufacturing_industries.

Bozkurt, V. (2014). Endüstriyel ve Post-Endüstriyel Dönüşüm: Bilgi, Ekonomi ve Kültür. Bursa. Ekin Kitabevi.

Buyruk, H. (2018). Gelişen Teknolojiler, Değişen İşgücü Nitelikleri ve Eğitim. Uluslararası Toplum Araştırmaları Dergisi. 8 (14). 599-632.

CIO. (2020). Emerging from COVID-19: How to Equip Hybrid Remote / in-Office Workforces for a Seamless Return. Access address: https://www.cio.com/article/3561756/emerging-from-covid-19-how-to-equip-hybrid-remote-in-office-workforces-for-a-seamless-return.html.

Claessens, S., Glaessner, T., and Klingebiel, D. (2002). Electronic Finance: A New Approach to Financial Sector Development. The World Bank Discussion Paper. No: 431. Washington. D. C.

Coates, D., and Warwick, K. (1999, January). The Knowledge Driven Economy: Analysis and Background. Paper Presented at a Conference Jointly Organized by The Department of Trade and Industry and The Centre for Economic Policy Research. London.

Çakmak, Z. (2016). Sanal Organizasyonların Yönetim Fonksiyonları Açısından Geleneksel Organizasyonlardan Farklılıkları. Florya Chronicles of Political Economy. 2 (2). 35-58.

Çanakçıoğlu, S., and Salepçioğlu, M. A. (2019). Sosyo-Ekonomik Açıdan Y Jenerasyonunun İnsan Kaynakları Üzerindeki Etkilerinin Değerlendirilmesi. Euras Academic Journal. 7 (2). 1-26.

Dalkılıç, E. (2017). İş'in Geleceği Dijital Dönüşümün Merkezi: İnsan. Access address: https://isingelecegi.com/isin-gelecegi-dijital-donusumun-merkezi-insan/.

Dikkaya, M., and Aytekin, İ. (2019). Bilgi İletişim Teknolojileri ve Dijital Ekonomi: Avrupa Birliği ve Türkiye Arasında Bir Karşılaştırma. Üçüncü Sektör Sosyal Ekonomi Dergisi. 54 (3). 1279-1299.

Erçakar, M. E., and Çolakoğlu, H. (2019). Bilgi Ekonomisinin Ekonomik Büyüme Üzerindeki Etkileri: BRICS Ülkeleri ve Türkiye İçin Bir Analiz. Yönetim ve Ekonomi Araştırmaları Dergisi. 17 (4). 248-268.

Gale, H. F., Wojan, T. R., and Olmsted, J. C. (2002). Skills, Flexible Manufacturing Technology. and Work Organisation. Industrial Relations. 41 (1). 48-79.

Gelgeç, G., and Hatırlı, S. A. (2018). Bilgi Ekonomisi ve Büyüme Arasındaki İlişki: Türkiye Örneği. Süleyman Demirel Üniversitesi İktisadi ve İdari Bilimler Fakültesi Dergisi. 23 (1). 97-122.

Houghton, J., and Sheehan, P. (2000). A Primer on the Knowledge Economy. Victoria University Centre for Strategic Economic Studies. CSES Working Paper. No. 18.

Işık, Ç. Y. (2019). Bilgi Ekonomisi ve Ekonomik Büyüme İlişkisi: Türkiye Üzerine Ampirik Bir Analiz. (Yayımlanmamış Yüksek Lisans Tezi). Namık Kemal Üniversitesi. Tekirdağ.

Kalkınma Bakanlığı. (2018). On Birinci Kalkınma Planı (2019-2023): Dijital Ekonomide Meslekler ve Yetkinlikler. (Yayın No: KB: 3000-ÖİK: 781). Çalışma Grubu Raporu. Ankara.

Kaya, A. (2005). Bilgi Ekonomisi ve Türkiye İçin Önemi. (Yayımlanmamış Yüksek Lisans Tezi). Uludağ Üniversitesi. Bursa.

Kelleci, M. A. (2003). Bilgi Ekonomisi, İşgücü Piyasasının Temel Aktörleri ve Eşitsizlik: Eğilimler, Roller, Fırsatlar ve Riskler. Yayın No: DPT. 2674. Ekonomik Modeller ve Stratejik Araştırmalar Genel Müdürlüğü. Stratejik Araştırmalar Dairesi. Ankara.

Kevük, S. (2006). Bilgi Ekonomisi. Journal of Yasar University. 1 (4). 319-350.

Koçel, T. (2014). İşletme Yöneticiliği. İstanbul.Beta Basım.

Margherio, L. (1999). The Emerging Digital Economy. The Heartland Institute: Freedom Rising. Access address: www.heartland.org/_template-assets/documents/publications/24388.pdf.

Meder, M. (2001). Bilgi Toplumu ve Toplumsal Değişim. Pamukkale Üniversitesi Eğitim Fakültesi Dergisi. 9 (9). 72-81.

Mikro Yazılım. (2020). Koronavirüs Sonrası İş Yerleri Nasıl Değişecek? Covid-19 Sonrası Öngörüler. Access address: https://blog.mikro.com.tr/koronavirus-sonrasi-is-yerleri-nasil-degisecek-covid-19-sonrasi-ongoruler/.

Nordhaus, W. D. (2000). Technology, Economic Growth, and the New Economy. Background Paper Prepared for a Conference on "R&D and the New Economy". Sweden.

Önder, M. (2019). Endüstri 4.0 Devrimi ve Haritacılık Mesleğine Yansımaları. TMMOB Harita ve Kadastro Mühendisleri Odası. 17. Türkiye Harita Bilimsel ve Teknik Kurultayı. 25-27 Nisan 2019. Ankara.

Öz, M. (2019). Lojistik faaliyetlerde dış kaynak kullanımı ve pazarlama tabanlı yetenekler üzerine etkisi. Konya. Eğitim Yayınevi.

Özdemir, L. (2010). Şebeke Organizasyon Nedir, Ne Değildir?. Dumlupınar Üniversitesi Sosyal Bilimler Dergisi. (26). 260-271.

Özgüler, G. (2002). Yeni Ekonomi Anlayışı Kapsamında Gelişmiş ve Gelişmekte Olan Ülkeler: Türkiye Örneği. (Yayımlanmamış Doktora Tezi). Anadolu Üniversitesi. Eskişehir.

Saatçioğlu, C. (2005). Yeni Ekonomi ve Finansal Piyasalar Üzerindeki Etkisi. Atatürk Üniversitesi İktisadi ve İdari Bilimler Dergisi. 19 (1). 151-165.

Salepçioğlu, M. A. (2000). Küreselleşme Süreci Bağlamında Yalın Kalite Analizi. (Yayımlanmamış Doktora Tezi). İstanbul Üniversitesi. İstanbul.

Salur, S. (2012). Bilgi Toplumu Parametreleri ve Ekonomik Büyüme Arasındaki İlişki: Panel Analiz. (Yayımlanmamış Doktora Tezi). Adnan Menderes Üniversitesi. Aydın.

Salvatore, D. (2003). The New Economy and Growth in the G-7 Countries. Journal of Policy Modeling. 25 (5). 531-540.

Sapancalı, F. (2001). Yeni Dünya Düzeni ve Küresel Yoksulluk. Dokuz Eylül Üniversitesi Sosyal Bilimler Enstitüsü Dergisi. 3 (2). 115-140.

Sturgeon, T. J. (2017). The New 'Digital' Economy and Development. United Nations Conference on Trade and Development. UNCTAD Technical Notes on ICT for Development. No: 8. 08 October 2017.

Talas, M., and Kaya, Y. (2014). Küreselleşmenin Ekonomik Sonuçları. Journal of World of Turks. 6 (2). 25-35.

Yılmaz, M. (2013). Küreselleşmenin Oluşumuna Zemin Hazırladığı Yeni Ekonomik Anlayış: Bilgi Ekonomisi. Atatürk Üniversitesi İktisadi ve İdari Bilimler Dergisi. 27 (1). 241-255.

Zagler, M. (2002). Services, Innovation and the New Economy. Structural Change and Economic Dynamics. 13 (3). 337-355.

CHAPTER 7

Developments in Cost Systems During the Industrial Revolutions and Cost Calculation at Smart Factories

Mustafa Çanakçıoğlu
{mustafa.canakcioglu@khas.edu.tr}

Assist. Prof., Kadir Has University, Faculty of Business, Fatih/Turkey

Abstract

It is widely accepted that humanity has a history of twelve thousand years on earth. As a result of the industrial and technological developments in the last two hundred and fifty years, we can now travel in space and plan the colonization of Mars. We experienced two industry revolutions after Charles Duell, the director of the patent office in the USA said in 1899, "There is nothing else that can be invented, it is practically over." Starting with the manufacturing methods developed and implemented by Frederick Winslow Taylor and Henry Ford in the early 20th century and until Industry 4.0, we developed many physical and mental methods, techniques and tools to overcome the bottlenecks and issues of traditional production lines. The purpose of this paper is to review the industrial revolutions and the development of cost systems during the process. In this sense, we will review the shift from mass production to lean and agile production and the technologies of Industry 4.0 which were introduced in 2011 as well as the production process and cost systems at smart factories.

Keywords: Smart Factories, Cost Calculation, Industrial Revolutions, Lean Manufacturing, Agile Manufacturing, Industry 4.0 Technologies.

Introduction

In the history of economics, we can talk about two major changes which have radically changed the societies and triggered growth through better economic performance. The first was agriculture and the second was the industrial revolution. Anthropological research which focuses on the historical evolution of humanity reveals that the fist society was a hunter-gatherer society (Society 1.0, Hunting Society). Starting with 13,000 BCE, humanity learned to cultivate land and settled to form the agrarian society (Society 2.0, Agrarian Society). Starting with the first and second industrial revolutions in the 18th century, the society turned into an industrial society (Society 3.0, Industrial

Society). With the third industrial revolution, we connected the data networks and turned into an information society (Society 4.0, Information Society) which creates added value. Shinzo Abe, the prime minister of Japan, thinks that the purpose of the smart systems of Industry 4.0 is not only to improve technology but also to increase the quality of life and education. In CeBIT 2017, he explained the concept of super-smart society (Society 5.0, Super Smart Society) built on the information society (Özsoylu, 2017:42; Eren, 2020: 171).

An economic industrial revolution requires the emergence of a new energy resource as well as new technologies in addition to needs. Industrial Revolution 1 was marked by mechanical manufacturing plants based on water, steam and coal power. Industrial Revolution 2 was based on oil and electricity as main energy resources. Its basic concept was mass production through new communication tools, division of labor and electric power. Industrial Revolution 3 is marked by internet as well as solar power, wind power and other renewables (Rifkin, 2014: 57-60). Industrial Revolution 3 was also marked by a digital revolution triggered by the microelectronics including nuclear energy, computers, fiber optics and chips. With the developments in IT, manufacturing was even more automated (Kagermann et al., 2013:14). Industrial Revolution 4 is also based on manufacturing based on cyber-physical systems (Özkan et al, 2018: 129-130).

Any of these industry revolutions changed the manufacturing strategies of the factories which focused on high quality to swiftly respond to the changing conditions, lowering the costs to meet the demand and improving the production and transportation costs for better profitability. A major change is the philosophy of "Lean Thinking", which was used in Japan since the 1950s and was introduced to the rest of the world in 1991. A report titled "21st Century Manufacturing Enterprise Strategy" and issued by Lehigh University's Iacocca Institute defines agile manufacturing as the capacity to cope with expected and unexpected changes and make use of them as opportunities.

As a result of the major changes in manufacturing strategies at manufacturing plants in 1991, the demands and expectations of customers have increased. The market life cycle of products has shortened and production costs have increased to include research & development, product & process design, capital investment, software development and training. With these developments, there is now greater focus on high quality, low cost, zero waste, high efficiency, manufacturing agility, high-quality customer services, fast response to changes, financial and non-financial performance measurement, efficient use of IT and automation. In this sense, market-and customer-focused systems including lean manufacturing and agile manufacturing reinforce the competitive power of companies and improve their capacity to meet market expectations. These are manufacturing systems which require comprehensive changes to make the manufacturing and organizational structure more flexible with the purpose of meeting the demands and expectations of the customers. These two manufacturing methods are the foundations of Industry 4.0 at smart factories.

Within the manufacturing systems, cost accounting can be defined as: A whole of procedures to determine the financial costs paid by a company to produce goods and services and offer them to buyers; log and monitor such costs in terms of type, function and place of expense; generate reports to allow reviewing and commenting on such costs; and control costs. These processes can also be considered as a cost management system. They are available since 2011 and allow communication of all units of industrial manufacturing as well as real-time access to data. Within the scope of Industry 4.0, how they will evolve at smart factories is an ongoing debate. This paper focuses on the types of manufacturing which evolved during the process from Industry 1.0 to Industry 4.0 and the evolution of costing methods from a traditional approach to strategic cost methods. It also deals with how manufacturing and costing systems will be built or organized at smart factories of Industry 4.0.

Development of Industrial Revolutions and Cost Management

It is not clear where, when, and how accounting started as a practice. However, written documents on accounting date back to 5000 BCE in Sumerians and 4000 BCE in Hebrews (Can, 2007: 2). The double-entry system which is still used was developed by Luca Pacioli. Luca Pacioli, a Franciscan friar and mathematician from Tuscany, wrote a book called "Suma Arithmetica" (1494) and defined the basics of the double-entry system in the section titled "Particularis di Compitus e Scripturis" (on book keeping and other documentation) (Köroğlu, 2015: 32). As is clear, accounting dates far back than the industrial revolutions. However, it is not the same for cost and administration management. Developments in this area started with the industrial revolutions.

Industry Revolution 1

Industry 1.0 was marked by a shift from an agrarian economy to an industrial economy with the invention of steam-powered machinery in the late 18th century. In the traditional agrarian economy, manufacturing was made at home and with handlooms. After the first industrial revolution, manufacturing shifted to factories with machinery (Genç, 2018: 237).

James Watt, while repairing the steam engine manufactured in 1698, improved it into a new and more efficient engine in 1763 and secured the patent for the engine in 1769. Replacement of wood with coal and steam and the introduction of machinery in manufacturing boosted the iron-steel and textile industries. Railroads and steamships allowed intercontinental trade (Schwab, 2016: 16).

The first industrial revolution ended in 1860 and the first steps in cost accounting were taken. However, this process was limited to calculation of unit costs and helped with certain organizational decisions. The textile company founded in 1855 in New England used certain costing methods to calculate and control the efficiency of wool used to manufacture textile products (measuring of capacity use ratio on unit cost). In 1860-1870s, railroad companies developed various accounting methods to help planning and control (ton-kilometer cost, passenger-kilometer cost, ratio of operating costs to operating revenues etc.). Costing methods developed by railroad companies were implemented at the steel factories founded by Carnegie (raw material and workmanship costs). Starting with 1880, various metal processing plants worked on the assignment of various general costs including depreciation to the final product (Önder, 2008).

Industry Revolution 2

The second industrial, also known as the "technology revolution", started in 1870 and continued until 1970s. In this period, use of electric power which is better than steam power at factories and replacement of coal with crude oil as the energy resource resulted in improved performance of industrial operations (Genç, 2018: 238). Defining factors of the second industrial revolution is the significance of crude oil and other raw materials in the economy. In addition to internal combustion engines which work with oil, new technologies invented in this period include telephone, telegraph and radio. These communication technologies provided new opportunities including stock exchange markets (Yüksekbilgili and Çevik, 2018: 423).

Adam Smith's book The Wealth of Nations published in 1776 had a profound impact on manufacturing shops. Frederick W. Taylor's scientific management approach as well as technological improvements in transportation, communication and manufacturing laid the foundations for current manufacturing factory systems and mass production (Çetin and Altuğ, 2005: 302). The first serial transport lines based on division of labor were established in 1870 at the butcheries in Cincinnati. With the development of the sliding assembly line, single-type mass production started (Alçın, 2016: 20). Initially implemented at Henry Ford's automobile factory in Rouhg, the world was introduced with the concept of mass production on October 7, 1913 with Ford's Model-T.

With the replacement of iron with steel in manufacturing, development of heavy industry and standardized and more efficient mass production, Industry Revolution 2 is marked by the significance of scientific information (Özkan et al, 2018: 5). Marketing increased consumption through strategic planning on distribution, promotion, pricing and product. New ideas on products and services became a strategy used by industries for competition. This resulted in the increased impact of innovation in economy and product diversity (Ovacı, 2017: 116).

After the Industry Revolution 2, the number of enterprises increased due to various factors including the replacement of labor with machines, improvement of the concept of services, increase in the diversity of products and better transportation and communication. The increase in the number of enterprises extended their purpose from solely making profits to lowering costs, planning production, making new manufacturing decisions, using new methods of cost accounting and analyzing profitability and costs (Bekçioğlu and Köroğlu, 2013: 55).

With the change in manufacturing methods, new accounting approaches were developed. With mass production, direct workmanship and general manufacturing costs became more important. It became necessary to register the labor costs, costs per part, division of direct-indirect workmanship, loss of time and transformation costs in the accounting logs in detail. Cost registry was used by Charlton Mills (England) in the 1800s, Boston Manufacturing Company in 1820 and Lyman Mills Company in the 1850s. These logs were inclusive of weekly and monthly payments to workers as well as the cotton conversion cost. With the expansion of the transportation business, increased manufacturing, increase in the number of distribution companies and developments in railways and textile business from 1850 to 1925, it became a requirement to coordinate processes, increase performance in certain internal operations and implement internal control (Yükçü and Atağan, 2014: 154). A standard approach to accounting as we know today was developed by Harsington Emerson in 1908. In Germany, cost accounting was introduced to the science community by a scientist named Schmalenbach in 1909 (Özel, 2010: 47). Andrew Carnegie made use of cost data for decision making at Carniege Steel, an American company, in the mid-1900s. In 1915, F.W. Harris developed the economic order model to control stocks.

Cost accounting as we know today dates back to the end of WWI. In the 1920s, General Motors developed modern cost accounting methods which helped the American economy. Beginning with the 1920s and 1930s, English iron-steel industry made extensive use of the standard costing system. In England, the idea of a "standard costing system" was proposed for the first time in 1929 at the annual meeting of the National Iron & Steel Manufacturers Federation. Many alternatives were proposed later. Workmanship was classified as direct or indirect and the raw materials and workmanship required for a product were standardized. The commission assigned in 1933 issued a report titled "Uniform Costing System for the Iron & Steel Industry" in 1935. In the 19th century, a prominent figure in cost accounting was Alexander Hamilton Church. A major contribution by Church was the full costing system. In the paper issued by The National Association of Cost Accountants (NACA) in 1947, it was argued that the full costing system is the most contemporary, effective, efficient and acceptable costing system. The concept of flexible budget emerged in early the 1940s. In the 1950s and 1960s, this was named variable budget. In 1950, Edwards Deming developed plant-wide control systems. General Electric used computers for business administration for the first time in 1954 and used the operation-based costing system to better distribute overhead manufacturing costs as of 1960. Break-even analyses were used in the 1950s and accountants developed Cost-Volume-Profit analyses in 1960s. In the same period, Joseph Orlicky and Oliver Wighy developed the Material Requirements Planning (MRP) system (Yükçü and Atağan, 2012: 39; Soba, 2008: 107).

In the 19th and 20th centuries, the methods of cost and management accounting were shaped by the expansion of the transportation business, scientific management approach in the American industry, increased output and the increase in the number of transportation companies. In the initial years of the concept of "Cost Accounting", the terms used included "industrial cost accounting" or "industrial accounting".

Industry Revolution 3

The starting point of Industry Revolution 3 was the use of semi-conductors in IT systems. They made data flow and control possible, expanded the use of personal computers (PC) and created the internet. With more extensive use of scientific data, the first programmable logic controller (PLC) (Madicon 084) was developed in 1969 and this marked the start of Industry Revolution 3 (Drath & Horch, 2014: 56). This accelerated the shift to Industry Revolution 3 where manufacture is more automation and technology-based and computer-aided integrated systems are used (Genç, 2018: 238). With the developments in communication, information, mechanics and micro-electronics as well as computers, the pace of the process of globalization also increased. This fueled a global transformation based on technology and created the information society (Bulut and Akçacı, 2017: 52). Industry 3.0 which marked the shift from the industrial society to the information society was shaped around semi-conductors, servers, PCs and internet so it is called the digital revolution or computer revolution. Another feature of this period is the search for a network to connect the machines within the computer system, the idea coming from mechanical power calculators. This is the start of the idea of the internet (Ziewitz and Brown, 2013: 22-23).

During Industry Revolution 3, machinery based on mechanical and electronics technology were replaced with machinery based on digital technology. Improvements in digital technologies, computers and the internet resulted with wider use of IT technologies and micro-electronic methods during the process of Industry Revolution 3 which continued until now (Kagermann et al., 2013:13). Automation of manufacturing processes through electronic and IT technologies changed the shape of these technologies. The internet facilitated the collaboration of designers in various areas. Industry Revolution 3 is also marked by an industrial organization where the communication and coordination with other stakeholders is stronger and the consumer has an impact in manufacturing (Ovacı, 2017:116).

The key factor in the changes in world globalization resulted with the international markets transforming into domestic markets. The increased pace of industrialization and removal of economic borders increased the diversity of products. Increased diversity boosted the demand for high-quality, low-cost and functional products as well as post-sales services. (Gürdal, 2007: 10).

This change in manufacturing technologies and IT resulted with an increase in the useful life of products and customer expectations. This triggered a high pace of change and renewal for the companies as well as more competitive markets. This competition required a reorganization of manufacturing processes in accordance with technological improvements. New manufacturing systems were built based on mechanization and automation, high quality, agile manufacturing and continuous improvement. New manufacturing systems used to plan and control manufacturing processes integrated the employees, machines and tools through automation (Yağmurlu, 2018: 4-5). With the increased use of computers and more automation, traditional labor-intensive manufacturing was replaced by capital-intensive manufacturing. This changed the method of manufacturing and had a major impact on the cost structure. As a result of this change, businesses were faced with a new manufacturing environment and a new cost structure (Çabuk, 2003: 110). The share of direct costs, especially direct workmanship costs in the general manufacturing costs decreased. On the other hand, the share of general manufacturing costs in total costs increased. Within general manufacturing costs, the share of variable costs decreased while the share of fixed costs increased (Altunay, 2007: 30).

In the 1970s, the Japanese company Toyota developed and deployed "just-in-time" (JIT) approach to ensure no-stock operations to boost efficiency. In the 1980s, Japanese companies developed and popularized the concepts of total quality management and efficiency improvement. The 1980s was a period also marked by robots, computer-aided design, computer-aided manufacturing, computer-integrated manufacturing, computer-aided process planning, agile manufacturing systems and other elements of factory automation. In the 1990s, the Total Quality Management approach became widely used and ISO 9000 quality certification system was introduced. Beginning with the mid-1990s, the age of "order-based mass manufacturing" (Mass Customization) started. Towards the end of the 20th century, globalization triggered the widespread use of various concepts including internet, planning of resources, learning organizations, international quality standards, supply chain management, lean and agile manufacturing (Soba, 2008: 108).

In the face of these developments, traditional costing methods became obsolete and companies needed a new costing system to ensure more efficient and timely data acquisition. In this sense, companies started to use a number of strategic costing methods including product lifecycle costing, target costing, kaizen costing, quality costing and operation-based costing to facilitate better decision-making in terms of competition, decrease the level of waste in terms of resource consumption, boost performance, accurately calculate product costs and offer better service quality to consumers (Bekçi and Özal, 2010: 81; Otlu and Demir 2005: 162).

Lean and Agile Manufacturing Before Industry 4.0

In the artisan manufacturing method, each product is manufactured for a certain customer. The product has no standards and the cost is high. After this, Fordism emerged as a manufacturing system based on a single type of product. The system started with Henry Ford's moving assembly line for automobile manufacturing and was improved for more complex products until the 1970s. Fordist manufacturing have produced very good results within the frame of its time. In those days, global demand was high. This required sequential placement of work stations for a high number of production in minimum time. This was exactly what Henry Ford did.

An English researcher invented the "flexible business system" in the early the 1960s. This system named "System 24" provided an automatic transfer of parts between machines for processing and was patented in 1965. With the improvements in computer control technologies in the 1970s, flexible manufacturing systems capable of manufacturing small or medium-sized volumes of products emerged (Gönen and Çelik, 2004: 135). The most important advantage of mass production is economies of scale and it has been unsupported by mass demand since customer demands and expectations are a lot more important. With flexible manufacturing systems which emerged from the integration of technological improvements to manufacturing systems, manufacturers can produce small batches of products with higher quality, diversification and safety. Flexible manufacturing systems consist of Computer Numerically Controlled or Numerically Controlled workbenches controlled by central computers, connected by automatic transfer systems and supported by work stations (Ronald and Charles,1993:128).

In the early 1980s and 90s, businesses focused on the strategy of increasing market share. This strategy requires a gaining competitive advantage through lower prices and diversification of products. Product diversification increases fixed costs and the amount of manufacturing at breakeven point, and reduces profitability (Ustasüleyman, 2008: 162). Starting with the early 1990s, the change in customer demands and expectations were not easy to meet through traditional manufacturing methods and systems. New manufacturing systems were required to manufacture fast, with high quality, in a short time and swiftly implement design and manufacturing changes (Akman and Keskin, 2012: 53).

Womack and colleagues published a book titled "The Machine That Changed the World" after some research at the Massachusetts Institute of Technology in USA. This introduced the philosophy of "Lean Thinking", basic principles of which were developed at Toyota in the 1950s under the leadership of engineers Eiji Toyoda and Taiichi Ohno (Bhasin, 2015:2).

Lean manufacturing based on lean thinking focuses on preventing waste and ensuring that the process consists only of value-adding steps. Waste is defined as anything which does not add value. Waste includes overproduction, unnecessary transfers, waiting, unnecessary stocks, unnecessary activities and errors. In lean manufacturing, businesses focus on customer satisfaction. Anything which does not have an impact of customer satisfaction is waste and unnecessary cost (Sezen et al, 2018: 51).

Lean manufacturing has 5 principles; namely customer value, value flow, continuous flow, traction system and excellence. Value is to manufacture the product or service customer is willing to pay for within a certain time and for a certain price. Value flow is the prevention of all activities which do not create value from the supplier to the customer. Continuous flow is ensuring the product or service flow for activities which add value. Traction system is the manufacturing of the value at the time and amount requested by the customer. Excellence is the operation of the process to provide the best possible performance and ensure continuous improvement (Terzi and Atmaca, 2011: 451).

Lean manufacturing focuses on preventing 7 wastes to improve customer value. These are overproduction, overstock, transportation, faulty manufacturing, unnecessary activity, unnecessary movement and waiting. A number of lean concepts and tools were developed to optimize operations and prevent waste in different areas. Some of them are listed below.

➢ SMED (Single Minute Exchange of Dies), a system for fast exchange of dies, was developed for the lean manufacturing of small batches. In this system, internal adjustments which are possible only when the machine is switched off were separated from external adjustments which are possible when the machine is operated (Tanık, 2010: 122).

➢ "Kanban" system for on-time manufacturing helps coordination between production lines and with the suppliers to receive the materials when and as required for the next operation (Özçelik and Cinoğlu, 2013: 85).

➢ Placement of the machines required for manufacturing of the final product in the order relevant to the workflow within the form of "Single Part Flow" system which prevents the time to wait for the shift between processes (Erol, 2012: 20-21).

➢ "U-lines" layout which is a combination of single-part flow and process-based line approach (Şeker, 2016: 468).

➢ 5S is a typical lean tool which optimizes the process and helps implementation of other lean tools; Sort (Seiri), Straighten (Seiton), Sweep (Seiso), Standardize (Seiketsu), Sustain and Self Discipline (Shitsuke) (Çakırkaya and Acar, 2016: 848-851).

➢ The philosophy of kaizen, which focuses on continual improvement in all areas,

➢ "Jidoka" approach which refers to the empowerment of the operators to stop the assembly line and the machinery in case of a problem or failure

➢ The concept of Poka-Yoke to develop preventive strategies against human error during the manufacturing process (Zerenler and Karaboğa, 2014: 266).

Use of lean methods including Just-in-time Manufacturing, Kanban, Kaizen, Continuous Flow, Total Productive Maintenance and SMED (Single-Minute Exchange of Dies) ensured several advantages including reduction of the rate of failure in manufacturing, increase in machine efficiency, proper use of equipment capacity, reduction of material losses, reduction of reprocessing and reduction of workmanship costs (Öksüz et al., 2017: 1-2).

The lean management approach promotes agility, prevents excessive stocks, reduces lead times and ensures high quality in goods and customer services. Its objectives include more output with fewer resources, short delivery times and low prices for a larger market share (Akman and Keskin, 2012: 54).

The basics of lean manufacturing was the elimination of any activity or process which does not add value to the final product. It increased performance but failed to adapt itself to the changing conditions. Therefore, the concept of agile manufacturing was introduced to ensure that an enterprise can adapt itself to unexpected changes and responds faster to customer expectations (Akman and Keskin, 2012: 55).

The concept of agile manufacturing was introduced by the report titled "21st Century Manufacturing Enterprise Strategy" published by Lehigh University Iacocca Institute in 1991. Iacocca Institute defines agility as "the situation where the manufacturing system is equipped with extraordinary skills (internal skills: hardware and software technologies, human resources, educated management and information) to swiftly respond to the changing needs in the market (speed, agility, customers, competitors, suppliers, responsiveness, infrastructure) (Baki, 2003:298)

Lean manufacturing is the capacity to make profit from change and competition in the markets, manufacturing methods and IT. Lean manufacturing designs products based on customer demands and its purpose is to meet unexpected customer requests in various times, with high quality and low cost in addition to the capacity to shift from one job to another (Ustasüleyman, 2008: 162). Lean manufacturing is beyond a single business and requires sharing of resources and technologies by companies. Lean manufacturing is in compliance with computer-integrated manufacturing, total quality management, planning of manufacturing resources, change engineering, empowerment of employees and optimized manufacturing technologies. It is a combination of known technologies and manufacturing methods (Baki, 2003: 298)

Lean manufacturing system ensures excellence in the manufacturing process from the supplier to the customer through operational methods. Agile manufacturing includes advanced technologies and scientific approach ensures sharing of resources and technologies. In fact, lean and agile production systems have created the infrastructure of the vertical and horizontal integration as well as manufacturing of smart factories. These two manufacturing systems were used to increase quality and efficiency in manufacturing as well as various methodologies and tools including just-in-time manufacturing, kanban, kaizen, continuous flow, six sigma, total productive maintenance and SMED. The remaining work is to replace humans with robots on the manufacturing line created by the lean manufacturing system and connect them with big data and IoT. Obviously, the elements of Industry 4.0 are not limited to robots, IoT and big data. However, these three are the required elements of Industry 4.0 for smart factories.

Industry 4.0 Technologies

Industry 4.0 was phrased for the first time in 2011 at Hannover Messe. Its first emergence as a concept was in an article titled "Industry 4.0: Towards Industry Revolution 4.0 with Internet of Things" in 2011 by Kagerman and others (Kagerman et al, 2011). Industry 4.0 will give rise to new types of advanced manufacturing and industrial processes through auto-controlled smart systems which check, organize and improve themselves (Thames and Schaefer, 2016: 13). These new and smart systems consist of high-tech components which include learning robots, big data, Internet of Things, cyber-physical systems, artificial intelligence, simulation, 3D systems, vertical/horizontal software integration, cloud technologies and cyber-security.

The main purpose of Industry 4.0, which refers to the integration of innovative IT with industrial processes, is to integrate the systems throughout the value chain from design and manufacturing to marketing and dispatch to organize more efficient processes (Barreto et al., 2017: 1246). This organization is the "smart factory" of the future where units communicate in real time and collaborate with each other as well as organizations and people through IoT, physical system processes are organized, a virtual copy of the physical environment is created and autonomous decisions are taken for self-organization (Sezen, 2018: 60). All "smart" things including smart communication, smart cities, smart buildings, smart homes, smart manufacturing and smart agricultural systems will use this structure through IoT. Industry 4.0 will continually improve automation technologies and radically change manufacturing and consumption relations. Its components are as follows.

Internet of Things (IoT): Internet of Things consists of network systems used for data communication between physical devices, machinery, vehicles and other tools with electronic equipment (Banger, 2017: 43) and it is the basis of smart factories, smart products and smart services. Internet of Things is defined as a network structure where devices and machines exchange data and make autonomous decisions without the need for human touch (Aktaş et al., 2016: 43). In other words, IoT is a communication network of devices, software and access services which control, monitor and analyze the data from physical events like manufacturing processes, logistics, power networks, customers, supply chain and recycling processes. Things also communicate through RFID (radio-frequency identification system) sensors and identifiers. This way, things can "think" and "talk" to update their information on status (Şekelli and Bakan, 2018: 206).

IoT database systems are scalable in terms of both performance and storage capacity and therefore they should be cloud-based (Dengiz, 2017: 40). IoT has layers of detection, communication, calculation and implementation. Actuators and sensors define the physical device accurately at the sensor layer. At the communication layer, data collected from the sensors are transferred to higher layers through wire and wireless system protocols. At the calculation layer, decisions are made based on the data collected with the sensors and communicated to the implementation layer. The calculation layer includes hardware, software, algorithms, big data analysis and security. The implementation layer sends the collected data to the user and management (Çelen, 2017: 12-13).

Cyber Physical Systems: Detection and control of the physical world with digital data have given rise to the concept of "Cyber Physical System". Cyber physical systems have two components. The first one is the network consisting of things and systems communicating via internet using and assigned internet address (Internet of Things) and the second one is the virtual platform created as a simulation of the things and behaviors in the real world. Without these cyber physical systems which can detect the smallest details in the manufacturing system, control them and solve possible problems, automation in smart manufacturing would not be possible (Özsoylu, 2017: 53). These systems which combine physical and virtual world are integrated communication, data processing, control and sensor systems. With the integration of IoT and cloud computing systems, the concept of "Digital Twin" which refers to the digital twins of cyber physical systems, physical things and systems was created in the next step (Dengiz, 2017: 39).

3D Printers: 3D printing, in other words additive manufacturing, is the printing of a digital 3D drawing and design in layers to manufacture a physical product (Soylu, 2018: 54). Traditional manufacturing is in the form of subtractive manufacturing. The raw material is cut, sliced and added to form the final product. In this process, a substantial amount of waste is generated. On the other hand, the manufacturing process in 3D printing is an additive process. During 3D printing, the software adds molten materials on top of each other to create layers and manufactures the product in a single part. This kind of manufacturing prevents raw material waste and improves efficiency and productivity. 3D printers store more than 100 materials (metal, plastic, stainless steel, polymer, resin, aluminum, ceramic, plaster, etc.) in solid, liquid and dust form. These printers help lower stock levels and support no-stock manufacturing systems. They can produce a single product or small batches of different product by changing the design based on orders without any additional cost (Bulut and Akçacı: 2017: 60).

Smart Factories: The concept of "smart factory" is the connection of cyber and physical worlds through cyber-physical systems and combination of resulting methods and business processes (Soylu, 2018: 46). The manufacturing process of Industry 4.0 is swift manufacturing of products at smart factories with the support of robot technologies based on customer requests and the analysis of data collected from the suppliers (Bulut and Akçacı, 2017: 46). A standard application at a smart factory is a high level of automation which means communication of machines to plan and control manufacturing processes. These smart factories operate 24/7 with full automation to ensure agile manufacturing and increase profitability and market share through special manufacturing. In addition to these benefits, companies can reach other objectives like high quality, instant access to accurate information, effective planning, integration of systems, cost benefits and process monitoring (Özsoylu, 2017: 52).

Smart Robots: Algorithms created to solve problems can be viewed in real time and the processes are much stronger than ever to analyze thousands of factors and variables. This resulted in robotic and learning machines. IoT allows robotic systems to communicate and guide each other. This means that the robots are autonomous. A device which is defined as a robot should be autonomous (Görçün, 2018: 358-359). The manufacturing process required by Industry 4.0 is based on fully-automatic production. Robots are used at smart factories to make efficiency analyzes using the data collected from the customers and suppliers (Soylu, 2018: 47). Improvements in sensors made robots capable of sensing the environment and response. With a more flexible manufacturing environment, smart robots can interact with other devices, materials and other manufacturing components to increase efficiency (Bulut and Akçacı, 2017: 58). Wider use of robots will prevent problems related to the people and human errors (Özsoylu, 2017: 54).

Big Data: Big data consists of informatics with high data generation rate and high data variability. It supports new data processing and analysis methods as well as process optimization (Özsoylu, 2017:51). In practice, Big Data means transformation of data collected from social media posts, network logs, blogs, photos, videos and log files into meaningful data available for processing. When analyzed properly, big data helps companies make strategic decisions, manage their risks, operate with high efficiency and innovate (EBSO, 2015: 19). However, big data systems are open to internet and this makes cyber security a major issue

Cloud Computing System: Cloud Computing is the general definition of internet-based configurable computing services which include data processing, storage and other systems with high processing power for computers and other devices (Yüksekbilgili and Çevik, 2018: 427). Cloud Computing refers to the whole body of services including the storage of all applications, programs and data on virtual server. These are accessible for any device via internet (EBSO, 2015: 22).

Simulation: Simulation is important for Industry 4.0 in terms of product design and development processes. Simulation is a method which provides logical and mathematical relations to understand the system structure and behaviors and allows testing with computers and tools which are nor embedded in the system. Virtual models built using real-time data create the virtual reality of the physical world with machines, products and people (Soylu, 2018: 48).

Augmented Reality: Augmented Reality digitizes physical objects as well as work-flow and information flow processes for the virtual environment and makes them a part of the virtual world in addition to the physical world. Augmented reality applications define physical environments in the virtual environment, create layers of various data and information, view them virtually to facilitate decision-making and augment the reality of the physical world.

Augmented reality is different from the virtual reality built by computers. Augmented reality is directly related with the physical world. Physical objects are replicated in the virtual world bur objects created in the virtual world do not necessarily exist in the physical world. Therefore, virtual environments are synthetic (Azuma, 1997: 356). Virtual reality creates them. However, no object which does not exist in the physical world is in the virtual world. AR can also be considered as an intermediary form between the physical world and virtual reality (Milgram et al., 1994: 44).

Horizontal & Vertical Integration: Horizontal integration within the scope of Industry 4.0 is the integration of organizations with the same type of customers. The final objective here is to increase the market share of the companies. Vertical integration is the integration of companies from various sub-industries in the same market (Yüksekbilgili and Çevik, 2018: 428).

Horizontal Integration at smart factories within the scope of Industry 4.0 refers to un interrupted flow manufacturing and planning steps within a single company and between multiple companies. This integration is inclusive of all points from raw material supply to design, manufacturing, marketing, dispatch and customers with integrated and end-to-end systems (Soylu, 2018: 48). Vertical integration deals with the internal processes of the business and uses various information technologies to integrate at various levels of hierarchy including sales, engineering, manufacturing planning, control and others for the optimization of material, product and data flow (Koçak and Diyadin, 2018: 112). This includes the integration of sensors, motors, control panels, production management systems, corporate resource planning software and others in manufacturing.

Cyber Security: It is important that data are transferred in a verifiable manner in Industry 4.0. With the improvements in vertical and horizontal integration, information security will be a major issue and a security system will be required to protect critical industrial systems and manufacturing lines against cyber threats. Verification of data from the devices within the manufacturing system and processability and accessibility to such data by the relevant people are important. The cyber security network will ensure ID coordination of the machines and access to and management of them through communication protocols (Numanoğlu, 2016: 28; Bulut and Akçacı, 2017: 57).

Manufacturing of Smart Factories

The most important result of Industry 4.0 has been the emergence of smart factories. The concept of smart factory is an integral part of a vast digital supply network. A smart factory is a flexible system which automatically adapts itself to changing conditions, learns, prevents human error, uses data acquired from connected operations and manufacturing systems, automatically regulates business flows, manages supply chain processes, improves energy consumption, prevents costs and waste and improves efficiency, quality and labor time. These factories operate 24/7 and are equipped with automation systems which allow real-time monitoring of and remote intervention to manufacturing processes. The consumers are involved in product development and manufacturing machines are reconfigured based on their demands. With this perspective, the National Institute of Standards and Technology defined smart manufacturing as "fully-integrated, collaborative manufacturing systems that respond in real time to meet changing demands and conditions in the factory, in the supply network, and in customer needs."

Smart factories are different from traditional factories in terms of flow systems, operation and manufacturing processes. On the other hand, the basic similarity is that they both have certain flow systems. As a result of this, key elements of both traditional and smart factories are work pieces and work stations. Work pieces are the outcome of a process of transforming the actions and movements in a manufacturing process into micro business units which are small, meaningful and highly efficient. The work station is the manufacturing or processing point where a business piece is produced. This ensures that a work piece divided into micro unit can be produced on a work station.

Another similarity between traditional and smart factories is that every flow system has a start and an end. A manufacturing process can start with an autonomous or worker-triggered work order for a raw material request and end with a dispatch to a customer or warehouse. With this perspective, a major difference of a smart factory is that flow processes are autonomous or semi-autonomous, independent of human factor. In smart factories, a manufacturing process starts with an order by a customer. In traditional factories, a manufacturing process start with the decision of a manager and is fully dependent on human factor. In a smart factory, it is independent of human factor and usually autonomous.

Individual or industrial customer requests are directly sent to the manufacturing site via cloud systems. These requests are transformed into autonomous work orders by cyber physical systems in the form of predefined algorithms for manufacturing processes. These orders are received and processed simultaneously and the initial manufacturing station is activated to perform the required function. After the performance of the basic function by the first manufacturing station (autonomous or semi-autonomous machine or a combination of machines), the next manufacturing station is ordered to operate. Other manufacturing stations are at stand by. This reduces or stops energy consumption when manufacturing stations are not in operation, resulting with significant cost reductions. Manufacturing stations involved in the process from start to end perform their functions sequentially and the final product is transferred to the warehouse or directly to the customer based on collected data. Data are processed and the activity is finalized by transferring data to transport vehicles or the warehouse.

All manufacturing stations within the process receive, process and send data. Therefore, manufacturing stations are autonomous systems independent of human factor and operate upon data sent by the previous station. Manufacturing stations are flexible within the manufacturing processes to a great extent. Various functions can be performed based on received data and predefined activities. A group of machines can tighten screws or assemble in various processes based on the received data. The basic elements which define the process are data features and work orders.

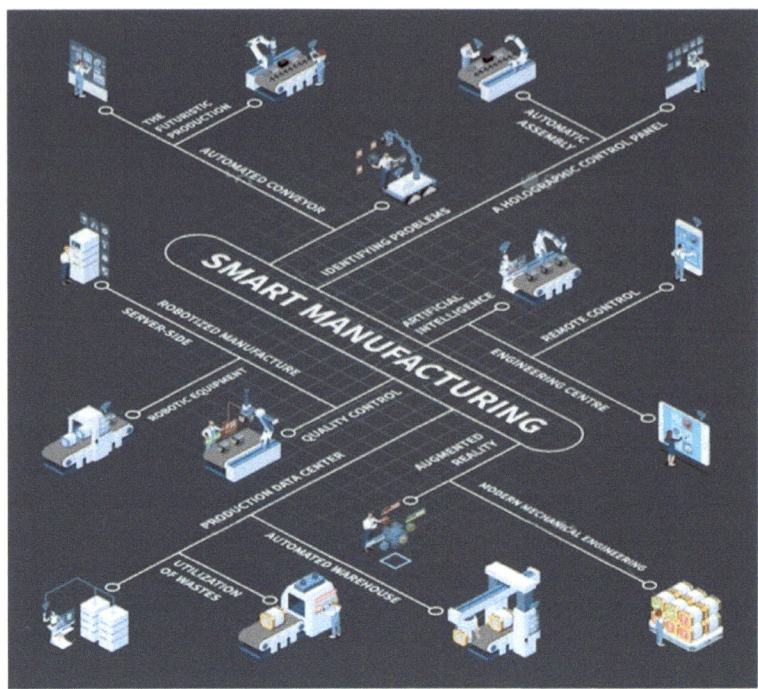

Fig.1. Manufacturing processes and systems at smart factories.

Manufacturing systems within the system are capable of performing task and operating in case of failure. These systems can receive and send data to and from the system also in case of failure to operate. In such case, cyber physical systems generate autonomous work orders and remove machines or devices from the process or assign works for the backup capacity. On the other hand, if the failure is unpredicted in terms of time or cause, the station sends the relevant data to the manufacturing station and the system and autonomously requests replacement of itself with another machine or station.

In conclusion, smart factories help optimize various assets and make the best use of them. It facilitates real-time determination of the labor force, equipment and performance and location of assets for instant realization of changes in inventory. Machine performance and general visibility of the manufacturing plant are extended beyond the factory site. A dynamic work flow which connects the supply chain to the manufacturing plant provides the information required by the team. In such cases, smart factories facilitate collaboration, increase efficiency and ensure seamless end-to-end operations.

Costing Systems at Smart Factories

Cost accounting consists of two sub-systems, namely the costing system and the cost registry system. The costing system is the basics and principles of the process of measuring the cost elements of manufacturing on a unit price.

Cost registry system is the basics and principles of the registry and monitoring of the cost elements and reporting the data (Özpeynirci and Şirin, 2018: 60; Karakaya, 2007: 9). In traditional cost accounting, total manufacturing cost is the sum of direct raw material cost, direct labor cost and overhead manufacturing cost. Direct raw material cost and direct labor cost can be directly allocated to the product cost. Overhead manufacturing costs are allocated not directly but through certain distribution costs. (Çabuk, 2003: 111).Unit price is calculated by dividing the total manufacturing cost by the amount of production. This cost will be the basis for determining the price of the product. In other words, it is a cost-based price determination. (Otlu and Demir, 2005: 165). As per the "Uniform Accounting System" which dominated Europe until 2000s, the traditional cost accounting registry flow is given in Figure 2 below.

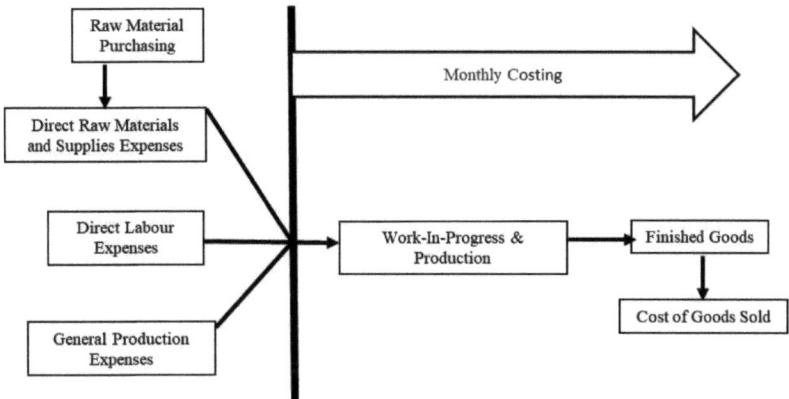

Fig. 2. Traditional Cost Registry System.

After the 1990s, lean and agile manufacturing systems which included just-in-time manufacturing had an impact on current traditional cost accounting registry flow. Although not widely accepted, the cost accounting registry flow in Figure 3 below is used by many businesses (Kaygusuz, 2006: 78).

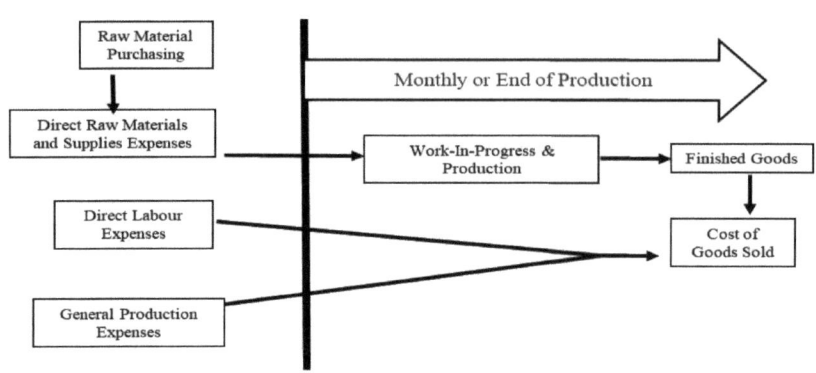

Fig. 3. Cost Registry System in Agile Manufacturing Systems.

Cyber physical systems will integrate the value chain digitally by connecting the physical world and the virtual world through sensors, actuators, computers, software systems and other IT tools. As it has always been the case, such integration is related with manufacturing. In the manufacturing process of Industry 4.0, smart devices in the industry and customer segments and the smart machines and systems which all connect to the internet acquire manufacturing data from "Big Data" systems on cloud. Stock control will be performed for raw materials based on the order by the customer. If the raw material is not available in stock, the supplier will be informed. Upon verification of the lead time for raw material, a timeline will be determined for manufacturing at the factory. Smart racks and sensors at the warehouse will check the entry of raw materials to the warehouse and the raw materials dispatched for manufacturing to determine the raw material cost. Auxiliary materials required for manufacturing will be printed by 3D printers. With advanced virtual visibility capability, robots on the manufacturing line will take the necessary action for each raw material and finish manufacturing with zero error. The products will be packaged and transferred to the warehouse with smart forklifts. The warehouse automation system and the integration of the warehouse with the supply chain optimize the dispatch and distribution processes. Through cloud computing and the sensors and actuators at the plant, expenses and repair costs of water, power, energy and air-conditioning systems as well as the depreciation of assets will be calculated and the costs will be associated with the order. Effective monitoring and reporting of costs and association with the sales in the income table will be in real-time.

These smart factories will possibly have technologies in sci-fi movies, including use of "artificial intelligence", "cyber-physical systems" and "Internet of Things" to ensure manufacturing processes which manage and control themselves. These factories will not only develop automation technologies, but also decision-making processes. The clear and foreseeable impact of these factories in the near future will be the elimination of direct labor costs. This estimation will prevent the applicability of the traditional costing at businesses which fully embrace Industry 4.0. An estimated cost registry system for a smart factory is given in Figure 4 below.

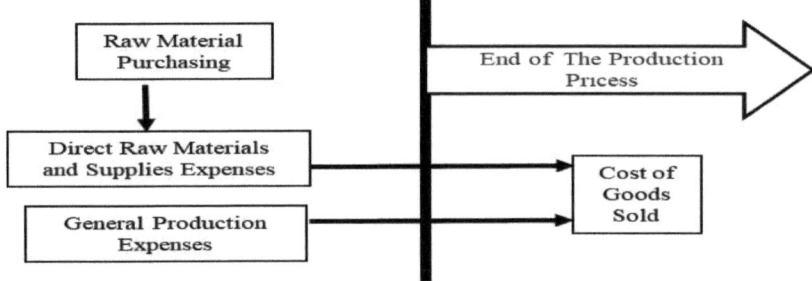

Fig. 4. Cost Registry System at Smart Factories.

The costing system is the grouping, control and association of the cost data with operations. Therefore, manufacturing cost of products are calculated by a combination of cost determination methods based on the scope of cost and the method of calculation. Therefore, there are various groups in a costing system built traditionally. There are three major criteria here; namely "management structure", "whether or not cost figures are actual" and "whether it covers all or some of the product cost". These three main groups and costing methods is given in Figure 5 (Kaygusuz, 2006: 42).

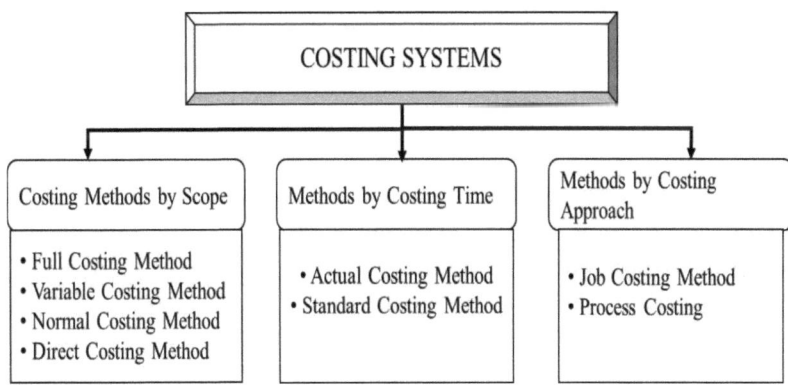

Fig. 5. Costing Systems.

Future smart factories will make use of artificial (AI) and it can be estimated that the manufacturing cost methods will not change. Among the time-based costing methods, only the actual cost method will survive. In an accounting system based on real time data, standart costing method will lose importance. Production planning and budgets will be instant in the future due to

IoT, cyber physical systems, AI, macro-economic and micro-economic data analyses, instant access to customer and market data, verified market and sales objectives as well as the analyses of current and previous capacity, manufacturing and cost data. Scope-based costing methods will also not be used. This is because the direct labor cost in all these methods will not be a part of smart factories where robots will be used. Furthermore, because smart factories are based on a model of uninterrupted production, the concept of capacity will also be eliminated. The future will be controlled by AI but full spread of smart factories on a global scale is not expected in the near future. Therefore, traditional costing systems will continue to exist for many years.

Conclusion

After hundreds of years of shifting from the agricultural revolution to industrial revolution, we saw four major industrial revolutions through change and development since the 18th century. Each industrial revolution resulted with huge social and industrial improvement and laid the foundation for the next. The outcome of the industrial revolutions include urbanization, emergence of the working class, increased economic welfare, and accelerated scientific and technical improvements among others. Improvements in manufacturing technologies which emerged with industrial revolutions triggered new manufacturing and management methodologies and tools for sustainable development and more efficient management of management processes. Specifically the improvements in digital technologies in the 1970s and onwards and lean and agile manufacturing systems developed at the end of 20th century triggered new approaches in accounting and cost accounting. Strategic costing methods developed to help companies gain a competitive advantage on a global scale are in accordance with the continuous improvement philosophy of agile manufacturing systems. These developments in manufacturing and costing triggered the process of Industry 4.0.

The main purpose of Industry 4.0 is to build smart factories capable of monitoring and analyzing and managing manufacturing processes with full automation. This will only be possible with "Cyber-Physical Systems" and "Internet of Thing" systems. The major advantage of this system is speed. In other words, data flow is in real-time. In such case, costing and accounting systems will also be real-time. The idea may look like science-fiction now, but the manufacturing lines of the smart factories of Industry 4.0 will be fully robotized in the future and there will be no direct labor cost in manufacturing or unit cost calculations. Therefore, a new costing method should be added to the traditional costing systems to cover scope-based costs. The name of this costing method without direct labor costs comes from the philosophy of Industry 4.0. Two major concepts are full automation and real-time data flow. Hence the name of this method can be "full-automation costing" or "real-time costing method".

The technology we will use tomorrow will be determined by the works of today. In other words, just like today, tomorrow's world will be shaped by history. An effect of the Covid-19 pandemic was the isolation of people at homes. Borders were closed, economies suffered and the winners seem to be companies with decent software and internet network. The question is what we should expect in the future, digital leadership of machines and digital slavery of humanity? It should however be noted that a machine wins a chess game with a human. But when human and machine make a team against another machine, the winner is the team of human and machine.

References

Akman, G., and Keskin, A.G. (2012). Evaluating Perception Level of Agile Manufacturing in Manufacturing Firms. Journal of Science and Technology of Dumlupınar University. 23: 53-66.

Aktaş, F., Çeken, C. and Erdemli Y.E. (2016). Internet of Things Technology Applications of Biomedical Field. Düzce University Journal Of Science&Technology. 4 (1), 37-54.

Alçın, S. (2016). A New Theme for Production: Industry 4.0. Journal of Life Economics. 3 (2). 19-30.

Altunay, M.A. (2007). Çağdaş Maliyetleme Sistemlerinden Faaliyet Tabanlı Maliyetleme Sistemi ve Bir Tekstil İşletmesinde Uygulanması. Yüksek Lisans Tezi, Süleyman Demirel Üniversitesi. Sosyal Bilimler Enstitüsü. Isparta.

Askin, R.G., and Standridge, C.R. (1993). Modeling and Analysis of Manufacturing Systems. John Wiley & Sons Inc. New York.

Azuma, R. T. (1997). A Survey of Augmented Reality. Teleoperators and Virtual Environments 6 (4). 355-385.

Baki, B. (2003). 21.Yüzyılın Üretim Paradigması: Çevik Üretim. Atatürk Üniversity Journal of Economics and administrative Sciences. 17 (1–2). 291-305.

Banger, G. (2017). Endüstri 4.0 Ekstra. Dorlion Yayınları. Ankara.

Barreto, L., Amaral, A., and Pereıra, T. (2017). Industry 4.0 Implications in Logistics: An Overview. Procedia Manufacturing. 13, 1245-1252.

Bekçi, İ., and Özal, H. (2010). Stratejik Maliyet Yönetiminin Sağlık Sektöründe Uygulanabilirliğine Yönelik Bir Araştırma. Akademik Araştırmalar ve Çalışmalar Dergisi. 2 (3). 78-97.

Bekçioğlu, S., and Köroğlu, Ç. (2013). 20. Yüzyılın Sonunda Maliyet Muhasebesinin Yerine Geçen Yeni Bir Yaklaşım: Stratejik Maliyet Yöntemi. Muhasebe ve Finans Tarihi Araştırmaları Dergisi. 4, 50-72.

Bhasin, S. (2015). Lean Management Beyond Manufacturing: A Holistic Approach. Springer International Publishing. Switzerland.

Bulut, E., and Akçacı, T. (2017). Industry 4.0 And Within The Scope of Innovation Indicators Analysıs of Turkey. ASSAM International Refereed Journal. 7. 50-72.

Can, A.V. (2007). Is Luca Pacioli "The Father of Accounting?" Akademik Bakış Uluslararası Hakemli Sosyal Bilimler E-Dergisi. (12). 1-15.

Çabuk, Y. (2003). Alternative Approach To Traditional Costing Systems: Activity Based Costing. Zonguldak Karaelmas University. Journal of Bartin Faculty of Forestry. 5 (5). 109-116.

Çakırkaya, M., and Acar, Ö. E. (2016). 5S Tekniği Aşamaları ve Makarna Sektöründe Bir Uygulama. Atatürk Üniversitesi İktisadi ve İdari Bilimler Dergisi. 30 (4). 845-868.

Çelen, S. (2017). Industry 4.0 and Simulation. International Journal of 3D Printing Technologies and Digital Industry. 1(1). 9-26.

Çetin, O., and Altuğ, N. (2005). Çevik Üretim. V.Ulusal Üretim Araştırmaları Sempozyumu. İstanbul Ticaret Üniversitesi. 25-27 Kasım 2005. 301-306.

Dengiz, O. (2017). Endüstri 4.0: Üretimde Kavram ve Algı Devrimi. Journal of Mechanical Design and Production. 15(1). 38-45.

EBSO, Aegean Region Chamber of Industry. (2015). Sanayi 4.0. http://www.ebso.org.tr/ebsomedia/documents/sanayi-40_81017283.pdf (Date of Access 01.06.2020).

Eren, Z. (2020). Toplum 5.0 ve Dijital Dünyada Toplumsal Dönüşüm ve Eğitim 5.0. Digital Transformation and Processes. Istanbul Gelisim University Press. İstanbul.

Erol, S. (2012). Yalın Yaklaşım ve Yalın Üretim. Anahtar Dergisi. 24 (278). 18-22.

Genç, S. (2018). Sanayi 4.0 Yolunda Türkiye. Sosyoekonomi. 26 (36). 235-243.

Gönen, S., and Çelik, M. (2004). Esnek Üretim Sistemleri Uygulayan İşletmelerde Üretim Maliyetlerinin Değerlendirilmesi. Ege Academic Review. 4 (1). 133-143.

Görçün, Ö. F. (2018). Technology Utilization in Logıstıcs And Robotic Systems. Mehmet Akif Ersoy University Journal of Social Sciences Institute. 10 (24). 351-368.

Gürdal, K. (2007). Maliyet Yönetiminde Güncel Yaklaşımlar. Siyasal Kitabevi. Ankara.

Gürdal, Kadir. (2007). Maliyet Yönetiminde Güncel Yaklaşımlar. Siyasal Kitabevi. Ankara.

Kagermann, H., Lukas, W. and Wahlster, W. (2011). Industrie 4.0 –Mit dem Internet der Dinge auf dem Weg zur 4. Industriellen Revolution. Inhalte der Ausgabe Nr. 13/2011.VDI Nachrichten. Berlin.

Kagermann, H., Wahlster, W., and Helbig, J. (2013). Securing the future of German manufacturing industry Recommendations for Implementing the Strategic Initiative Industrie 4.0. Final Report of the Industrie 4.0 Working Group. Ed:Ariane Hellinger ve Veronika Stumpf, Acatech-National Academy of Science and Engineering, https://www.din.de/blob/76902/e8cac883f42bf28536e7e8165993f1fd/recommendations-for-implementing-industry-4-0-data.pdf (Date of Access 14.05.2020).

Karakaya, M. (2007). Maliyet Muhasebesi. Gazi Kitabevi. Ankara.

Kaygusuz, S.Y. (2006). Yenilikçi Yönetim Muhasebesi. Aktüel yayınları Alfa Akademi. İstanbul.

Koçak, A., and Diyadin, A. (2018). Evaluation of Critical Success Factors in the Transitional Processes of Industry 4.0 using DEMATEL Method. Ege Academic Review. 18 (1). 107-120.

Köroğlu, Ç. (2015). The Developments in Accounting Audit From the Foundation of Turkish Repulic Toward Present. Niğde Üniversitesi İktisadi ve İdari Bilimler Fakültesi Dergisi. 8 (3). 31-44.

Milgram, P., Takemura, H., Utsumi, A. and Kishino, F. (1994). Augmented Reality: A Class of Displays On the Reality-Virtually Continuum. SPIE Proceedings Vol. 2351: Tele-manipulator and Telepresence Technologies. Boston. 282-292.

Numanoğlu, N., Eynehan, M. E., Morkoç, N. G. and Aksoy, E. (2016). Türkiye'nin Küresel Rekabetçiliği İçin Bir Gereklilik Olarak Sanayi 4.0 Gelişmekte Olan Ekonomi Perspektifi. Turkish Industry & Business Associatin and The Boston Consulting Group. Yayın no; TÜSİAD-T/2016-03/576. İstanbul. http://www.tusiad.org/indir/2016/sanayi-40.pdf (Date of Access 07.06.2020).

Rifkin, J. (2014). The Third Industrial Revolution How Lateral Power is Transforming Energy. the Economy and the World. (Çeviren: Murat Başhekim ve Pelin Sıral). İletişim Yayınları. Yayın no: 2089. İstanbul.

Otlu, F., and Demir, Ö. (2005). Cost Systems From The Dimension Of Strategic Decision Making. Fırat University Journal of Social Science. 15(1). 155-170.

Ovacı, C. (2017). Open Innovation in the Era of Industry 4.0. Maliye Finans Yazıları. 108. 113-132.

Öksüz, M. K., Öner, M., and Öner, S. C. (2017). Evaluation of Lean Manufacturing Techniques from the Perspective of Industry 4.0. 4th International Regional Development Conference (IRDC'2017). 21-23 September 2017. Tunceli/Turkey. 1-9.

Önder, E. (2008). Maliyet Muhasebesi Ders Notları. İstanbul Teknik Üniversitesi. Tekstil Teknolojileri ve Tasarımı Fakültesi Tekstil Mühendisli Bölümü. İstanbul.

Özçelik, T. Ö. and Cinoğlu, F. (2013). Yalın Felsefe ve Bir Otomotiv Yan Sanayi Uygulaması. İstanbul Ticaret Üniversitesi Fen Bilimleri Dergisi. 12 (23). 79-101.

Özel, S. (2010). Maliyet Muhasebesi. Maliye ve Hukuk Yayınları. Yayın No:89. Ankara.

Özkan, M., Al, A., and Yavuz, S. (2018). The Effects of Fourth Industrial Revolution with respect to International Political Economy and Turkey. Marmara University Journal of Political Science. 6 (2). 126-156.

Özpeynirci, R., and Şirin, B. H. (2018). Forming the Cost System in Business Firms Making Industrial Machine Manufacturing and a Relevant Application. Karamanoglu Mehmetbey Unıversity Journal of Social And Economic Research. 20 (35). 59-71.

Özsoylu, A. F. (2017). Industry 4.0. Journal of Çukurova University Faculty of Economics and Administrative Sciences. 21 (1). 41-64.

Schwab, K. (2016). Dördüncü Sanayi Devrimi. (çev.) Zülfü Dicleli. Optimist Yayınları. İstanbul.

Sezen, H. K., Sert, F. C., and Şenaras, A. E. (2018). Teknoloji, Yalın Yönetim ve Ötesi. Ekonometride Güncel Konular. Editör: M. K. Terzioğlu. Gazi Kitabevi. Ankara.

Soba, M. (2008). Flexible Manufacturing Systems and the Effects to the Rivalry Power of the Companies. Usak Üniversity Journal of Social Sciences. 1 (2). 103-124.

Soylu, A. (2018). Industry 4.0 and New Approaches to Entrepreneurship. Pamukkale University Journal of Social Sciences Institute. 32. 43-57.

Şeker, A. (2016). Yalın Üretim Sisteminde Kanban. Tek Parça Akışı ve U Tipi Yerleştirme Sistemleri. The Journal of Academic Social Science Studies. 50 (Autumn II). 449-470.

Şekkeli, Z. H., and Bakan, İ. (2018). Smart Factories. Journal of Lıfe Economıcs. 5 (4). 203-219.

Tanık, M. (2010). Kalıp Ayar Sürelerinin SMED Metodolojisi ile İyileştirilmesi: Bir Yalın Altı Sigma Uygulaması. Muğla Üniversitesi Sosyal Bilimler Enstitüsü Dergisi. 25. 118-140.

Terzi, S., and Atmaca, M. (2011). Examination of Value Stream Costing in Terms of Lean Manufacturing System. Suleyman Demirel University The Journal of Faculty of Economics and Administrative Sciences. 16 (3). 449-466.

Thames, L., and Schaefer, D. (2016). Softwaredefined cloud manufacturing for industry 4.0. Procedia CIRP. 52, 12-17. https://doi.org/10.1016/j.procir.2016.07.041 (Date of Access 20.05.2020).

Ustasüleyman, T. (2008). Çevikliğin İşletme Performansına Etkisine Yönelik Yapısal Bir Model Önerisi. Gazi Üniversitesi İktisadi ve İdari Bilimler Fakültesi Dergisi. 10 (2). 161-178.

Yağmurlu, N. (2018). İmalat Sanayiinde Stratejik Maliyet Yönetimi Uygulamaları ve İşletme Performansı Üzerindeki Etkileri: Borsa İstanbul'da Bir Araştırma. Doktora Tezi, Süleyman Demirel Üniversitesi. Sosyal Bilimler Enstitüsü. İşletme Anabilim Dalı. Isparta.

Yükçü, S., and Atağan, G. (2012). 20. Yüzyılın İlk Yarısında Maliyet Muhasebesinin Gelişimi. Muhasebe ve Finans Tarihi Araştırmaları Dergisi. 2. 39-67.

Yükçü, S., and Atağan, G. (2014). Maliyet Muhasebesi Tarihinin Üretim Teknolojisi Tarihine Bağımlılığı. Muhasebe ve Finans Tarihi Araştırmaları Dergisi. 6. 142-173.

Yüksekbilgili, Z., and Çevik, G. Z. (2018). With Respect to Industy 4.0 an Analysis on Turkey's Current and Future State. Research of Financial Economic and Social Studies. 3 (2). 422-436.

Zerenler, M., and Karaboğa, K. (2014). Müşteri Memnuniyetinin Sağlanmasında Hataların Önlenmesine Yönelik Üretim Odaklı Bir Bakış Açısı: Poka-Yoke Sistemleri. Selçuk Üniversitesi Sosyal Bilimler Enstitüsü Dergisi. Dr. Mehmet Yıldız Özel Sayısı. 263-275.

Ziewitz, M., and Brown, I. (2013). Research Handbook on Governance of the Internet. Edited by Ian Brown. Edward Elgar Publishing Limited. UK.

CHAPTER 8

The Role of Nanotechnology for Antimicrobial Agents

Figen Özyıldız[1], Elif Alyamaç Seydibeyoğlu[2], M.Özgür Seydibeyoğlu[3,4]
{seydibey@gmail.com }

[1] Dr., Ege University, Department of Biology, İzmir/Turkey

[2] Assist. Prof., Izmir Katip Çelebi University, Department of Petroleum and Natural Gas Engineering, İzmir/Turkey

[3] Professor, Izmir Katip Çelebi University, Department of Materials Science and Engineering, İzmir/Turkey

[4] Ege University Sciencepark, Filinia R&D, Izmir, Turkey

Abstract

Antimicrobial agents are substances that kill microorganisms or prevent their reproduction. Antimicrobials are used in the treatment of infectious diseases. Microorganisms can resist antibiotics used as antimicrobial agents and cause side effects. This has increased the interest in natural herbal antimicrobial agents as an alternative to synthetic antimicrobial agents. Many studies have been conducted, especially on the antimicrobial effect found in the essential oil part of the plants. In recent years, the spread of microorganisms has increased significantly and started to seriously threaten public health. As a result, the researchers' search for new antimicrobial agents has increased studies on antimicrobial activities of nanoparticles. The production of nano metals has gained importance with its antimicrobial properties. Metal oxides such as silver nanoparticles ZnO and TiO_2 have begun to be used, especially in the production of antimicrobial particles. Scientists continue to explore the risk factors for COVID-19, which is a serious threat to the world, which was first noticed in December 2019 in Wuhan, China. It has been stated with the current research of nanotechnology, it can also be used to fight this new corona virus. It has been emphasized that nanotechnology tools can play an important role in the diagnosis, treatment, and advancement of the vaccine development of COVID-19 infection. In this section, antimicrobial agents and their effects on Corona and COVID-19, the nanotechnology, in particular, the antimicrobial effects of nanoparticles and their effects on Corona virus are emphasized.

Keywords: COVID 19, Nanotechnology, Nanomaterials, Antimicrobial.

Introduction

Antimicrobials are drugs used to treat infectious diseases caused by microorganisms. Their common disadvantage is that they have side effects and cause resistance development in microorganisms. Therefore, if necessary, they should be selected and used considering the factors of the element and host (Saran and Karahan 2010). In addition, essential oils obtained from parts of plants such as stem, leaf, bud, fruit, flower and seed and extracts prepared with water or alcohol; has antimicrobial effects on many microorganisms. Plants contain compounds with various antimicrobial effects, such as saponins, coumarins, terpenoids, alkaloids, flavonoids, thiosulfinates, phenolics and organic acids. The antimicrobial activity of these compounds varies depending on many factors, especially with their chemical structure and concentration (Sengün and Oztürk, 2018). In addition, many studies have been conducted on antimicrobial activities of nanoparticles in recent years. Nanoparticles may be small, but they have a wide ratio of surface to volume, which brings them special, remarkable characteristics. With these characteristics, nanoparticles were used in the areas of medicine, sensors, biotechnology, DNA labeling and drug delivery, and are used as a connection among bulk materials. Nano techniques have been widely used to increase the distribution and effectiveness of antiviral drugs, especially with nucleoside analogs in conjunction with systems of delivery that have possible uses against drug-resistant human immunodeficiency virus diseases. For newly designed drug formulations, the many available nano delivery systems can be used to deliver the drugs effectively to COVID-19 for quicker therapy indices. But this research is continuing, and there are still no nano-drugs available to treat COVID-19. Nanotechnology also has a role in the COVID-19 diagnosis (Waris, et al., 2020). Nano-sized metal and metal oxides, especially silver (Ag), titanium dioxide (TiO_2), zinc oxide (ZnO) and Copper II oxide(CuO_2) are among the new generation biocides. As the contact surfaces of the particles with increasing specific surface area increase with their contact with microorganisms, their antimicrobial activity increases. Silver(Ag) compounds and nanoscale silver particles are used in medical applications and medical implants due to their broad-spectrum antimicrobial activity against bacteria, fungi, and viruses, and as they are non-toxic. Ag + ions have been found to be ineffective by binding to electron-bearing compounds such as thiols, carboxylates, amides and imidazole's in the structures of enzymes and DNAs in microorganisms. In semiconductor metal oxides, TiO_2, the band gap of which is closest to visible light, is widely used because it is easy to find and does not show toxin properties. O_2, HO_2 and especially OH radicals resulting from TiO_2 photocatalytic processes neutralize microorganisms. These radicals oxidize organic compounds in the structure of microorganisms, causes them to die

(Dural, Erem and Ozcan, 2013). In this section, antimicrobial materials, role of antimicrobials for corona and COVID 19, nanoparticles and nanotechnology for antimicrobial uses, the use of nanotechnology for corona viruses are discussed.

Antimicrobials

We use antimicrobial term for synthetic or organic substances, which in certain amounts they can inhibit or destroy microorganisms (Bhatia et. al., 2014).

Antimicrobials are substances which used in many areas, which involves areas with interaction with human skin, plastics, food, food manufacturing, prevention of the growth of microbials or annihilation of the organisms. A worldwide concern is that efficacy of the antimicrobials and antimicrobial resistance. For many sectors like agricultural, medical, or other related, antimicrobial resistance in bacteria is an increasing issue. With microbial resistance to conventional antiseptics and antibiotics growing in prevalence, antimicrobial agents are developed from compounds of natural origin (Kara, 2016). Antimicrobials, in addition to the compounds of origin from which they originate, are classified into the microorganisms by their effect rates. Biocide and biostatic are 2 categories in which microorganisms are categorized according to the impact rate of antimicrobial agents. Biocides are antimicrobial agents that have a significant impact on microorganisms and antimicrobials that have a microorganism-inhibiting function named biostatic al (Kara, 2016).

Characteristics of antimicrobials

Antibacterials

The term bacteriostatic is used as materials that prevent reproduction of the bacteria. By removing the bacteriostatic from the atmosphere, bacteria can then replicate (Kara, 2016). Bactericidal is a term used for substances that kill bacteria. The difference between bactericidal and bacteriostatic impact lies in the irrevocability of this method. It is not reproducible even a killed organism is evacuated from the agent. It has a melter impact on the active cell in certain situations. In other situations, cell may stay intact and may also stay active due to metabolic form (Kara, 2016). Antimicrobials can classify into categories by their mechanism of antimicrobial activity. Classes of antimicrobials are inhibition of the synthesis of cell walls, inhibition of nucleic acid synthesis, depolarization of the cell membrane, inhibition of bacterial metabolic pathways, inhibition of protein synthesis. Even worse, the excessive use of antimicrobial substances has helped lead to the massive resistance issue we deal today. Factors that contributed to the the problem of resistance include increased intake of antimicrobial substances by humans and animals, and excessive prescribing of antimicrobials (Reygaer, 2018).

Antifungals

Species, particularly plants, compounds and extricates determined from distinctive characteristic assets have moreover been a effective instrument for anticipating contagious diseases and spoilage. Since of the greatly routine utilize of turmeric in nourishment items, in arrange to ponder turmeric and curcumin with the objective of overseeing parasitic deterioration and contagious pathogens, numerous works have been carried out. (Moghadamtousi et al., 2014). Antifungals can be divided into three groups, based on their sites of activity: azole, which inhibits the synthesis of ergosterol (the principal fungal sterol), 5-fluorocytosine, which inhibits macromolecular synthesis, polyene, which interacts physiochemically with fungal membrane sterols. There are numerous types of systems that contribute to the development of antifungal resistance. Such systems include medicine target adjustment, adjustment of sterol biosynthesis, lowering of the target enzyme's intercellular concentration, and antifungal target's high expression (Ghannoum and Rice, 1999).

Antiviral

Viruses are nonautonomous species unlike bacterial, fungal, and parasitic pathogens and thus allow living cells to reproduce. Most replication processes consequently require typical cellular metabolic pathways, making it even harder to develop a drug that can specifically target the virion without any negative effects on infected cells (Jassim and Naji, 2003). Viral diseases with developing and constant viruses are a increasing health problem globally. Consequently, the discovery of novel antiviral agents derived from plants has gained greater importance than in the past. A variety of native Amazonian medicinal herbs are known to have an antimicrobial and anti-inflammatory feature, but only a few have been reviewed for their antiviral activities and immunomodulatory characteristics. (Williams, 2001). A couple of hundred plant and herb organisms that have activities as modern antiviral agents were studied, with surprisingly mild commonality. A large range of active phytochemicals that are terpenoids, proteins, lignans, polyphenolic flavonoids, furyl compounds, coumarins, alkaloids, sulphides, polyins, saponins, thiophenes, and peptides were discovered. A significant degree of antiviral action has demonstrated some volatile essential oils from commonly used kitchen herbs, spices, and herbal teas (Jassim and Naji, 2003).

Antiprotozoal

Human protozoan pathogens cause both symptomatic and asymptomatic illnesses which at some stage will affect virtually every human being. Through the long-standing discovery of antiprotozoal chemotherapy, much of which predates the current antibiotic age, the main impact of diseases resulting from these pathogens is expressed worldwide. Yet, despite the replication of antibacterial products over the past few years, we might suggest that the progression of effective protozoal infection treatments has had a slow effect, not only due to the complexity of protozoan growth processes and host-parasite-drug interactions but also due to the low economic ability to manufacture new medicines. Gladly, that international travel and immigration in the 1990s, along with an increasing awareness of antiprotozoal drug resistance and acute and chronic protozoal infections in immunocompromised species, led to a renewed interest in antiprotozoal treatment (Khaw and Panosian, 1995).

Identification methods of Microorganisms

The methods used to describe, characterize, and classify the microorganisms' structure and functions are classified into two as cultural methods and molecular methods.

Cultural Methods

The common tecnique of cultural counting is the cultural count made in the petri dish by the process of spreading. If the number of microorganisms to be identified in food is 1000 kob /ml or 10000 kob /g and more, then the technique of smear cultural counting is applicable. The bulk cultural count is used if the amount is 100 kobs / ml or 1000 kob / g, if less than such values are used, MPS (Most Probable Quantity) method, or membrane filtration method if the food to be analyzed is sufficient Pre-enrichment in a non-selective general medium, enrichment in selective medium, transformation to selective solid medium, isolation, and recognition of typical colonies are made in cultural analysis. (Figure 1). The figures are from our own study.

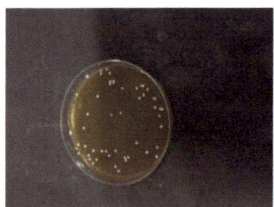 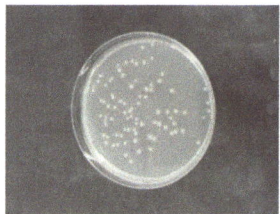 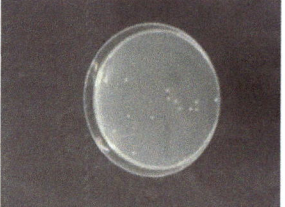

Fig.1a) *Candida albicans* (DSMZ5817) colony on Sobaroud Dextrose Agar (SDA)
b) *Staphylococus aureus* (RSKK95047) colony on Mueller-Hilton Agar (MHA)
c) *Escherichia coli* (0157H7(RSSK232)) colony on MHA

Molecular Methods

The application of molecular instruments is important if specific strains are to be identified, the margin of error of traditional approaches minimized and findings obtained in a short period. A 16S rRNA (ribosomal RNA) bacterial with an amount of 1500 nucleotides carries sufficient information for accurate phylogenetic study and rRNA is present in all organisms (Figure 2).

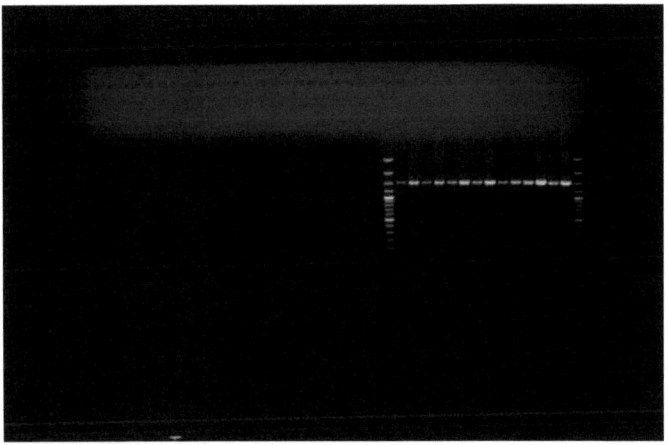

Fig. 2. The figure shows the image of 100 bp DNA marker agarose gel obtained from the result of the amplification of universal primers that are targeting the area of 16 S rDNA that is 11F and 1492 R primers (Thermo Fisher Scientific).

From the very beginning of evolution its function has not changed and hence its nucleotide sequences and secondary structures have remained strongly conserved. rRNA often includes variable regions that influence the evolutionary inter-organism relationships. Variable regions can be used as regions suitable for the targets of primers or hybridization probes for PCR (Polymerase Chain Reaction). Other reasons for targeting probes and primers to the 16S /18S rRNAs of the small subunit of the ribosome or to the 23S / 28S rRNAs of the big subunit; lack of lateral gene transfer; having very long nucleotide sequences which are about 1500 nucleotides for 16S and about 3000 nucleotides for 18S; large rRNA databases are available for 6 comparative sequence analysis (Isman, 2011).

The basic array of techniques used to treat viral infections in the laboratory includes a number of methods for viral isolation and detection of viral antigens, nucleic acids, and antibodies (serology), though many other protocols are also used.

Viral cell culture isolation is most frequently done in approved virology laboratories. Most procedures can also be done in these labs, but may also be done in different laboratory facilities, such as general microbiology, blood bank, serology, pathology, medicinal chemistry, or molecular virology. The movement towards viral diagnostic research outside from standard virology laboratories is expected to intensify as fast diagnostic methods focused on methodologies of immunological and nucleic acid are gradually replacing the viral culture.

Cell culture

The modern era of medical virology starts with the first observations of viral isolation in cell culture by Weller and Enders in 1948 and Enders et al. in 1949. The requirement for methods of cell culture is also a need for virology laboratories as distinct institutions from other labs in general clinical microbiology. Although the relative importance of viral isolation as a diagnostic technique is slowly diminishing, it is still essential because it is the only approach that can provide a living isolate that can be used for potential research, such as a test of phenotypic antiviral susceptibility. A significant benefit is that compared to other forms of identification of antigen and nucleic acid, viral culture enables the identification of several viruses, not all of which could have been detected at the time the culture was ordered.

Antigen detection

Antigens identification approaches involve fluorescent anticorps (FA), immunoperoxidase staining, and EIA staining. FA staining is the most used diagnostic virology amongst these. Liu originally described FA staining for influenza identification in 1956 for rapid viral diagnosis, and pioneered Gardner and McQuillan for several viruses. In the 1980s, clinical laboratories broadly embraced the technique especially for the detection of respiratory viruses. Those monoclonal antibodies were essential to commercial availability. Cytocentrifugation focuses on improving the techniques of FA staining to prepare samples and stain multiple antibodies labelled with multiple fluorescent labels at the same time.

Detection of nucleic acids

The PCR technique introduced in 1985 allowed the identification of viral infections by correctly identifying different viral nucleic acids. It can possibly detect any virus and helps to develop applications in PCR analysis and other techniques for nucleic acid amplification. There seems to be no question that nucleic acid detection methods will dramatically change the world of diagnostic virology over the next period. The PCR analysis can be modified to detect viral RNA by taking a step using the enzyme reverse transcriptase (RT). Examples of techniques for quantitative detection of nucleic acid include HIV and hepatitis C virus (HCV) viral load analysis. Multiplex methods allow more than one virus, or even a virus and another type of pathogen to be detected at the same time. For example, a multiplex PCR procedure, which detects the DNA of Epstein-Barr virus (EBV) and Toxoplasma gondii, was used to diagnose large lesions in AIDS patients' brains (Storch, 2000).

The Function of Corona and COVID 19 Antimicrobials

More than 70,000 cases of Corona Virus Disease 2019 (COVID-19) have been identified since it was first described in December 2019, where 2000 cases are deadly. The disease continues to spread so far, and new export cases have been recorded in China and other countries. This appears the outbreak poses a major public health threat. Medical treatment for people with COVID-19 consists of support interventions, strict application of required infection prevention activities, and antimicrobial therapy for all associated bacterial or viral diseases. The number of this pandemic has already increased and thus there is a vital need for effective antiviral therapy. It was assumed that the viral antigen triggered the immunopathological reaction; thus, initially, the most successful strategy is to prevent viral replication, to minimize peak viral load, and subsequent immunopathological damage. One possible result may be that arbidol may help slow growth of lung lesions in conjunction with LPV / r and the likelihood of respiratory and gastrointestinal spread to reduce COVID-19 viral load and yield high fecal concentrations (Deng et al., 2020).

Pregnancy is a partially immune deficiency condition that makes pregnant women more vulnerable to respiratory infections, and seasonal flu deaths are much more severe. Antiviral therapy has commonly been used in China to treat COVID-19 patients and is often recommended for pregnant women. The suggested treatment regimen was combined therapy with Lopinavir / Ritonavir antiproteases, as it is safe during pregnancy When using investigational medicinal agents in pregnant women beyond clinical trials, WHO recommends caution and careful risk-benefit evaluation. Remdesivir, an analog nucleotide, and chloroquine, an antimalarial drug, are promising medicines against COVID-19 since they are established to suppress in vitro SARS-COV-2 viruses (Liang and Acharya, 2020).

Copper is a significant micronutrient for the viral diseases that is effective on the hosts and pathogens. Copper (Cu) can kill a range of infection viruses including, human immunodeficiency virus 1 (HIV-1), poliovirus, bronchitis virus and more single, or double chain, or developed or non-developed RNA and DNA viruses. Cu also has the strong potential to destroy other contact viruses, including SARS-CoV-2. Since this current outbreak of COVID-19 is expanding, and no drugs or vaccines are presently available, the critical alternative now is to improve the immune system capable of battling SARS CoV-2. Copper exposure to human coronavirus 229E disrupted the viral genomes and the anatomy of viruses irreversibly disturbed, including disintegration of the membrane and dispersal of surface spikes (Raha et. all., 2020). Microbe contact with Cu is mediated by destruction of the micro-organism by genomic and plasmid DNA.

Several Cu alloys a quickly inhibited coronavirus in humans. Cu/Zn brasses were very efficient at the lower concentration of Cu, where the Cu (I) and Cu (II) portions made greater inactivation by ROS production on alloy surfaces. Novel coronavirus (SARS-CoV-2), which is responsible for the current pandemic COVID-19, is particularly susceptible to copper surfaces. In cell-based research, $Cu^{2}+$ has been shown to block papain-like protease-2, a protein necessary for replication by SARS-CoV-1 (Raha et. all., 2020) Based on many preclinical experiments and observational data in humans, Acute Respiratory Distress Syndrome (ARDS) may be increased by vitamin D deficiency and decreased by vitamin D receptor activation. Many randomized clinical studies are continuing, through using either oral vitamin D or oral calcifediol(25OHD) (Quesada-Gomez et. al., 2020). An effective antimicrobial/virucidal technology on air filtering media is vital to preserving a clean air environment and protecting people, particularly as lockdown has been shown to have a virucidal impact on the silver nanocluster/silica composite coating formed on facial masks. In the study conducted by Balenge et. all, silver nanocluster-silica composite coating results were shown on the FFP3 mask. In the circumstances mentioned here, this coating will lessen the titre of SARS-CoV-2 to 0 altogether. As has been noted, this coating can be deposited on virtually any filter media, as well as on surfaces made of metal, ceramic, polymeric, and glass (Balagna et. al., 2020).

Nanoparticles and Nanotechnology for Antimicrobial Uses

In recent years, the development in nanotechnology has drawn considerable interest by developing practical nanomaterials using new characteristics for future modifications in the biology, technology, and chemical areas. ZnO is widely used in different applications including piezoelectric devices, thin-film transistors, dye-sensitive solar cells, UV/ozone sensors, and glucose sensors. ZnO nanoparticles display amazing photocatalytic properties to reduce environmental contaminants. ZnO is developing as a potential option for treating and disinfecting wastewater. ZnO nanorods also act as agents of anticancer, antibacterial, or antifungal. Various studies have shown that ZnO induces important cytotoxicity, apoptosis, and autophagy in many human cancer cells by the production of reactive oxygen species (ROS) and preferential disintegration of Zn^2+ ions in the microenvironment of mild acid cancer, while saving normal cells due to pH differentiation. ZnO's antibacterial effects are associated with its electrostatic interaction among the bacterium's nanoparticles and cell surface/membrane. By using the ion channels and carrier proteins, nanoparticles penetrate the cell wall of microbes, can bind to various intracellular organelles, and thus influence the metabolic processes by shaping and accumulating ROS. Because of the association of ZnO and cell membrane, the fungal and bacterial lipid bilayer gets destructed resulting throughout the leakage of cytoplasmic content. Nevertheless, the nanoparticles' size and shape again play an important function in conferring their cytotoxicity. ZnO performs significantly in treatment operations like bioimaging and drug carrier. Lately, nanostructures based on zinc oxide have received significant interest in preclinical drug delivery systems (DDS) study. The FDA and USA, indicated ZnO as safe in various reports. The successful treatment usage of ZnO in DDS, unfortunately, seems to be in the preliminary stage. Few studies use acid-degradable ZnO nanoparticles for effective doxorubicin transmission to cancer cells. Also, several other studies have confirmed that the anti-cancer efficacy of ZnO nanoparticles, filled together with isotretinoin, curcumin, and paclitaxel. Quercetine is a naturally present bioactive substance with powerful antioxidant, an anticancer activity that can modulate cascades of cell-specific pro-survival signals. It has many other pharmacological impacts involving cardioprotective, bacteriostatic, and antiviral activity (Sadhukhana et. al., 2019). Given the various biomedical uses, the metal nanoparticles have attracted significant interest.

Instead of Pt, Au MnO_2, ZnO_2, Pd, etc., among different metals, silver (Ag) is a precious metal because of the possible biomedical uses in the medicine sector. Much more focus has been given to silver nanoparticles (AgNPs) in various medical applications while possessing special properties such as antimicrobial function, therapeutics, biomolecular identification, nanosilver-coated medical equipment, and optical receptors. Many metal and oxide nanoparticles were synthesized using biological materials. Therefore, the biogenic approach has given a solution that is efficient, simple, non-toxic, and environmentally friendly, particularly for the use of natural species. The research conducted by Bhat et al demonstrated biosynthesis silver nanoparticles from fungi Candida albicans. The nanoparticles were also tested independently, in combination with Ciprofloxacin, for their bactericidal properties against selected pathogenic bacteria. In combined form with Ciprofloxacin, the relative value of particle-specific impact silver nanoparticles has shown increased bacterial activity. Silver nanoparticles can appear to be greater drug choices and can theoretically replace the higher antibiotic doses (Bhat et al., 2015). Infectious diseases outbreaks caused by different pathogenic bacteria and fungi, and the development of antimicrobial resistance, contributed to the look for new antimicrobial agents. A review of the literature showed the antiviral activity of silver NPs, bactericidal, and fungicidal. It was shown in the study by Salvodori et all. The Ag/Ag_2O NPs showed significant antimicrobial activity against Gram-negative multidrug-resistant (MDR) Escherichia coli (E. coli) strains, Gram-positive Methicillin-resistant Staphylococcus aureus (MRSA) and the yeast Cryptococcus neoformans (C. neoformans), as shown by the process of the disc diffusion, the minimal concentration of bactericides (MBC), the minimal concentration of fungicides (MFC) and minimum concentration inhibitory(MIC). The Ag/Ag_2O NPs toxicity tests in mammalian cells demonstrated decreased cytotoxicity, a significant aspect of biomedical use. The Ag/Ag_2O NPs synthesized by the nanobiosorbent R. mucilaginosa applies a strong inhibitory impact on microorganisms and is secure for eukaryotic cells, bringing nanomedicine a possible use and, at the same time, reusing contaminating content (Salvadori et al., 2019).

There are many publications discussing the bactericidal effect of TiO_2 photocatalysts on many microorganisms. But there are only a few publications that reveal several ways of TiO_2 effect. There are many possible mechanisms that ensure cell death through the photocatalytic process. The first of these mechanisms was revealed by Matsunaga et al. In this study, evidence of the oxidation of Co A was obtained in which Saccharomyces cerevisiae was exposed to light in the presence of platinized TiO_2. When the cells were irradiated under a halogen lamp for 120 min. in the presence of TiO_2 / Pt, it was revealed that more than 97% of the intracellular CoA was lost, in comparison it was revealed that 42% disappeared when TiO_2 was not present (Matsunaga et al., 1985). Since the TiO_2 photocatalyst functions as both an antibacterial as well as detoxifying agent, the researchers concluded that it is exceptional throughout the setting. E. coli cells mineralization has also been reported by Jacoby et al., (1998). Sunlight has been reported to have enough light to activate TiO_2. This has been used in disinfection applications (Blake et al., 1999).

In a study, Escherichia coli, Pseudomonas aeruginosa, Staphylococcus aureus, Enterococcus faecium and Candida albicans, which are hygienic organisms, were tested on plaques coated with TiO_2. The reduction coefficient was as follows, respectively; E. coli> P. aeruginosa> S. aureus> E. faecium> C. albicans. (Kuhn et al., 2003). TiO_2 photocatalysts draw great attention as a material for photocatalytic sterilization in the food and environmental industry as well. In a study, a new photobioreactor was designed and tested for sterilization applications of some food-borne pathogenic bacteria (Salmonella choleraesuis subsp., Vibrio parahaemolyticus and Listeria monocytogenes). The photocatalytic reaction was carried out at different concentrations of TiO_2 and due to different UV irradiation time. A synergistic effect was observed when TiO_2 was used with UV irradiation, and it was found that the bactericidal effect was much higher than irradiation without using TiO_2(Kim et all.,2003). It has been determined that HeLa cells (cervical carcinoma) die when exposed to the light of a 500 W mercury lamp with the presence of TiO_2 (Blake et al., 1999).

Oral bacterial adhesion is an important problem for oral hygiene. A number of studies have been conducted that examined the impact of photocatalytic applications on mouth bacteria. Bacteria tested include Streptococcus sobrinus, Strepttococcus mutans, Strepttococcus rattus, Streptococcus cricetus, Candida albicans and Actinomyces viscosus. In a study with Porphyromonas endodontalis, Porphyromonas gingivalis, Provotella intermedia, Provotella melaniogenica, Actinomyces actinomycetemcomitans, Actinomyces naeslundii and Actinomyces viscous, in vivo antibacterial tests performed on titanium metal was one of the most effective in dental metal implants (Blake et al., 1999).

A coated plastic film was developed for use in the fruit packs for practical uses. The antifungal activity demonstrated by a TiO_2 coated film was able to control fruit rot in lemons. Lemons stored in uncoated films had higher post-harvest rot than those stored in TiO_2 coated films. The average number of casualties was 3.2 and 1.9, respectively, for the uncoated and TiO_2 coated film. This result confirmed that a thin layer of TiO_2 on plastic film produced a photocatalytic reaction against P.expansum. TiO_2 coated film did not cause any surface damage on lemon (Maneerat and Hayata, 2005).

Corona Nanotechnology

Nanotechnology products are already being used to provide solutions to fight COVID-19 in many different areas: products of nanotechnology are already being used to find solutions for fighting COVID-19 in various fields: (i) nanocomposite, nanofiber, nanoparticle technology implemented into respiratory masks, offering filtration efficiency, high breathability, washing opportunity, and antiviral and antibacterial properties: (ii) nanofibers and nanoparticles for air filters and air cleaning systems; (iii) nanoproducts as effective as surface cleaning products and disinfectants, and nano silver-incorporated dishwashing and laundry detergents and soaps; (iv) medical products (gloves, bandages, scrubs, wipes, aprons, etc.) are created with nanosilver technology; and (v) for diagnosis of SARS-Cov-2 RNA and host antibody response, diagnostic tests that uses magnetic nanoparticles and nanorods (Valdiglesias and Laffon, 2020). Finally, at the phase of treatment, nanomedicines are at the focus of the more researchers' interest, several of which are currently being studied in clinical settings. Thus further, nanotechnologists are acting out their social obligation to address the current public health issues (StataNano, 2020). Furthermore, the inactivation of viruses through using modified nanomaterials (acid functionalized multi-walled carbon nanotube containing photo-activated molecules) and induction of viral binding with the host cell surface receptor are significant aspects of nano-based techniques towards viruses (e.g., particularly for the issue of SARS-CoV-2 angiotensin-converting enzyme 2(ACE2) receptor). The related feature of nanostructured materials having a large surface to volume proportion and allowing the inclusion of ligands on their surfaces can, therefore, meddle with viral contact and block their entry through cells (Nasrollahzadeh et. all., 2020). With the obvious likelihood of tremendous outbreaks, the situation is very rapidly becoming more urgent, and the need for the production of rapid diagnostics and efficient prevention methods is getting larger. The reverse transcription-polymerase chain reaction (RT-PCR) has been typically used as a standard diagnostic method for the identification of CoVs. Unfortunately, particularly for the case of COVID-19, some false positive or false negative results have been reported. Notably, for clinic purposes, in one research, a double-operational plasmonic biosensor combining the localized surface plasmon resonance (LSPR) sensing transduction and the plasmonic photothermal (PPT) effect provided a promising alternative for the diagnosis of COVID-19. Sensitive identification of the particular arrangements of SARS-CoV-2 via nucleic acid hybridization has been achieved through 2-D gold nanoislands equipped with complemental DNA receptors (Nasrollahzadeh et. al., 2020). Vaccination is usually the most cost-efficient method and inexpensive technique for preventing, monitoring, and fighting against infections, particularly those contributing to certain respiratory or pulmonary diseases. The latest vaccine development studies have primarily concentrated on the CoV transmembrane spike(S) glycoprotein, which ranges from the viral surface and intervenes host cell entry. SARS-CoV-2 S needs angiotensin-converting enzyme 2 (ACE2) to transfer onto cells. The SARS-CoV S and SARS-CoV-2 S receptor-binding regions are connected to human ACE2 with identical affinities, thereby allowing the successful distribution of SARS-CoV-2 across wide human populations. SARS-CoV-2 S glycoprotein protects a furin cleavage site at the margin of subunits S1/S2 that separates this virus from SARS-related CoVs and SARS-CoV. Also, the ectodomain trimmer SARS-CoV-2 S was selected to establish a model for the development of viral entry inhibitors and vaccines (Nasrollahzadeh et. al., 2020).

Concluding Remarks

Corona virus especially COVD 19 has been affecting the whole world including each and every country. It has been one of the most severe health problems creating more than 10 million cases and more 500,000 deaths across globe.

Within the scope our book, we tried to summarize the antimicrobial materials used for various purposes and the role of nanotechnology for this important technology group. We have presented an updated and recent review on new Corona COVID 19 findings as well.

We believe that these findings can be used for making new anti-viral and antimicrobial products and also helping the researchers to find new solutions for the health care problems of the world. There are many researches going on to make more effective sanitizers and masks. The findings in this chapter will help to formulate novel products for the COVID disease.

References

Balagna, C., Perero, S., Percivalle, E., Nepita, E. V., and Ferraris, M. (2020). Virucidal effect against Coronavirus SARS-CoV-2 of a silver nanocluster/silica composite sputtered coating. Open Ceramics, 100006. https://doi.org/10.1016/j.oceram.2020.100006.

Bhat, M. A., Nayak, B. K., and Nanda, A. (2015). Evaluation of bactericidal activity of biologically synthesised silver nanoparticles from Candida albicans in combination with ciprofloxacin. Materials Today: Proceedings, 2(9), 4395-4401.

Bhatia, A., Kalra, J., Kohli, S., and Kaushik, R . (2014). Antimicrobials is a general term for natural or synthetic compounds which at certain concentrations inhibit growth of or kill microorganisms, Journal of Applied Chemistry, 7(5):01-06.

Blake, D. M., Maness, P. C., Huang, Z., Wolfrum, E. J., Huang, J., and Jacoby, W. A. (1999). Application of the photocatalytic chemistry of titanium dioxide to disinfection and the killing of cancer cells. Separation and Purification Methods, 28(1), 1-50.

Deng, L., Li, C., Zeng, Q., Liu, X., Li, X., Zhang, H., Hong, Z., and Xia, J. (2020). Arbidol combined with LPV/r versus LPV/r alone against Corona Virus Disease 2019: A retrospective cohort study. Journal of Infection, Volume 81, Issue 1, July 2020, Pages e1-e5. https://doi.org/10.1016/j.jinf.2020.03.002.

Dural, Erem, A., and Ozcan, G. (2013) Polimer Esaslı Nanokompozitler ve Tekstil Uygulamaları, Journal of Textiles and Engineer, Cilt (Vol): 20 Say (No): 89.

Ghannoum, M. A., and Rice, L. B. (1999). Antifungal agents: mode of action, mechanisms of resistance, and correlation of these mechanisms with bacterial resistance. Clinical Microbiology Reviews, 12(4), 501-517.

Isman, B. (2011). FISH ve standart mikrobiyolojik yöntemlerle gıda ve sulardaki önemli bakterilerin belirlenmesi. Adnan Menderes Üniversitesi Fen Bilimleri Enstitüsü Biyoloji Anabilim Dalı, Doktora Tezi.

Jassim, S. A., and Naji, M. A. (2003). Novel antiviral agents: a medicinal plant perspective. Journal of Applied Microbiology, 95(3), 412-427.

Kara, H. (2016). Olive Leaf Powder and Boron Doped Polypropylene Composites, Department of Material Science and Engineering, Izmir Katip Çelebi University Graduate School of Science and Engineering.

Khaw, M., and Panosian, C. B. (1995). Human antiprotozoal therapy: past, present, and future. Clinical Microbiology Reviews, 8(3), 427-439.

Kuhn, K. P., Chaberny, I. F., Massholder, K., Stickler, M., Benz, V. W., Sonntag, H. G., and Erdinger, L. (2003). Disinfection of surfaces by photocatalytic oxidation with titanium dioxide and UVA light. Chemosphere, 53(1), 71-77.

Liang, H., and Acharya, G. (2020). Novel corona virus disease (COVID-19) in pregnancy: What clinical recommendations to follow? Acta obstetricia et gynecologica Scandinavica, 99(4), 439-442. Acta Obstet Gynecol Scand. 2020; 00:1–4.

Maneerat, C., and Hayata, Y. (2006). Antifungal activity of TiO_2 photocatalysis against Penicillium expansum in vitro and in fruit tests. International Journal of Food Microbiology, 107(2), 99-103.

Matsunaga, T., Tomoda, R., Nakajima, T., and Wake, H. (1985). Photoelectrochemical sterilization of microbial cells by semiconductor powders. FEMS Microbiology Letters, 29(1-2), 211-214.

Moghadamtousi, S. Z., Kadir, H. A., Pouya, H., Tajik, H., Abubakar, S., and Zandi, K. (2014). A review on antibacterial, antiviral, and antifungal activity of curcumin. BioMed research international, Volume 2014, Article ID 186864, 12 pages.

Nasrollahzadeh, M., Sajjadi, M., Soufi, G. J., Iravani, S., and Varma, R. S. (2020). Nanomaterials and Nanotechnology-Associated Innovations against Viral Infections with a Focus on Coronaviruses. Nanomaterials, 10(6), 1072. https://doi.org/10.3390/nano10061072.

Quesada-Gomez, J. M., Castillo, M. E., and Bouillon, R. (2020). Vitamin D Receptor stimulation to reduce Acute Respiratory Distress Syndrome (ARDS) in patients with Coronavirus SARS-CoV-2 infections: Revised Ms SBMB 2020_166. The Journal of Steroid Biochemistry and Molecular Biology, 105719. https://doi.org/10.1016/j.jsbmb.2020.105719.

Raha, S., Mallick, R., Basak, S., and Duttaroy, A. K. (2020). Is copper beneficial for COVID-19 patients?. Medical Hypotheses, 109814. https://doi.org/10.1016/j.mehy.2020.109814.

Reygaert, W. C. (2018). An overview of the antimicrobial resistance mechanisms of bacteria. AIMS Microbiology, 4(3), 482.

Sadhukhan, P., Kundu, M., Rana, S., Kumar, R., Das, J., and Sil, P. C. (2019). Microwave induced synthesis of ZnO nanorods and their efficacy as a drug carrier with profound anticancer and antibacterial properties. Toxicology Reports, 6, 176-185.

Salvadori, M. R., Monezi, T. A., Mehnert, D. U., and Corrêa, B. (2019). Antimicrobial Activity of Ag/Ag$_2$O Nanoparticles Synthesized by Dead Biomass of Yeast and their Biocompatibility with Mammalian Cell Lines. International Journal of Research Studies in Microbiology and Biotechnology, Volume 5, Issue 1, PP 7-15.

Saran, B., and Karahan, Z. C. (2010). Antimikrobiyal ajanlara genel bakış. Turk Urol Sem, 1, 216-20.

Sengün, I. Y., and Oztürk, B. (2018). Bitkisel Kaynaklı Bazı Doğal Antimikrobiyaller. Anadolu University of Sciences & Technology-C: Life Sciences & Biotechnology, 7(2).

StataNano (2020). Nanotechnology in battle against coronavirus. Available from: https://statnano.com/nanotechnology-in-battle-against-coronavirus Accessed 30 May 2020.

Storch, G. A. (2000). Diagnostic virology. Clinical infectious diseases, 31(3), 739-751.

Valdiglesias, V. and Laffon, B. (2020). The impact of nanotechnology in the current universal COVID-19 crisis. Let's not forget nanosafety!. Nanotoxicology, 1-4. https://doi.org/10.1080/17435390.2020.1780332.

Waris, A., Ali, M., Khan, A. U., Ali, A., and Baset, A. (2020). Role of nanotechnology in diagnosing and treating COVID-19 during the Pandemic.

International Journal of Clinical Virology, https://doi.org/10.29328/journal.ijcv.1001017.

Williams, J. E. (2001). Review of antiviral and immunomodulating properties of plants of the Peruvian rainforest with a particular emphasis on Una de Gato and Sangre de Grado. Alternative Medicine Review, 6(6), 567-580.

CHAPTER 9

A Comparative Study of Privacy Policies and Data Protection During the COVID-19 Pandemic Within Different Countries

Seldağ Güneş Peschke[1], Ömer Fatih Sayan[2]
{seldag.peschke@gmx.net ; fatihsayan@hotmail.com}

[1] Professor, Ankara Yıldırım Beyazıt University, Department of Comparative Law, Ankara/Turkey

[2] Deputy Minister, Ministry of Transport and Communications of /Turkey

Abstract

In many countries, including Turkey, various precautions and measures are being used to protect the public against the COVID-19 caused by the novel coronavirus SARS-Cov-2 which spreads worldwide. At this point, besides the traditional measures such as quarantine, social distance and social isolation, technological opportunities are also used. In this context, to prevent the spread of coronavirus in various countries; mobile applications, or some other technological tools, are developed. In most of these applications, personal data such as the health, location and contact information of the persons are stored to prevent the disease. These data help to identify the people at risk, follow the treatment process, show the spill map of the virus, control the quarantine and the curfew, detect crowded places, which have major importance during the pandemic. In such cases, it is legally possible to apply different methods by authorized institutions and organizations in order to protect public health and thus to ensure public order and public security. At this point, the security of personal data is indisputable. In this context, personal data such as tracking of location data, health data and people's mobility activities need to be carried out within the framework of the basic principles of data protection laws in each country. In this article, the usage of personal data in mobile applications and other technological tools during the COVID-19 pandemic is analyzed in different countries, in terms of their privacy policies and data protection laws.

Keywords: COVID-19 pandemic, SARS-CoV-2, data protection, privacy.

Introduction

Since the discovery of SARS-CoV-2 in December 2019, the living standards of the people all around the world have changed. People had to give up their habits and a new way of life style has been formed. This situation has also affected the business relations and privacy of people. Legal regulations regarding privacy policies, data security and data sharing have been revised and adapted according to current conditions. In some states the privacy policies have become stricter and in others, the governments have taken the control on individuals.

During the pandemic, the primary focus for the countries was to protect the public from the disease. For that reason, many applications are provided via smart phones. Most of the countries have developed new applications under the limits of their legal regulations. Within the usage of these tools, the authorities have the power to keep the balance between public health and personal privacy.

Extraordinary measures, like tracing people, recording their data or restrictions on movements of people are taken into consideration in each country by public health authorities and governments. COVID-19 pandemic requires the creation of new legal rules, as well as the development of cost-effective practices and applications to reduce social transmission, which is a start of new practices and regulations that require a reassessment of the confidentiality of data under emergencies.

Privacy Policies in the Apps During the Pandemic in Europe

We are living in a global world where the transfer of knowledge is becoming very fast in the scope of ICT. In the last years within the development of IT, the communication habits of the society have changed into media-based communication via internet. As a result of these technologies, online media have become a central point in our communication. A huge amount of information and personal data are uploaded, downloaded, stored or transferred from one place to the other, sometimes without the consent of the data owners or their knowledge. Peschke could show that the usage of digital devices changed the perception of private and public spheres. Digital privacy could be identified as a kind of public privacy with a high permeability to the public sphere (Peschke, 2016).

Personal data are one of the fundamental human rights, which was first mentioned in the international level under the UN Universal Human Rights Declaration in 1948 and the European Human Rights Convention in 1950 (Güneş Perschke, 2014). Then the European Union and many other international organizations have passed many regulations in this regard. The regulations introduced by the United Nation, Council of Europe and the European Union are crucial to constitute consistency in this field. Also, judgments or decisions given by the supervisory bodies of these organizations have strengthened the legal character of data protection and privacy.

By enforcement of the European General Data Protection Regulation (GDPR) in 2018, the institutions had to increase their data awareness. The new regulation has brought stricter rules on privacy and data protection according to 95/46 EU Directive, which was in force for more than 15 years (EU, 2020a).

As GDPR is broad legislation, it provides rules which processes different types of personal data in emergencies like pandemic such as COVID-19. Processing of personal data can create risk of violating the fundamental rights and liberties of the people at a high level. For that reason, the data protection impact assessment must be carried out before the processing activities (GDPR, Article 35). Under these conditions, the measurements are taken strictly by governments, public and private organizations throughout Europe.

After the appearance of the virus, during the pandemic the EU adopts new privacy and data protection policies against the spread of the disease. The borders of privacy and security of the data are the main issues to be discussed during the pandemic period. The rights and the freedoms of the individuals have changed, according to ordinary times. However, legality, transparency and proportionality are kept as essential elements in EU in the coordination of measures against COVID-19.

For instance, in Bulgaria, The State of Emergency Law, which was put into force on 24 March provides guidance for the possible actions and measures which could be taken during the pandemic. The measures enable the Ministry of the Interior, its regional directorates and the police to request from the electronic communications' providers' networks or services (ECS) access to data required for establishing an identifier of the cells used (i.e. location data), to enforce the mandatory isolation of persons who refused the mandatory isolation; and ECS providers are obliged to save for six months such data and to provide direct access to law enforcement authorities when requested. These measures will remain in place until the end of the state of emergency period.

In Slovakia, following a decision by the Constitutional Court, ECS providers are required to share personal data with the permission of the user, in a written request by the health authorities. In the Czech Republic, for obtaining and processing these data the GDPR requires the user's consent. In Poland and Spain mandatory data-sharing is defined as anonymous and aggregated data (Almeida et al., 2020)

On April 8, European Commission announced the eHealth Network, which is used voluntarily as a platform of the Member States' competent authorities to deal with digital health. A week later, a common EU Toolbox is published for Member States on contact tracing mobile applications (EU, 2020b)

In some European countries, the aims of the use of voluntary smartphone applications are contact tracing, collecting information on signs and symptoms from each person and giving support regarding mandatory quarantine. As an example of this, Spanish Ministry of Health has requested to be developed an application shows that citizens are not sick or carrying the COVID-19. This application is a pandemic isolation tracking project that allows users to verify their location. The Ministry of Health collects the users' data to prevent future spread of the coronavirus. Additionally, in order to provide verified answers to questions about COVID-19, WhatsApp chatbot or other chat application helpline service are developed.

Furthermore, The UK Government has been published a Coronavirus Information service on WhatsApp platform on 25th of March, 2020. This technology allows users to trust the app is beneficial for the maintained public health purpose. It is efficient at decreasing infection risk, and also using it will not create any kind of inconvenience for the individuals or their friends and family. Slovakia has launched a new quarantine application for people who arrived the country and prefer to spend the mandatory quarantine period at home instead of the government quarantine facilities.

Accordingly, travel applications in Turkey will be made through the Hayat Eve Sığar (Life Fits into Home) mobile app that was developed in collaboration with BTK (Information Technologies and Communication Authority) and the Ministry of Health and that will be used to detect and track COVID-19 cases. This app also shows risky areas and violations of social distancing using Bluetooth technology. Besides, risks will be analyzed quickly. While contact tracing during intercity travel reduces many risks, it will help the foresight of infected people.

With the collaboration among the Ministry of Health and BTK, when the people, who are asked to self-isolate due to the coronavirus pandemic, moving from their home or residence, the data by the GPS phone tracking will be passed onto the Ministry of Health. Thereafter, telecom operators will share both the physical and digital logs collected by the Life Fits into Home app, as well as the location timelines with BTK. Thus, the risk of spreading the infection is minimized.

In the Czech Republic, the Ministry of Health issued an extraordinary measure to observe the movement and contacts of COVID-19 infected individuals on March 19, 2020. With the consent of the infected person, the location data of a particular SIM card must be sent by the mobile operators to the Ministry of Health (Kouřil and Ferenčuhová, 2020).

Apple and Google produced a tracking app for COVID-19 which consists of application programming interfaces (APIs) and operating system-level technology. Actually, Austria has already developed contact tracking application before launching Google and Apple technologies, developers are now trying to combine this technology into the application originally launched by the Red Cross.

On 15 April, Ursula von der Leyen, the President of European Commission and the Charles Michel the President of the European Council, announced a <u>Joint European Roadmap which contains some precautions to ban the spread of SARS-CoV-2. These measures</u> include recommendations to the EU Member States to protect public health, to reactivate the economy and to form strategies for the EU member states.

This roadmap guided public health authorities for data gathering and sharing in harmonization on the spread of the virus at the national and subnational level. In addition, the data of people who are infected and cured are recorded. By this Roadmap, the privacy barriers overcome to share patient information for public purposes.

Data have a very high value for companies, institutions, governments, because of their credibility in the commercial and social world. In the pandemic, it is clearly understood that the data play an important role and it could be used to prevent the spread of the virus. For that reason, mobile apps are designed which trace people according to their locations, social distancing, movements, contacts with other people, etc. According to the GDPR, organizations must take convenient technical and organizational precautions to demonstrate that they have considered data compliance measures into their data processing activities. It means that organizations must integrate these measures into design features, work policies and physical infrastructure of products and services, which can affect ethical and moral aspects of protection of personal data and privacy.

In the pandemic, the apps in the smart phones are approved by the national health authorities. One of the main characteristics of these apps mostly is that, they are used by individuals voluntarily, but also there are exceptions like China. With the help of smart contracts, it is also easy to direct people as participants inside the application.

For the data users, the consent of the data owner is needed and this consent must be obtained separately for each data processing activity. Within the scope of GDPR, it has been stated that data protection impact assessment must be carried out especially before the sensitive data will be processed (GDPR, Par. 91) (EU, 2020a). The rules about data protection, such as GDPR do not prevent the measures, taken in the fight against coronavirus pandemics. Actually, GDPR provides legal assurance to the employer and the authorized public health authorities to ensure that they process personal information in a pandemic-related manner without the consent of the data owner.

In Slovakia, on 24 March 2020, an emergency law is adopted by the Public Health Agency (PHA) requiring Telecom operators to share data on user ID (name and address), location and time, upon request. According to this law, personal data can also be processed by operators to identify users who will get messages from PHA. Nevertheless, users should be notified ahead of time. In Slovakia, however, the Constitutional Court has suspended the relevant provisions by not taking sufficient measures for the protection of personal data. Later, Parliament amended the act and now ECS providers can share data with health authorities upon written request and written or otherwise verifiable consent of the user.

Therefore, there is a quite close relation between the recording of personal data and personality rights. Accordingly, unlawful usage and storage of personal data cause a violation of personality rights (Güneş Perschke and Perschke, 2013). For that reason, most of the data, which are used during the pandemic in the applications are anonymized. The data are collected in two centralized institutions in Joint Research Center and the European Center for Disease Control which keep the data to model and give notice about the disease; to develop common measures and to develop strategies inside the EU.

In Spain, on March 28, 2020, the Ministry of Health issued a decision from the digitalization and artificial intelligence secretariat to analyze the mobility of citizens before and during the restriction. The analysis will be based on anonymous and aggregated data provided by mobile operators. In contrast, in France, a proposed amendment to France's emergency law of 22 March 2020, which would allowed public authorities to adopt any measures to collect and process location and health data for a period of six months, was rejected by Parliament (Almeida et al., 2020).

In Belgium, the government announced on March 20, 2020 that telecom operators will share their data with the Ministry of Health to increase coronavirus precautions. Government has set up a scientific committee to look into changing the government's coronavirus testing approach from restricted testing to a more systematic method. This committee examines ways to use anonymized mobile location data from telecom operators to combat the spread of the infection.

Privacy is considered as a basic human right and a necessity for the European Union which is regulated specifically in Privacy Directive. It is declared by the European Commission that during the pandemic personal data is processed lawfully and all the fundamental rights of the individuals are respected

In most EU countries, the access to data for authorized experts is limited. Some new rules are applied for the processing of electronic communication data, such as mobile location data. Telecommunication providers have used the data of individuals to track COVID-19 in different ways. Adequate measures are applied to ensure the secure transmission of data from telecom providers, as the data protection rules are flexible enough to allow various measures in emergencies

The national laws of the Member States should respect the EU regulations including the ePrivacy Directive which provides that location data can only be used by the operators when they are anonymized or with the consent of the individuals.

Allowing disclosure of location information out continuously can create several privacy issues. Data protection authorities (DPA) in most countries have made statements or published guidance documents on data processing and sharing in the matter of the pandemic. Austria, Italian and the Czech Republic Data Protection Officers generally recommended the processing of such anonymous information including location data. On the other hand, Dutch Data Protection Officers argue that it is not possible to anonymize location data due to the possibility of identifying users, while Spanish Data Protection Authorities recommend that privacy issues may be adjusted when there is a lack of anonymization.

When the terms and the conditions of these apps are accepted by the data owners, the personal data are started to be recorded, encrypted and anonymized securely. In the data collection and usage process, the respect for all fundamental rights, especially for privacy and data protection, prevention of surveillance and stigmatization are accepted as priorities for the European Commission.

The system generates reports on the collection of mobile devices at a certain location. If it is not possible to process anonymous data, ePrivacy Directive (Art. 15) enables the Member States to take legal measurements for national security and public safety. This legislation is used in emergency situations under the condition that it constitutes a necessary, appropriate and proportionate action within the fundamentals of a democratic State. When these precautions are taken, a Member State is obliged to put in place sufficient protections. Mapping and tracking people with effectively anonymized data, fall outside of the scope of data protection rules in the EU.

Nevertheless, the European Data Protection Supervisor (supervisory authority of the EU institutions and bodies) proposed that these measures are temporary till the end of the crisis. The data which is recorded in this period is justifiable and they will be deleted which are obtained from mobile operators as soon as the current emergency ends. And also the apps will be deactivated, when the pandemic is over and the prior regulations will continue to be used again.

As an example, the Czech Republic Ministry of Health published an exceptional measure for telecom operators on March 19, 2020, aimed at collecting and sending location data for a particular SIM card (individual's name and phone number). That information should be erased within 6 hours. The data is sent to the Ministry of Health upon request and with the specific permission of the user infected by COVID-19. Mobile network operators must provide location data collected for the past three weeks (Kouřil and Ferenčuhová, 2020).

Privacy Policies in the apps in other OECD Countries during the Pandemic

Many states are practicing remarkable steps to track and trace the spread of the virus, by switching their system to digital technologies. Thus, OECD countries are examples of those countries that take efficient measures for the coronavirus without applying to strict lockdowns. However, the main reason that some countries' coronavirus success is a wide range of web of digital surveillance, as the governments have supported the applications.

For instance, South Korea gave so much effort for the data – such as cell phone and GPS, to locate the path of individual coronavirus infections. The data owners who got the disease and uncovered are informed and isolated. Contact tracing also permit the South Korea government to combat coronavirus without closing down its economy as a whole, while critical financial difficulties appear in EU during the pandemic.

Singapore is another example of the countries that extended the role of digital technologies to allow the tracking of the public's symptoms, contacts with the others and their movements. Singapore has used Bluetooth technology and has permited contact tracing devices to slow down the spread of the coronavirus. The application called TraceTogether is an alternative to the government's contact tracing smartphone app for the people who do not use a mobile phone. These devices are in action by exchanging Bluetooth signals with other active nearby participant or smart phones that are using the same applications. The users of these devices will be alerted in a contact tracing if they are detected to have been near someone infected with the virus. If the user is interviewed by the officer as part of the contact tracing process, then they should consent that the data will be downloaded from their device. The authorities informed the data owners that tracing apps are not designed to track user's movements and rejected concerns and critics regarding mobile phone users' privacy. The government announced that the data and the data owners' detailed information are collected by the devices will be encrypted and kept at the most 25 days (Bashir, 2020a).

In India, digital technology has to offer massive advantages for Indian health care professionals during pandemic. Aarogya Setu ('Bridge to Health') is a COVID-19 tracking mobile application which is developed by the Ministry of Electronics and Information Technology (Upadhyaya et al., 2020). This app uses smartphone's GPS and Bluetooth features to track the disease and tries to discover the risk if the app user is near a person who has been confirmed or suspected of having the COVID-19 by scanning through the database of known cases across India (Bashir, 2020b).

Furthermore, because of the increase of questions and challenges, the public's trust to the responsibles of processing personal data in the government, is decreased. These concerns do not aim to stop the usage of data against the virus, but a balance is tried to be created between personal and public interests to increase societal trust in the public institutions for health purposes.

In 2018, in Brazil, the General Data Protection Law (LGPD), which describes many significant changes in personal data rules, was put into force. These changes involve personal data processes such as digital media used either by individuals or by public and private organizations. The LGPD was devised to protect the fundamental rights of freedom and privacy (OECD, 2020).

During the pandemic COVID-19, China has produced apps for the smart phones to track people, like it is in the other countries. Taiwan, South Korea and Singapore, from far east have also used smartphone location data to track individuals. These apps track the people, and aim to show the locations of the people if they are connected with the people who carries the virus or they are at a risky situation. These apps are mostly part of high-tech, surveillance-based tools which China has developed against the spread of COVID-19.

Wuxi health code is the most common app used by the Chinese government. It creates an QR code for each person, after they are registered to the system. Without having the QR code it is impossible for the people to travel, to use the public transportation, to be inside the social life. In all the locations which the people visit, they should show the QR code to the authorities.

In Wuxi health code there are 3 colours, red, yellow and green. The green code allows people to travel freely, besides, it scans them everywhere wherever they go. With the yellow code people should stay at home for at least seven days. Red code requires a two-week quarantine. In Hangzhou and Wuhan cities, it is obligatory to be registered in Wuxi health code (Zwitter and Gstrein, 2020).

China is using surveillance technology in these apps to track people's movements. For that reason, its policies on privacy and data protection under the authoritarian regime are criticised very often. It is pointed out by the legal experts that these technologies could endanger fundamental rights. Privacy policies are discussed in different ways, if the location data plays a key role during the pandemic, as the data inside the mobile phones are very personal.

The data from apps is often part of a package of measures taken by governments. So it is difficult to pinpoint if these data are used to control the disease or to monitor the individuals. Data protection rules must be balanced with the fundamental rights, public health and public interest. If not, it seems as the people give up their liberties to the governments.

Moreover, facial recognition system is used in Russia to track people who break the rules of mandatory quarantine. However, by using of facial recognition app, a vast number of security and privacy concerns occur. Especially, by using these technologies without having specific guidance. Users may also have issues practicing an extensive range of fundamental rights, including the right of access to their data without their permission (OECD, 2020).

Lastly, privacy enforcement authorities (PEAs) have an important role in guiding on proposed new government legislation which provides transparency existing privacy and data protection situations. PEAs should provide advanced devices, especially when a person has important questions including the use of personal data, reversibility of new government controls, and the practice of their investigation.

PEAs of Hong Kong, China have released general guidance, including the details about the rules that are applied to the use of data on social media in order to track the potential carriers. The question about what kind of precautions are taken by government regarding COVID-19 frauds and invalid claims about products that can treat the virus (For example in Spain and the United States).

Poland, Ireland, Switzerland Slovakia, the United Kingdom and New Zealand have published extensive guidance for data controllers and processors in order to inform the public, about regulations on data protection and privacy during the pandemic.

Conclusion

The pandemic period has brought new regulations, that have caused significant changes in the protection of data within the context of privacy and security. As COVID-19 is becoming a new arena for the current research activities, the existing ethical and legal framework is needed to be reviewed. There is a big need for the protection of data within the scope of ethical rules in different socio political and economic realities with basic human rights principles. Today, in the age of new technologies, it is difficult to keep the balance between freedom of information, privacy, security with public health and public interest. As a contribution to the tradeoff these different interests, there is a need for intensive multidisciplinary investigation and research according to the new challenges of ICT technologies.

The current regulations on data protection and privacy, especially on research and innovation activities, should be collected in a comparative way to set new regulations for emergencies.

The existing ethical and legal framework in different European countries should be adopted to EU regulations within the future needs of the pandemic to ensure a single Bill of European Ethical Rules on Research and Innovation Activities (BERORIA).

During the pandemic each country tried to find governmental technological solutions against the spread of the virus. Most of the countries implemented digital surveillance to track their citizens. They produced apps for the smart phones to trace their movements, locations, contacts. In all the countries, privacy should be the biggest priority. While taking temporary measures against coronavirus, great attention should be given to civil and fundamental rights of the individuals. It is so fragile that legality, proportionality and necessity should be kept as the main elements of the personal data collection, while tracing, tracking and recording the lives of the individuals. The states should respect the data protection regulations, how long they keep these data and with whom they share these data are the most important issues. For that reason, the governments should create solutions and balance the personality rights with public interests and public health.

References

Almeida, B., Doneda, D., Ichihara, M. Y., Barral-Netto, M. Matta, G. C., Rabello, E. T., Gouveia, F.C., and Barreto, M. (2020). Preservação da privacidade no enfrentamento da COVID-19: dados pessoais e a pandemia global. Ciência & Saúde Coletiva. 25 (1). 2487-2492. Epub June 05, 2020.https://doi.org/10.1590/1413-81232020256.1.11792020.

Bashir, E. (2020a). COVID-19 update 4: mobile apps by public authorities and data sharing by providers of electronic communications services. Cullen International.

Bashir, E. (2020b). Data sharing by providers of electronic communications services with public authorities to fight COVID-19. Cullen International.

EU. (2020a). Data Protection Rules Inside and Outside the EU. Brussels: European Coımission. (https://ec.europa.eu/info/law/law-topic/data-protection_en)

EU. (2020b). Coronavirus: Recommendation for the Use of Mobile Data. Brussels: European Coımission. (https://ec.europa.eu/digital-single-market/en/news/coronavirus-recommendation-use-mobile-data-response-pandemic)

Güneş Peschke, S. (2014). The Protection of Personality Rights From Roman Law Till Today. Yetkin, Ankara.

Güneş Peschke, S., and Peschke, L. (2013). Protection of the Mediatized Privacy in the Social Media Aspects of the Legal Situation in Turkey and Germany. Gazi University Law Journal 17 (1-2). 857-883.

Kouřil, P., Ferenčuhová S., (2020). Smart" quarantine and "blanket" quarantine: the Czech response to the COVID-19 pandemic. Eurasian Geography and Economics, Doi:10.1080/15387216.2020.1783338

Peschke, L. (2016). The Relevance Patterns of Public Privacy for Digital Natives in Turkey. TRT Akademi Digital Media. 01 (02). 366-386.

OECD. (2020). Ensuring data privacy as we battle COVID-19. Paris: OECD.

OECD. (2020). Tracking and tracing COVID: Protecting privacy and data while using apps and biometrics (COVID-19). Paris: OECD.

Upadhyaya, G. K., Iyengar, K., Jain, V. K. and Vaishya, R. (2020). COVID-19 and applications of smartphone technology in the current pandemic. Diabetes&Metabolic Syndrome: Clinical Research&Reviews.

Zwitter, A., and Gstrein, O. (2020). Big Data, privacy and Covid-19-learning from humanitarian expertise in data protection. Journal of International Humanitarian Action. 5 (4).

CHAPTER 10

The Impacts of Outbreaks on External Trade and Macroeconomic Structure: The Case of Covid-19 Pandemic in Turkey

Ali Osman Balkanlı
{aobalkan@yahoo.com}

Assist. Prof., Istanbul University, Economics, Faculty of Political Sciences, Istanbul/Turkey

Abstract

With the industrialization which started in the 1600s, the world economy moved towards the industrial sector and industrial production step by step from the classical agriculture-based economy that had existed for thousands of years. The increasing share of industrial production within the national income gradually revealed the services segment connected to the industrial sector. As the industrial sector developed and expanded over time, the services sector rapidly increased its share in the economy. When we look at today's economies, we can observe this development. It has also been observed that the services sector has an increasing rate of growth from the 1950s and beyond. In a sense, the services sector in economies has become a supportive sector for the industrial sector.

While this reality speaks of the growth and stability of the economies today, it is required to emphasize the growth and stability of the services sector along with the growth and stability of the industrial sector. When we talk about the services sector here, we have to consider not only the banking and finance sector, but also the small and medium-sized enterprises that dominate the whole economy. In a sense, it can be said that this section constitutes the sector directly facing the consumers in an economy. Although this segment varies according to the structure and development of economies, it forms weaker, undersized and small capital and more labor-based organizations than industry in most countries. With this aspect, such organizations have more social content and affect social-economic balances more.

When the world economy is analyzed in the historical context, the pandemic or other causes of crisis conditions refer to the periods in which the economies suffered great traumas. Obviously, this trauma means huge losses for these economies. However, the growth levels achieved for these economies are not an easy and rather difficult process. And their growth, in the context that they can bring about structural changes in these economies, means advancement in the path of economic development for these countries. In such a difficult and troublesome process, unusual and unavoidable pandemics and other causes of crises are evident, which explains the weakening of these economies. And this weakening may in some cases mean collapse for these economies.

With the Covid-19 Outbreak, significant changes have occurred in the whole economy. While these changes from production to consumption affect the life processes of a society, they have also created serious problems in tradesmen workplaces. These problems meant the decrease or disappearance of work efficiency on one hand, and on the other hand, it meant the unemployment of both the employer and the workforce in these workplaces. In result, while countries' economic growth rates decrease, people suffered serious unemployment and income problems. These developments are not limited to certain economies and every country had to live through these problems. In this article, it will be determined how and to what extent the crisis situations such as pandemic affect the conditions of world and especially in Turkey.

Keywords: Covid-19, Pandemic, Endemic, Outbreak, Economic Growth, Unemployment, Recession, World economy, Turkish economy, Endemic, Income Shrinkage, Economic Crisis.

"The COVID-19 crisis has become more predictable in a sense. What was widely viewed as a 'Chinese problem,' and then an 'Italian problem' has become an 'everybody problem'".

[Baldwin, R. and Di Mauro, B.W., "Mitigating the COVID Economic Crisis", CEPR Press, (London, 2020):8].

Introduction

With the industrialization process which started in the 1600s in the world economy, classical agriculture-based economic structure that had existed for thousands of years left its place to the industrial sector and industrial production. In this process, the increasing share of industrial production within the national income has gradually brought the development of the services sector depending on the industry segment. In other words, as the industrial sector developed and expanded over time, the share of the services sector in the economy increased rapidly. In a sense, while transitioning to modern life, the services sector in economies has become a supportive sector for the industrial sector and has become increasingly important.

Therefore, based on this reality, it can be said that the growth and stability of the services sector also supported the growth and stability of the industrial sector, being important in the growth and development of economies today. In general, this sector is the sector directly facing the consumers. Although this sector varies according to the structure and development of economies, it forms from relatively weaker, undersized, and small capital and more labor-based organizations than the industry in most countries. Evaluated in this aspect, it can be said that such organizations have more social content and affect social-political and economic balances more. These sectors are the ones which interacts with people the most, and therefore these sectors are more affected by crises, as compared to other sectors. At this point, it can be said that the Covid-19 pandemic as an economic crisis factor creates relatively worse effects on the services sector. Therefore, the services sector has an important place in examining the effects of economic crises. However, this statement does not mean that other production sectors are not affected or affected very little by economic crises and outbreaks.

Looking at the world economy in its historical context, it can be said that the economic crisis conditions due to epidemic or other reasons refer to the periods in which economies suffer great traumas (1889-1892, 1918 Pandemic conditions). Obviously, this trauma means huge losses for these economies. Because the growth levels achieved for these economies are growth levels that are not at all easy and achieved as a result of intense efforts. And this growth, which they have achieved, means the progression on the road to economic development for these countries. In such a difficult and troublesome process, crises that occur unexpectedly and are unavoidable (based on economic or health, ecological, environmental, and so on) are clear traumas for these economies. This weakening, according to the degree of deepening of crisis, may in some cases also mean a collapse for these economies.

The problematic of today is the economic crisis caused by Covid-19's health crisis. With the Covid-19 Outbreak which started in 2020, significant changes have occurred. While these changes from production to consumption affect the life processes of societies in countries, they have also revealed serious problems in the services sector of economies. While these problems meant the decrease of work or disappearance of work efficiency on one hand, it also meant unemployment of both the employer and the laborers in the workplace. Covid19 pandemic health crisis has brought up an intense unemployment problem in the world economies. While this situation brought about a decrease in income in societies, it caused the decrease of continuous income flow, which were thought to be stable. At this point, the focus of this article will be the effects of Covid19 Outbreak on the macroeconomic structure and external trade.

Possible Effects of Outbreaks on Macro Economic Processes and Foreign Trade as an Item of Economic Recession and Crisis

The word "pandemic", which is basically referred to as a global outbreak, consists of the combination of the word "pan", and "demi". In Greek Language, "pan" means "all" and "demi" refers to "demos" in the Greek language.(παν-δημία). The pandemic, which is formed by the combination of these two words, is used in the meaning of the outbreak that concerns all peoples, globally. In this condition, the word "epidemic" describes localized outbreaks. These terms aren't a term of new modern life. These terms have been used since old times. In the 17th and 18th centuries, the terms epidemic and pandemic were used frequently instead of each other. The first known use of the word pandemic is in 1666 and it was also used in the years 1831–1832 for the cholera pandemic disease. (Morens et al., 2009:1018). The term pandemic was then used for the influenza outbreak 1889-1892 and for the 1918 outbreak.

Humanity has faced a pandemic outbreak in 2020 (according to some sources, it is started from December 2019) after a long break, apart from the minor outbreaks after the 1918 epidemic. When they have been analyzed, we can see that all of the outbreaks have one thing in common: Human interactions are important determinants in the transport and transmission aspects of viruses (Jordan, 1927: 257).

At the long term analyses, outbreaks are more dangerous for humanity than economic crises. In detail, we can say that influenza pandemics have badly effected about three times every century since the 1500s. In the 20th century, there were 3 influenza pandemics named "Spanish influenza" in 1918-1919, "Asian influenza" in 1957-1958 and "Hong Kong influenza" in 1968-1969. All pandemic-epidemic problems not only damaged economic development of countries, but also affected human life. For instance, the influenza pandemic in the 1918-1919 period killed more than 50 million people and it was a big problem for global economy (Qiu et al., 2017:4).

Behind the economic balances in a country, the thoughts and behaviors that societies and individuals in the society realize with the subconscious and conscious are of great importance. Therefore, it can be said that in economies, the processes that individuals experience behind the consumption, saving, and investment decisions are important determinants. In one aspect, this situation has found a place in J. Maynard Keynes' approach to "future prospects", in M. Friedman's "continuous income hypothesis" (or other economists' descriptive approaches (Rational Expectations, etc.), too. And we can say that outbreaks have the power to influence people's thoughts and behaviors. The changing of people's thoughts and behaviors will change their economic decisions. The changing economic decisions will clearly change economic magnitudes, gravities, and in result the macroeconomic balance.

At this point, Baldwin and Mauro, in their own words, say this on the subject: "Efforts to flatten the curve reduce economic activity. The recession, so to speak, is a necessary public health measure. Keeping workers away from work and consumers away from consumption both reduce economic activity". (Baldwin and Mauro, 2020:8). These variables can be related to economics as well as social, technological, ecological, and health issues.

Epidemic or pandemic outbreaks should also be considered as items that may have the power to influence macroeconomic balance. Because when the epidemic arises, the developments experienced affect the production, consumption, saving, and investment decisions of individuals, societies through the social subconscious and conscious thoughts and behaviors. This influence manifests itself especially in the form of worrying about the present and the future. This state of concern directs the economic decisions of these individuals or society as a whole. After this influence, production contraction may be seen more clearly in some of the production sectors and/or in all sectors in general.

According to Baldwin and Mauro, "the COVID-19 pandemic creates all manner of economic shocks,

1) First are the purely medical shocks – workers in their sickbeds aren't producing GDP.

2) Second are the economic impacts of containment measures.

3) Third are the expectation shocks. As in the Global Crisis of 2008-09, the COVID-19 crisis has consumers and firms all around the world putting off spending; they are in wait-and-see mode" (Baldwin and Mauro, 2020:9-10). The fluctuations in economies will eventually affect the economic development indicators (Mikalauskiene et al., 2018: 62). In the Covid19 pandemic process, economic development indicators of countries, especially GDP per-capita growth rate, resource productivity and efficiency have decreased.

Negative subconscious or conscious thoughts about today and/or the future may bring new decisions not only on production and consumption but also on savings, investment, and the financial markets. It can be said that in the negativity of future expectations, individuals and communities will try to reduce their consumption. This development means that in sectors that produce and/or import these products, demand will decrease. Indeed, consumers will generally try to reduce their consumption, depending on the level of their consumption flexibility, although there may be an increase in some areas, such as safety and basic needs.

It is obvious that it can have important effects on macroeconomic balance and foreign trade, depending on the magnitude of the impact. This effect, on the other hand, may bring production shrinkage in the factories that produce these products, and shrinking production may mean shrinking employment. While unemployment increases, this situation may bring a decrease in general economic activity due to the risk of income reduction at the effect of decreasing of consumption. With the contraction which starts at some point in general economic activity, its decline will affect production and consumption decisions on the general economy one step later. Social psychology and its management are important here. In these situations, in some countries, governments want to manage the problems and social images of the problem (for socio-psychological effect). And it can be thought that there are economic concerns and need for control to the economy at the background of this administration demand.

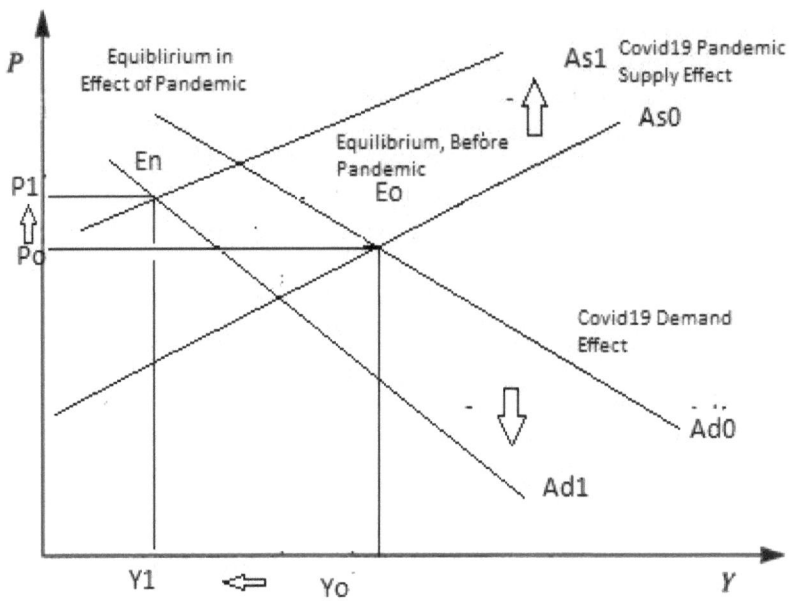

Diagram 1: National Income Equilibrium, Before and After Pandemic (Predictive)

In the event that the pandemic has a high risk of spreading, on the one hand, production factor owners can refrain from participating in the production, and on the other hand, firm owners can shrink production to avoid risk and risk-based costs. In this case, it can be said that production may be adversely affected due to the epidemic. According to G.Gopinath "the coronavirus epidemic involves both supply and demand shocks. Business disruptions have lowered production, creating shocks to supply. And the reluctance of consumers and businesses to spend has lowered demand. On the supply side, there is a direct reduction in the supply of labor from unwell workers, from caregivers who have to take care of kids because of school closures, and sadly, from increased mortality. But an even larger effect on economic activity occurs because of efforts to contain the spread of the disease through lockdowns and quarantines, which lead to a drop in capacity utilization" (Gopinath, 2020:43-44).

It is expected that these developments, which may occur in the countrys' economies, will also show their effects in foreign trade relations and figures. Especially in a situation where the epidemic is global (presence of pandemic state), it may bring shrinkage in countries' imports and exports. In the presence of an outbreak, the contraction in the market (in the production), for example, in the tourism sector, may be a serious problem, with the risk of exposure to too much contamination risk. This situation may be in many sectors, as entertainment, eating and drinking sectors, barbers and make-up, hair-dressers, education, and etc. (generally in services sectors). Therefore, it can be said that economies cannot avoid being affected by pandemics. This effect may be low or high depending on the size of the pandemic. Decreasing the effects of pandemic in the economy will depend primarily on the flexibility of consumers and producers, the availability of protection opportunities, time and treatment methods.

1918 Influenza Outbreak and Its Effects

The 1800s are years that mankind has begun to make more research and knowledge as compared to previous centuries. In this period, at the end of the century, (1889-1892) humanity faced an influenza pandemic (Park and Williams, 1919:45). This situation urged researchers to investigate and understand the microorganisms. Humanity faced other diseases (SARS, cholera, tuberculosis, plague, smallpox, dengue, AIDS, influenza) but they were more regional, not worldwide. But pandemic illnesses are worldwide. In the literature, although the 1918 pandemic is called the Spanish epidemic, mainly the Spanish people say that the epidemic came from the battlefields from the Alps and Pyrenees (from France) to Italy and Spain during the war. Here, Spain's problem was that when the disease started, many countries hid it from the world and said that it was Spaniards' disease with 8 million deaths (in May and June) (Crosby, 2003: 26).

The 1918 pandemic and the 1890 pandemic's emergence and development consisted of 3 stages (Royen and Rhodes, 1948: 567). In the Spanish flu, the disease appeared in the form of headache and fever and runny nose and cough, hoarseness in the first stage (first wave), and later triggered diseases such as the pharynx, larynx, trachea and conjunctivitis. These are the effects (most prominent) in the first wave of the virus. While the virus was evolving, it caused more pneumonia (20%) and deaths in the 2nd and 3rd waves. However, the first wave remained as rare events. The 2nd and 3rd waves (80 percent of influenza cases for France are in the 2nd wave) first started in autumn 1918 (September) and appeared in the third wave in the spring of 1919. The disease started mildly in the second wave, then turned into pneumonia. "The remaining 20 per cent, however, suffered from pneumonia and nearly half died" (Royen and Rhodes, 1948: 562).

According to other countries, Great Britain was impacted more in the 1918 June from Flu pandemic. It was first seen in Portsmouth. The outbreak then leaped to the southern coastal areas. The first area outbreak's spread was the British military (British soldiers). The number of infected soldiers was 31,000 in June 1918. Influenza disease, which was named Blitzkatarrh as a nickname in Germany, was first seen among soldiers as in England (Crosby, 2003: 26). After June, it started to become widespread (turn into a pandemic) and become evident in Europe and America (Crosby, 2003: 27).

Spanish flu is surely not limited to Western Europe and North America. While the Epidemic spread in the British military in mid-June, it also spread to Russia at the same time. And then again in June, the influenza epidemic began to manifest itself in Mumbai and Calcutta (and all over India). In the same period, the epidemic splashed to China and the flu outbreak occurred in half of Chingking region. It also leaped to New Zealand and the Philippines after the outbreak. In fact, influenza has transformed from an epidemic disease to a pandemic disease in 4 months and has also surrounded the U.S. (Crosby, 2003: 28).

Of course, each outbreak (relative to other outbreaks) has relative significance in itself, depending on the impact of the troubles it causes for people. At this point, the global epidemic problem experienced by humanity in 1918 should be defined as a serious problem. Considering the number of deaths caused by the epidemic and their effects on the country's economies, the 1918 pandemic has been a very serious trauma for humanity. In the effect of this trauma, the world economy has received serious injuries from production to consumption. Similar things can be said for the 1890 global epidemic. For example, in this regard, when the 1918 epidemic began to flare-up (in October, 1918), people in the US were comparing the Spanish epidemic of 1918 with the epidemic they experienced in 1890. And they were stating that the 1890 epidemic was not milder than the 1918 epidemic and stated that it caused serious devastation (Albany Evening Journal, 1918: 6). And again, as in today, the discourses of "vaccine found" were frequently encountering in 1918 (Albany Knickerbocker Press, 1918: 2)

The influenza pandemic of 1918 was very dramatic in the world. Especially on 1918 pandemic of USA, it can be said that the United States Influenza pandemic emerged in three waves at the period of 1918-1919. The first wave came up in March 1918 and this wave continued until the summer of 1918. In here it must be noticed that the worse effect occurred at the second and third waves, especially in the fall of 1918 and the spring of 1919 (Brahmbhatt, 2005:4-5; Garrett, 2007:8).

Interestingly, Spanish flu has splashed across the axis from Massachusetts to Virginia, following the paths, railways in the United States. It leaped to the Appalachians… So much so that influenza began firstly to appear in North American ports in early summer. (Crosby, 2003: 29). When the virus entered the United States in the summer of 1918, it had reached millions of mansions, and at the same time, the virus displayed genetic change (Crosby, 2003: 30). The effects of the virus were different in the summer of 1918, and the next two waves were different. Especially in the later waves, pneumonia began to appear (Royen and Rhodes, 1948: 662).

In the next step, the pandemic leaped to Rockies, Los Angeles, San Francisco, and Seattle. The virus reached almost every part of America and all areas considered as safe areas were infected. So much so that if the virus made special efforts to infiltrate every niche and corner of America, it could not be so effective. (Crosby, 2003/1989: 63-64). In fact, it is a fact that war is an important determinant in this period in this diffusion. The virus, under the influence of the mobility of the First World War, was transported from Europe to America via humans and goods in thousands of ships (Crosby, 2003:30).

The influenza virus, which became a global outbreak in 1918, was first seen in 1915. This is a cycle spoken in the 2020 Covid19 Pandemic (as seen in November-December 2019), too. It was seen in America, England and other countries in the following years. The influenza pandemic of 1918 started to draw attention firstly in 1917 in the form of "pus bronchitis" in England. And the disease manifested itself primarily in soldiers, especially commandos (Royen and Rhodes, 1948: 561). Outside of England, in Continental Europe, this outbreak which was primarily seen in soldiers has occurred frequently in the military. In the U.S.A., it has occurred in the military, even in military schools (Jordan, et al., 1919:74–95).

According to Thomas Garrett, "the economic effects of the 1918 influenza pandemic were short-term effects and changes according to sectors. For example, many businesses, especially those in the service and entertainment industries, suffered double-digit losses in their revenue. Other businesses that specialized in health and health care products experienced an increase in their revenues" (Garrett, 2007:21). On the other hand, in a newspaper dated 19th October 1918, the economic negativities of the pandemic were described under a headline with "How Influenza Affects Business" as follow : "Merchants in Little Rock say their business has declined 40 percent. Others estimate the decrease at 70 percent. The retail grocery business has been reduced by one-third. A department store that has a normal business of $15,000 daily is doing only half of that. Bed rest is emphasized in the treatment of influenza. As a result, there has been a demand for beds, mattresses and springs. Little Rock businesses are losing $10,000 a day on average" (The Arkansas Gazette, October, 19. 1918, cited by Garret, 2007).

Again in a newspaper of those days, the economic breakdown of the period was expressed as follows: "Physicians report they are kept too busy combating the disease to report the number of their patients, and have little time to devote to other matters. Industrial plants are running under a great handicap. Many of them were already short of help because of the draft. Out of a total of about 400 men used in the transportation department of the Memphis Street Railway, 124 men were incapacitated yesterday. This curtailed service. The Cumberland Telephone Co. reported more than a hundred operators absent from their posts. The telephone company asks that unnecessary calls be eliminated" ("Influenza Crippling Memphis Industries." The Commercial Appeal, Oct. 5, 1918: 7 cited by Garret, 2007).

In another newspaper of the pandemic period, the economic collapse in the pandemic process was depicted as follows: "Fifty percent production decrease reported by coal mine operators. Mines throughout eastern Tennessee and southern Kentucky are on the verge of closing, owing to the epidemic that is raging through the mining camps. Coalfield, Tenn., with a population of 500, has "only 2 percent of well people. ("Tennessee Mines May Shut Down." The Commercial Appeal, October 18, 1918:12, cited by Garrett, 2007). Obviously, the negative course of the economy experienced in the 1918 Pandemic process is somehow also seen in the 2020 covid19 pandemic.

Impacts of Covid19 Pandemic on the World Economy and Turkey

Covid19 outbreak started in China and first death was on 9 January 2020. And after, epidemic position of the outbreak transformed fast to pandemic. Outside China, first case was seen on 13 January 2020 in Thailand. And later, also all the G7 economies faced covid19 cases by the end of the January and in February. In Europe, the tragic country of Covid19 was Italy at the end of February or early March, and after covid19 outbreak spread to all the G7 countries (Baldwin and Mauro, 2020:2).

At the 20th and 21st centuries, by far the greatest pandemic threat comes primarily from influenza viruses, such as the H5N1 virus outbreak in 2003, the H1N1 epidemic in 2009, and the ongoing H7N9 epidemic in China. It was thought that the Covid19 pandemic, which was defined as an epidemic when it first appeared in China, would remain regional like SARS. However, the outbreak splashed very quickly all over the world. With the spread, the World Health Organization has described the outbreak as a pandemic (Okdah and Snyder, 2016:4).

As of June 20th, 2020, 24.00, the number of Covid19-infected people in the world is 8,894,711. As of this date, the number of people who died from the Covid19 virus is 465,944. Recovered people are 4,724,625. As of now active cases are 3.704.142, closed cases are 5,190,569 (https://www.worldometers.info/coronavirus/,2020). With the Covid19 epidemic, the manufacturing industry and services sectors in China were seriously affected. However, in particular, there have been more severe declines in the services sector (Gopinath, 2020: 42). With an optimistic scenario, the expected global GDP growth for 2020 ranges between -8.8 % (WTO) and 1 % (UNDESA). According to IMF reckoning is the main reference point for assessing the economic impact of COVID-19. In this forecasting limits, global growth will reduce by -4.2 percent (UNIDO, 2020).

Table 1. Worldwide, Covid19 Pandemic Data, According to 2020, 20.06, 23:59

Country	Total Cases	Total Deaths	Total Recovered	Active Cases	Population
World	8,894,711	465,944	4,724,625	3,704,142	7,780,000,000
USA	2,326,251	121,900	966,048	1,238,303	330,944,050
Brazil	1,067,579	49,976	543,186	474,417	212,512,836
Russia	576,952	8,002	334,592	234,358	145,932,745
India	411,727	13,277	228,181	170,269	1,379,567,062
UK	303,110	42,589	N/A	N/A	67,875,356
Spain	293,018	28,322	N/A	N/A	46,754,281
Peru	251,338	7,861	138,763	104,714	32,956,067
Italy	238,275	34,610	182,453	21,212	60,464,181
Chile	236,748	4,295	196,609	35,844	19,111,018
Iran	202,584	9,507	161,384	31,693	83,956,634
Germany	191,216	8,961	174,700	7,555	83,776,217
Turkey	186,493	4,927	158,828	22,738	84,309,377
Pakistan	171,666	3,382	63,504	104,780	220,732,413
Mexico	170,485	20,394	127,332	22,759	128,888,616
France	160,093	29,633	74,312	56,148	65,269,418
Canada	100,959	8,410	63,450	29,099	37,731,670
China	83,352	4,634	78,410	308	1,439,323,776

https://www.worldometers.info/coronavirus/#countries, (06.21.2020).

The Covid19 outbreak crisis effected and will effect the economy. Because, "on the demand side, the loss of income, fear of contagion, and heightened uncertainty will make people spend less. Workers may be laid off, as firms are unable to pay their salaries. These effects can be particularly severe for some sectors such as tourism and hospitality – as seen for example in Italy. Since the start of the recent US equity market selloff on 20 February 2020, airline stock prices have been hit disproportionately, in line with the post-9/11 terrorist attacks but lower than after the global financial crisis. In addition to these sectorial effects, worsening consumer and business sentiment can lead firms to expect lower demand and reduce their spending and investment. In turn, this would exacerbate business closures and job losses" (Gopinath, 2020:44).

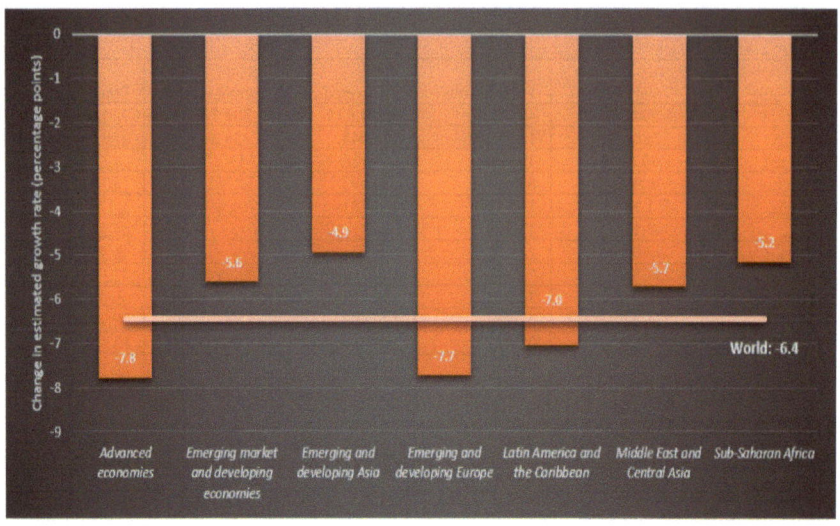

Fig. 1. At the world economy regional differences of GDP growth rates projected for 2020 in the IMF's WEO Oct 2019 and Apr 2020, https:// www.unido.org/ stories/ coronavirus-economic-impact-26-may-2020, (06.10.2020).

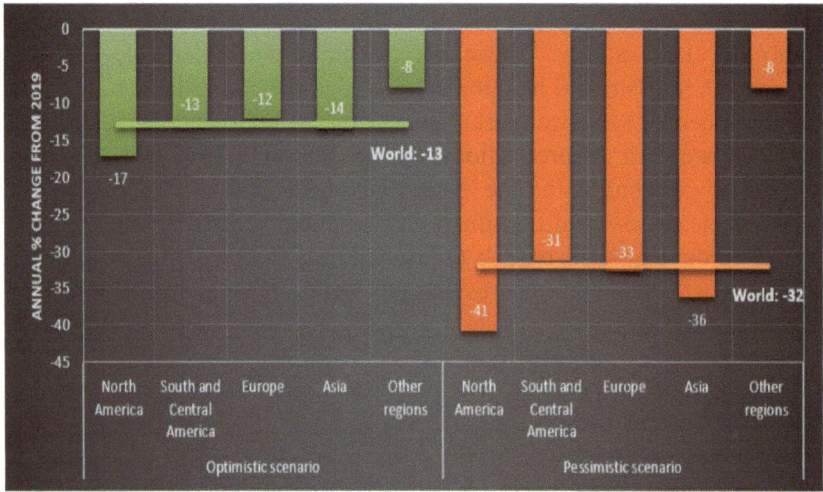

Fig. 2. Projected Annual Change in The Volume of Global Trade, By Region, https:// www.unido.org/ stories/ coronavirus-economic-impact-26-may-2020 (06.10.2020).

Table 2. Average change in Index of Industrial Production across world regions by income level

	High Income	Upper Middle Income	Lower Middle Income	Upper and Middle Income
Number of Countries	30	15	3	18
March 2020 Vs December 2019	-4.2	-5.8	-5.8	-5.8
March 2020 Vs March 2019	-47	-4.8	-4.4	-4.7

https:// www.unido.org/ stories/ coronavirus-economic-impact-26-may-2020 (06.10.2020)

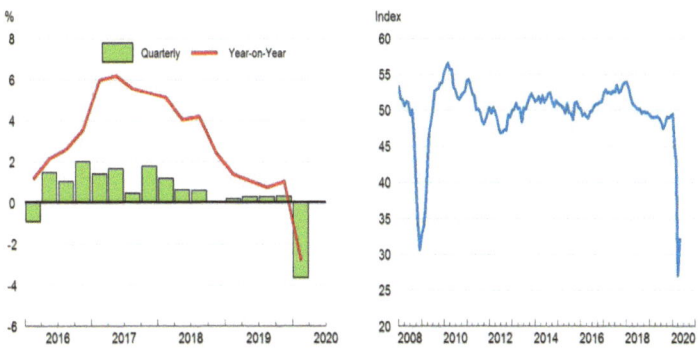

Fig. 3. World trade's Collapsing Figure in the Covid19 Pandemic Process, (OECD, 2020).

Essentially, economists and historians state that major outbreaks occurring in the world economy and the world society have a modifying effect on the world economy and societies. At this point, it can be said that the "black death, plague epidemic" that appeared in Europe in the last millennium had such a change (Jordà, et al., 2020: 1). It can be said that the 2020 Pandemic will have such a modifying effect. As a result, outbreaks will have a modifying effect on economies and societies to the extent that they affect the production and consumption, savings, and investment decisions of people who are subjects of the economy. In Figure 3, the effect of Covid19 on world trade can be seen. Clearly, world trade has collapsed in the Corona process. Considering the pandemic process in Turkey, changes occurring in certain sectors and data, effects of Coronavirus on the economy are clear.

In fact, while the balance of payments, the current account yielded a deficit of 469 million dollars in April 2019, in April 2020 the deficit was 5.062 million US dollars with effect by Covid19. In this negative development, we observed an increase of $ 3.810 million in the April in the foreign trade deficit and also a deficit of 240 million dollars in April (2020) in the balance of services. The interesting point here is that while the current account excluding gold and energy yielded a surplus of $ 3.257 million in April 2019, in April 2020 a net

209

deficit of $ 3.315 million occurred (www.tcmb.gov.tr). This obviously shows the Covid19 effect to a large extent. This negativity has also manifested itself in investments. Such that, direct investment, which were $ 433 million in April 2019, dropped to $ 133 million in April 2020. At the same time, there was an exit of 2.365 million dollars in portfolio investments, and a net decrease of 8.605 million US dollars in official reserves (www.tcmb.gov.tr). As can be seen in the table, the effect of Covid19 on foreign trade was seen in March, but essentially in April 2020.

Table 3. Turkey External Trade Between 2019-Jan-April and 2020-Jan-April. (Billion USD)

Monts	2019			2020		
	Export	Import	%	Export	Import	%
January	13.875	16.165	85,8	14.694	19.207	76,5
February	14.323	16.057	89,2	14.605	17.633	82,8
March	16.336	18.250	89,5	13.373	18.812	71,1
April	15.341	18.073	84,9	8.990	13.553	66,3
Cumulative	2019			2020		
	Export	Import	%	Export	Import	%
January	13.875	16.165	85,8	14.694	19.207	76,5
Jan-Feb.Cumulat.	28.198	32.221	87,5	29.299	36.840	79,5
Jan-March Cumulat.	44.534	50.472	88,2	42.673	55.652	76,7
Jan-April Cumulat.	59.874	68.545	87,4	51.662	69.205	74,7

(%) Import/Export Ratio
www.ticaret.gov.tr, (06.15.2020).

Table 4. Turkey, Exports by ISIC, Rev.4, (general trade system), (2019-2020, Montly, Jan-April)

	Total 19	Total.20	%Δ	Jan.20	Feb20	March19	March20	April19	April20
Total	59.875	51 662	-13.7	14 694	14 605	16.336	13 373 264	15.341	8 989 535
Crop and animal	3.620	1 688	-53.4	516	424	1 293	406	1 413	342
Manufacturing	56.745	48 692	-14.2	13 817	13 876	15.554	12 665	14.620	8 334
Other manufactur.	2.187	1 569	-28.3	497	599	619	371	604	103
Motor vehicles trailers and semi-t.	9.748	7 019	-28.0	2 245	2 374	2.723	1 902	2.453	498
Manufacture of wearing apparel	5.558	4 327	-22.1	1 378	1 389	1.559	1 082	1.383	476
Manufacture of textiles	3.825	3 262	-14.7	970	969	1.024	881	1.003	442
Other transport equipment	1.237	1 055	-14.7	357	366	389	173	306	160
Basic metals	5.744	4 930	-14.2	1 336	1 235	1.516	1 301	1.376	1 059
Mining and quarrying	998	878	-12.0	251	183	261	204	263	241
Electrical equip.	3.608	3 223	-10.7	889	901	978	846	939	586
Rubber&plastics	2.654	2 387	-10.1	628	644	710	642	687	473
Machinery and equipment n.e.c.	3.696	3 395	-8.1	884	915	1.024	904	965	691
Fabricated metal products(-machi.)	2.842	2 675	-5.9	711	712	765	696	755	556
Agriculture, forestry and fish.	1.859	1 862	+	570	476	453	443	388	373
chemicals and chemical products	2.955	3 005	+1.7	765	765	775	769	763	707
Manufacture of food products	4.384	4 713	+7.5	1 151	1 133	1.149	1 242	.1114	1 188

www.tuik.gov.tr, (06.15.2020).

Turkey's export rate in the world export is 0,9 percent according to 2019 data (Erginbay, 2020:2). But Covid19 pandemic has affected negatively to this rate and absolute export values decreased dramatically in 2020. Turkey's exports in 2020 (January-April) decreased by 13.7 percent as compared to 2019 (January-April). In this decline in exports, crop and the livestock sector took the lead with a decline of 53.4 percent in agricultural exports. Manufacturing industry exports followed this sharp decline with 14.2 percent. While exports of the motor vehicles sector decreased by 28 percent in the manufacturing industry, the decrease in the exports of the other manufacturing industry was 28.3 percent. The extraordinary decline in exports of the motor vehicles sector continued with a 22.1 percent decrease in the clothing sector and a 14.7 percent decrease in the textile sector. In this period, the export of food products industry, chemical and chemical products exports displayed a positive trend.

This situation can be followed from the sectorial development of production. At this point (in analyzing consumption fluctuations) white goods sector can be considered as an indicator sector. Generally speaking, the Turkish White Goods sector is the number 1 producer in Europe with its production capacity exceeding 30 million units and is the second producer in the world after China. Turkey is the 2nd manufacturer in the market after China. Brazil, USA, Poland, Germany and Italy follow Turkey. 75% of the sector's production is exported to more than 150 countries. Thus, Turkey left behind Germany and Italy, which are accepted as the white goods production bases with their share in the market. As the durable consumer goods manufacturing industry, the sector, which is the driving force of economic growth, employs 60 thousand people, and 600 thousand people in total. In the sector, which had a stagnant year in 2019, with the beginning of March when the effects of the epidemic started to appear in 2020, significant decreases in production started to be observed. The contraction in production in the durable goods sector was realized in February as 3%, in March as 15.7%, and in April, when the effects of the crisis became evident as 49.3%. When evaluated with the developments of the first 5 months of 2020, it is predicted that there will be a 10% contraction in domestic white goods sales and a 15% decrease in export volume due to the negative effects of the corona epidemic in 2020 (Türmob, 2020: 9).

Table 5. Percentage change of industrial production index over the previous month in Turkey, 2019-2020 (Economic activity (NACE Rev.2), Total Industry (2015:100))

Years	January	February	March	April
2019	1.3	1.1	2.3	-0.7
2020	-0.3	1.9	-6.8	-30.4

www.tuik.gov.tr, (06.10.2020).

The decreases in foreign trade, (both in imports and exports) that started with March and became tragic with April showed itself in manufacturing industry production. As can be seen in Table 4, the production index fell 6.8 percent in March 2020, and this decline was -30.4 percent in April 2020. The manufacturing industry capacity utilization rate confirms this situation.

As such, seasonally adjusted (%) (Weighted-NACE REV.2) monthly capacity utilization rate decreased from 76.90% in December 2019 to 75.80 in January 2020, 76.60% in February 2020, 76.20% in March 2020 and it decreased to 61.90% in April.2020. In May 2020, this rate increased to 62.70% with a small recovery (www.tcmb.gov.tr).

Regarding this change in trend in capacity utilization rates, as listed by the Turkey Statistics Institution in March, the unemployment rate appears to be in compliance with the recovery. According to Turkish Statistical Institue data, while the unemployment rate (for 15 age and up ages) is 13.6 % in February

2020, this rate decreased to 12.8 % in April. (www.tuik.gov.tr). It is seen that the extraordinary covid19 effect to decrease capacity utilization rate in April exhibited a relative recovery (61.90% to 62.7%) in May. Therefore, it can be predicted that this recovery will continue relatively in June and the following months. But what is decisive here is how the Covid19 global outbreak (pandemic) will trend in the second half of the year. Here, the country effect of Covid19 pandemic is clearly observed. In fact, the effect of Covid19 pandemic on society is not only impressive on production and consumption trends. In addition, due to the risk of infection in daily life, it is seen from the increase in the use of credit (debit) cards instead of cash.(https://evds2 .tcmb.gov.tr). In this period, in the financial markets, the interest rates have trended low according to the past periods. However, the same trend did not apply to exchange rates and gold prices. During the Covid19 period, remarkable rises in exchange rates and gold prices emerged. (https://evds2.tcmb.gov.tr)

In the first period of Corona days in the Turkish economy, official unemployment rates did not increase fast. On the contrary it decreased. Especially, for 14-64 ages unemployment rate was 14 % on December 12, 2019. In 2020, January 1, this rate was 13.8 %. This rate is 13.2 % in 2020, March and 12.8 %, in 2020, April (tuik.gov.tr) . These rates show to positive trend at the covid19 process. But it must be specified that at the backside of these rates, there are public intervene and seasonal effects of employment. It is reality that in the process, unemployment increased in the first days but the government fastly intervened to process, some policies have been implemented. Especially, in the Covid19 pandemic process, the Turkish government declared to "Short Term Working Allowance/Grant" and layoff banned via act. These factors affected unemployment conditions in the Covid19 process in Turkey. And also, we know that the Industry production index and Industry capacity using rates did not reflect the corona effect in production until the end of March in this surround, the unemployment rate didn't increase dramatically and on the contrary, it decreased. Here, the main effective factor was "layoff banning" and "Short Term Working Allowance/Grant" and (especially) seasonal effect. The short-time work allowance is the salary-like payment made to the worker for periods not worked to complement the weekly working time applied at the workplace. And the central government pays (grants) it. In here, unemployment data show directly the general unemployment level. But these data include seasonal effects. The examined period is the spring season and in this period there is a seasonal effect in increasing employment in Turkey conditions. So, when, the seasonally adjusted, unemployment rates look, the Covid19 effect on employment maybe see more discernible.

Looking at the labor force indicators, seasonally adjusted, the effect of covid19 can be clearly seen even after the effect of government policies. Thus, while the number of the labor force employed in January 2020 was 28.007

thousand people, this number is decreased to 27.512 thousand people in February, 26.509 thousand people in March, and 25.541 thousand people in April. According to this, the seasonally adjusted unemployment rate was 2020, 12.7% in January, 12.8% in February, 13.1% in March, and 13.8% in April. While the labor force participation rate was 51.8% in January, it was 50.8% in February, 49% in March, and 47.5% in April (www.sbb.gov.tr). In this seasonally adjusted employment data, despite government intervention, the effect of Covid19 can be clearly seen.

While the effects of Covid 19 increase, governments have been more aggressive for the social-rehabilitation of Covid19. And these activities of governments affected increase of public expenditures and these developments affected countries' budget balances. This development applies also to Turkey. In this sense, Turkey Central Government Budget's public expenditure were high especially in April. It increased from TL 91.161.877 in March to TL 108.443.227 in April. Increase in expenditure is observed in April. (From February to March there is decrease). This increase in public expenditure is reversed in May to 85.446.203 TL (www.hmbgov.tr). These data show that in Turkey, public expenditures increase extraordinary in April 2020 by the effect of the Covid19 pandemic. This upward trend in public spending seen in the Covid19 process in Turkey is also an improvement observed in most countries of the world. Most governments have provided similar support to their citizens. Surely, these supports were more intensively and in larger amounts in developed economies.

Conclusion

Covid19 virus has created a pandemic in the world by starting its journey from China to all over the world. Especially in the European countries and America, the Covid19 pandemic, a pandemic that caused the death of thousands of people and caused serious psychological traumas in those who were ill and not, seems relatively to have reduced its severity in May and June 2020. Considering the 2nd and 3rd waves and their effects in the 1890 and 1918 pandemics, it cannot be said that the Covid19 pandemic has ended.

The epidemic conditions of the first wave of the Covid19 pandemic during the January-April period did not only affect the health conditions of people. At the same time, as a reflection of the pandemic feature, it has pushed economies and societies around the world into a contraction and withdrawal process. During the epidemic, people "pulled their hands and feet" from everything and, of course, the economy, while being drawn to their shells in order to protect and sustain their lives. Indeed, the Covid19 pandemic is a very important outbreak in the history of mankind, which people feel the "risk of life". Especially with the support of communication opportunities developed in the globalizing world, the pandemic process has been followed by all humanity "moment by moment" and almost the whole world has lived in the same "social-psychological atmosphere". These developments in the world and Turkey has brought a period of more state intervention in the economy and society. And this situation has been supported by the private sector in societies and societies (even if they are opposite).

In order to prevent the economic deterioration and stagnation caused by the Covid19 pandemic, it is necessary to wait for the states to develop and maintain various policies to protect their economies and societies, as a solution to possible 2nd and 3rd Covid19 pandemic attacks. In this case, fiscal and monetary policies will be the primary policies that can be implemented. While fiscal policies are more important for medium and long-term orientation and influence, monetary policies will give governments an important power in short-term orientation and influence. In addition to fiscal and monetary policies, governments will also be able to implement production support policies to support their industries, agriculture, and services sectors. And since this period expresses a "social disaster period", governments will tend to wrap their peoples more in the context of social security. These policies have to be considered in the possible 2nd and 3rd waves of the Covid19 pandemic, too.

References

Albany Evening Journal. (1918). Epidemic of 1899-90 Was Much Worse. October 14. https://quod.lib.umich.edu/cgi/t/text/idx/f/flu/02z0flu.0000.020/1/--epidemic-of-1899-90-was-much-worse? rgn=full+text;view=image;q1=Subject+--+influenza+history.

Albany Knickerbocker Press. (1918). New Influenza Vaccine Found by State Scientists. October 9,https://quod.lib. umich.edu/cgi/t/text/idx/f/flu/0450flu.0015.540/1/--new-influenza-vaccine-found ?rgn=full+text;view=image;q1=Subject+--+influenza+history.

Baldwin, R. and Mauro, B. (2020), Mitigating the COVID Economic Crisis. CEPR Press. London.

Brahmbhatt, M. (2005). Avian and Human Pandemic Influenza–Economic and Social Impacts. https://www.worldbank.org/content/dam/Worldbank/ document/HDN/ Health AHI-SocioImpacts.pdf.

Crosby, A.W., (1989), "America's Forgotten Pandemic: The Influenza of 1918", University of Texas (2003), Cambridge University Press, Austin.

Edwin O. J. and Dudley B. R. and Fink, E.B.(1919), *Influenza in Three Chicago Groups*, The Journal of Infectious Diseases, Volume 25, Issue 1, July 1919, Pages 74–95,Published:,01 July 1919, https://quod.lib.umich.edu.

El-Okdah, O. and Snyder, M. (2016), Global Pandemics and Global Public Health, www.ipinst.org wp-content/uploads/2017/10/Global-Pandemics-and-Global-Public-Health1.pdf, ICM.

Garrett, T. A., (2007), Bird Flu Pandemic: History Warns of Economic Pain, Though Some Might Gain, https://www.stlouisfed.org/~/media/files/pdfs/ publications/pub_assets/pdf/re/ 2007/ d/ bird_flu.pdf.

Garrett, T. A., (2007), "Economic Effects of the 1918 Influenza Pandemic Implications for a Modern-day Pandemic", November, https://www.researchgate.net/ publication/ 237365204_ Economic_Effects_of_the_1918_Influenza_Pandemic_Implications_for_a_Modern-day_Pandemic.

Qiu,W and Rutherford, S. And Mao,A,. And Chu,C., (2017), The_Pandemic_and_its_Impacts, http://hcs.pitt.edu, The Pandemic and its Impacts, December,(18), Culture and Society Vol 9–10.

http://www.sbb.gov.tr/istihdam/#:~:text=%C4%B0%C5%9Fg%C3%BCc%C3%BC%20202020%20y%C4%B1l%C4%B1%20Nisan%20d%C3%B6neminde,d%C3%B6neminde%20y%C3%BCzde%202013%2C8%20oldu (2020).

Mikalauskiene, A., Narutaviciute-Cikanauske, R., Sarkiunaite, I., Streimikiene, D. and Zlateva,

r., (2018). Social Aspect of Sustainable Development: Issues of Poverty and Food Shortage. Montenegrin Journal of Economics. Vol. 14. No.2.

Morens, D. M. & Folkers, G. K. and Fauci, A. S. (2009), *What Is a Pandemic?,* Perspective, 1018, JID 2009:200 (1 October), https://watermark.silverchair.com/200-7-1018.pdf.

Jama Network, (1927), 1689-1693, https://jamanetwork.com/journals/jama/article-abstract/251741.

Edwin O.,J., (1927) *The Influenza Epidemic Of 1918*, Ipreventive Measures, (November 12, 1927).

Jorda, O. and Sanjay, D. and Singh, R., Alan,D. and Taylor, M., (2020), *Longer-Run Economic Consequences of Pandemics*, Federal Reserve Bank Of San Francisco Working Paper Series, NBER and CEPR March 2020 Working Paper 2020 https://www.frbsf.org/economic-research/publications/working-papers/2020.

OECD, (2020). Economic Outlook 2020. Volume: 2020. Issue 1 (June). https://doi.org/ 10.1787/888934140088.

Park,W.H., and Williams, W., Studies on The Etiology of the Pandemic of 1918, https://quod.lib.umich. edu/cgi/t/text/idx/f/flu/6060flu.0016.606/1/--studies-on-the-etiology-of-the- pandemic-of-1918?rgn= full+text; view=image;q1=Subject+- -+influenza+history.

Royen C.E. V. ve Rhodes, A.J., (1948), *Pandemic Influenza (1918 - 1919)* Chapter LIV), Virus Diseases of Man, https://quod.lib.umich.edu/ cgi/t/text/ idx/f/ flu/0260_flu.0016.620/-- chapter-liv-pandemic-influenza-1918-1919? q1=Subject+--+influenza+history& view =imag e&seq=1&size=100.

Uğurlu, E., (2020), Covıd-19 Salgını Ardından Türkiye İhracat Sektörlerinde Çin'e Karşı Hangi Sektörlerde Rekabet Avantajı Sağlayabilir? (Uluslararası Ticaret Bölümü Araştırma Raporu), İstanbul Aydın Üniversitesi, İstanbul.

UNIDO, (2020), Coronavirus: The economic impact, https://www.unido.org/stories/coronavirus-economic-impact-26-may-2020.

www.physio-pedia.com/Endemics,_Epidemics_and_Pandemics (2020).

www.worldometers.info/coronavirus (2020).

www.tcmb.gov.tr (2020).

www.tuik.gov.tr (2020).

www.turmob.org.tr (2020).

Additional-Table 1. Turkey, Imports, by ISIC, Rev.4, 2013-2020 (general trade system (2020, Montly) in Turkey

	Total2020 (3 montly)	Jan19	Jan20	Feb19	Feb20	March19	March20	April19	Apl20
Total	69 205	16.165	19 207	16.057	17 633	18.251	18 812	18.073	13 553
Agriculture, forestry and fishing	3 560	680	915	646	819	1.005	885	971	943
Crop and animal production hunting	3 540	675	909	642	813	1.000	879	966	939
Mining and quarrying	8 933	3.127	3 137	2.714	2 483	2.875	2 196	2.566	1 118
Confidential data	7 572	2.667	2 754	2.353	2 206	2.412	1 785	2.171	827
Manufacturing	54 342	11.894	14 557	12.337	13 737	13.764	15 105	13.807	10 942
Manufacture of food products	2 011	399	523	483	490	505	503	518	495
Manufacture of textiles	1 467	341	398	344	409	366	395	398	264
chemicals and chemical products	9 308	2.279	2 303	2.200	2 290	2.328	2 431	2.445	2 284
rubber and plastics products	1 550	340	389	371	422	402	430	420	310
Manufacture of basic metals	10 960	2.057	3 323	1.913	2 656	2.568	3 244	2.488	1 737
computer electronic and optical products	3 916	924	1 074	864	908	1.018	997	1.000	937
electrical equipment	2 678	598	708	646	716	705	690	762	564
motor vehicles trailers and semi-trailers	4 817	894	1 110	988	1 367	1.177	1 566	1.117	775
other transport equipment	2 141	288	514	914	483	438	791	283	353

www.tuik.gov.tr (06.15.2020).

CHAPTER 11

An Alternative Method of Growth for Turkish Companies:
A Discussion over the Defense Industry

Tuncay Turan Turaboğlu
{turaboglu@mersin.edu.tr}

Assist. Prof., Mersin University, Faculty of Economic and Administrative Sciences, Department of Business Administration, Yenişehir/Mersin

Abstract

The shortage of financial resources is one of the main challenges facing the deep-rooted Turkish private sector. This concerns the economy as a whole and, also applies to public spending. However, companies need to have access to adequate financial resources and accumulate capital to be able to have a well-functioning structure and keep up with a sustainable trend of growth. From this perspective, growing based on a planned effort, allocation of funds on regular bases, learning by doing (producing) and purchasing guarantee could be a new alternative for the defense industry, which is portrayed as a case of success in Turkey. It is plausible to apply the template or the model structure used in the defense industry to some other industries with priority and get successful results. The organizational structure based on a foundation is a significant component of this success achieved by the defense industry. This forms of structure which is called industrial foundations, could be an alternative for Turkish companies to overcome challenges of financial resource shortages and have a well-functioning trend of growth.

Keywords Defense Industry, SSB, Offset, TSKGV, Industrial Foundations.

Introduction

A great deal of issues is now debated in different contexts in today's world that shaped by the coronavirus pandemic. The issues at hand are now wide-ranging from crisis management, healthcare industry, relations between individuals and societies, digital technologies, work from home and distance learning to production-distribution-consumption relations, from companies to the overall economy. While the debate is usually focused on how to overcome the current challenges, it also dwells on how it will shape our future. As the access to production factors has become more difficult under these circumstances, the production-distribution-consumption chains tend to be disrupted, with economies downsizing while it is judged that the problem could be eliminated only with government intervention. The programs rolled out by countries as a result corroborate this argument. However, the significant thing in reality, is to perpetuate production-distribution-consumption chains since only printing money would not be sufficient to overcome the problem.

A great deal of efforts have been exerted over the years to salvage the Turkish economy that had started an economic take-off long time ago, fell into financial crises from time to time, failed to overcome shortages of resources and capital accumulation, and to make effective and efficient use of available resources, and now appear to suffer from current account deficit and high inflation. A considerable portion of such efforts is focused on the foundation and growth of private companies based on domestic capital. In retrospect,

- a mixed economic system was adopted due to the shortage of capital accumulation in 1920s.
- Import substitution policies were introduced based on a planned economy perspective that is acknowledged in 1960s, and they protected national private companies against devastated competition, and put them on a track of incremental growth.
- The liberal policies of the 1980' supported the economy to compete in the international market-place.
- Mergers and acquisitions, which became common upon the advent of globalization in 1990s, led to grift relations with foreign capital.

Because of the pandemic, the argument that Far Eastern countries including China in particular are no longer a reliable partners for the West in the logistics chain, and that Turkey could serve as a new partner is still relevant while the debate is concentrated on whether the Turkish economy fits this role or not. To sum up what is debated,

- Major chemical, pharmaceutical and packaged food manufacturers are usually from developed countries, and they rather operate with focus on domestic markets, and
- the iron-steel industry heavily relies on scrap iron and runs operations based on mills that create goods with poor value added, and
- some considerable competitiveness is created in industries that rely on stones and soil while their value added tends to be low, and
- the automotive industry is embedded in the global production-distribution-supply network of major automobile manufacturers, and unique brands and models along with critical technologies such as engine and transmission seem to bounce back whereas a competent sub-industry has flourished, and
- cutting-edge technologies such as laminated object manufacturing and CNC machining with over 5 axes are still relevant for machinery business while they are still taking baby steps, and

- textile and shipbuilding industries have been shifted to developing countries such as Turkey as a result of delocalization policies adopted by developed countries while a considerable portion of their value added activities remain outside the country, and
- imported goods play a major role in production while consumer durables electronics industries have amassed substantial technological know-how, and
- the defense industry has absorbed the technology and started manufacturing unique products, and this now tangibly comes to reap its fruits in domestic and international markets.

One of the salient developments amid the pandemic is the production and launch of masks and ventilators at a short notice. This also applies to the use of unique defense industry products in a way to make an overwhelming impact in practice, and to achievements of software-based companies. Such developments suggest that Turkish companies have a more resilient structure than their counterparts in countries with advanced industrial infrastructure and manage to offer their own solutions to respond to various needs in a short time span. Could this structure of the defense industry and surrounding ones serve as a case in point to eliminate financial shortcomings and build a well-functioning future where companies can grow?

Turkish Defense Industry

Rolled out by the Ottoman Empire to regain its deteriorating power against Europe, some reform arrangements were originally taken in military training and equipment. To this end, foreign consultants, and arms and military equipment recommended by them began to be imported from a variety of countries as a part of offset policies. While they were occasionally interrupted, the efforts to restore the military balance against Europe went on but they yielded no lasting success. The defense industry, which failed to go beyond military uniforms, equipment, vessel and submarine mounting, maintenance and repair operations, gained momentum following the proclamation of the Republic. Private entrepreneurs such as Şakir Zümre, Nuri Demirağ and Nuri Killigil were the early momentum drivers of the time in addition to MKE, TAMTAŞ and public enterprises such as renovated military shipyards. Such efforts were interrupted by the military aids of the US after the World War II and Turkey's accession to the NATO. Having become more and more apparent prior to the peace operation to Cyprus (1964) and following the embargo imposed in the aftermath of the operation (1974), actions in contrary to the spirit of alliance imprinted the need to have a domestic defense industry on minds. To this end, the Turkish Naval Society (1965) was founded as a part of the Build Your Own Ship initiative, and manufactured domestic escort and landing ships while the Turkish Air Forces Foundation (1970) was founded as a part of the Build Your Own Aircraft initiative, and it was followed by the foundation of the Turkish Land Forces Foundation (1974) (aydin.edu.tr, 23.06.2020).

The Defense Industry Support Fund was rolled out in 1985, and then the Defense Industry Development and Support Administration Office (SAGEB), the High Coordination Council, and the Defense Industry Executive Committee were founded. This was a major step taken to run defense industry operations, which had been previously run by public enterprises such as MKE (Mechanical & Chemical Industry Company), promoted by military plants and created by the companies established by the aforementioned foundations, as a part of a much better plan and allocate more resources. Individually founded as a part of the plan, the Land, Air and Naval Forces Foundations were renamed (1987) as the Turkish Armed Forces Foundation (TSKGV) upon a merger based on the Law No. 3388 (Turaboğlu and Yılmaz, 2017: 741). SAGEB was reorganized under the title of the Undersecretariat for Defense Industries (SSM) and then of the Presidency of Defense Industry in 2018. Led by the foundation companies, this structure has promoted foundation of companies with private equity in time to run key and sub-industrial operations partly thanks to the contribution of offsetting applications, and to a considerably large defense industry ecosystem. The ecosystem exponentially expands through technological parks, clusters and organized industrial zones (OIZ) and begins to focus on critical technologies.

The fact that the briefly-aforementioned success of the defense industry's current structure is not coincidental becomes more evident when one takes a look at the following roles of the Defense Industry Executive Committee founded under the Law No. 3238 to serve as a decision-making body of the Presidency of Defense Industry (ssb.gov.tr, 23.06.2020):

- Making decisions based on the fallowing items in kline with strategies and principles established to improve the defense industry:
- Production of defense industry products needed for Armed Forces based on priorities, and imported supply,
- Analyzing, guidingi monitoring and engaging when necessary in means to establish manufacturing plants for the defense industry coupled with the foreign capital and technology of the public-private sector,
- Export, offsets and reciprocal trade of defense industry products,
- Designation of the sum of aids to be granted to improve human resources for the defense industry, and payments to be made to staff members,
- R&D for defense industry products to be supplied, productions of their prototypes, making an advance payment, placing long-term orders and giving an instruction to the Presidency of Defense Industry to designate financial incentives,
- Establishing coordination among organizations involved in the defense industry,
- Setting principles of usage for the Defense Industry Support Fund,

A closer look at these aforrementioned-statements reveals the following factors that lies behind the success of the defense industry:
- A planned effort carried out by public organizations while it is occasionally interrupted,
- Public organizations and foundations deliver the role of transferring funds on regular basis and,
- Monitoring direct procurement, offset, licensed productions and original productions stages, and give a guarantee of purchase.

A Planned Effort

The defense industry is described as a reflection of the scientific circles in a country, and an indicator of its industrial infrastructure and original technology-production capacity (Şenol, 2007: 34). The characteristics of the defense industry are well defined in the Principles of Turkish Defense Industry Policy and Strategy (www.resmigazete.gov.tr, 24.06.2020):
- Need for precise production techniques based on high technology,
- Requiring high quality standards,
- Requiring qualified labor force,
- Requiring high-cost R&D operations on a continuous basis,
- Requiring a high initial investment cost,
- Forcing to produce/sell products in most cases to meet a limited requirement for few buyers,
- Requiring focus on exports for sustainability and growth,
- Forcing to operate under high security and confidentiality conditions.

Having these characteristics the defense industry had been distinguished from other industries and has achieved considerable growth especially during the period of the Turkish Republic. The growth of the defense industry during the Republican Era can be addressed in four periods:
- From 1923 to 1952
- From 1952 to 1965
- From 1965 to 1985
- From 1985 to present.

In the period between 1923 and 1952, the main objective was set to eliminate the main shortcomings and for that purpose some plants, which merged under the title of MKE (later on), were established. Over this period, revised and new-built shipyards provided maintenance services for the *Yavuz* battle cruiser and manufactured submarines while THK (Turkish Aeronautical Association) and TAMTAŞ (Aircraft and Engine Company) were founded to manufacture aircrafts and aircraft engines. Mobilized in 1941, military aids led to the extinction of these achievements in naval and aviation industries after the accession to NATO in 1952. How devastating were the consequences became clear when the USA threatened to impose an embargo during the Cyprus disputes in 1964. Then, public monetary aids were collected as part of various campaigns as done by the Ottoman Empire to reinforce the naval forces in its twilight years, and by the Republic of Turkey to improve the air power in early years of its foundation. At the time, there were some attempts to set the military shipbuilding industry back on its feet to begin with. The embargo imposed in the aftermath of the Cyprus peace operation in 1974, negatively impacts the efforts to build a domestic defense industry. Harnessing the power to create funds thanks to public donations and aids, the foundations began to establish one company after another (Ziylan, 2001: 1-2).

Despite all the steps taken, it was not until the 5th Five-Year Development Plan approved by the Turkish Parliament in 1984 that a planned period was kicked off with operations run in a body and a defense industry ecosystem created over time. Covering the period from 1985 to 1989, the plan mentioned a focus on investments to foster the defense industry (DPT, 1984: 41). To this end, the Defense Industry Development and Support Administration Office (SAGEB) was founded by the Defense Industry Support Fund in 1985 under the Law No. 3238, and it was followed by the Undersecretariat for Defense Industries (SSM) in 1989, and reorganized as the Presidency of Defense Industry (SSB) in 2018. Adopted in 1998, the Principles of Turkish Defense Industry Policy and Strategy gave a fresh impetus to the whole process.

Currently, 178 organization are member of the Defence Industry Manufacturers Association (SASAD) while the total number of firms producing goods and services for the defence industry are 213 (sasad.org.tr, 27.06.2020; ssb.gov.tr, 27.06.2020). In fact, one can infer that the industry signifies a remarkable power given the companies that promote organizations to manufacture defense industry products as a sub-industry.

Allocation of Funds on a Regular Basis

Defense expenditures in Turkey are financed by funds allocated out of the general budget for the Ministry of National Defense and the Ministry of Interior, and funds created by the Defense Industry Support Fund (SSDF) and the Turkish Armed Forces Foundation (TSKGV). Funds created by SSDF and TSKGV become essential for the supply of modern equipment since nearly half of the funds allocated out of the general budget is spent on wages and salaries of the staff members.

The revenue items of SSDF affiliated to SSB and expenditures to be made by SSDF are set out in the Law No. 3238. While SSDF's revenue items vary from time to time, expenditures are made in secret based on the Law No. 5202 and the applicable regulations (Saygılı, sbb.gov.tr, 27.06.2020). In addition, PDI runs and/or promotes R&D and manufacturing projects via 14 companies within its body (ssb.gov.tr, 27.06.2020).

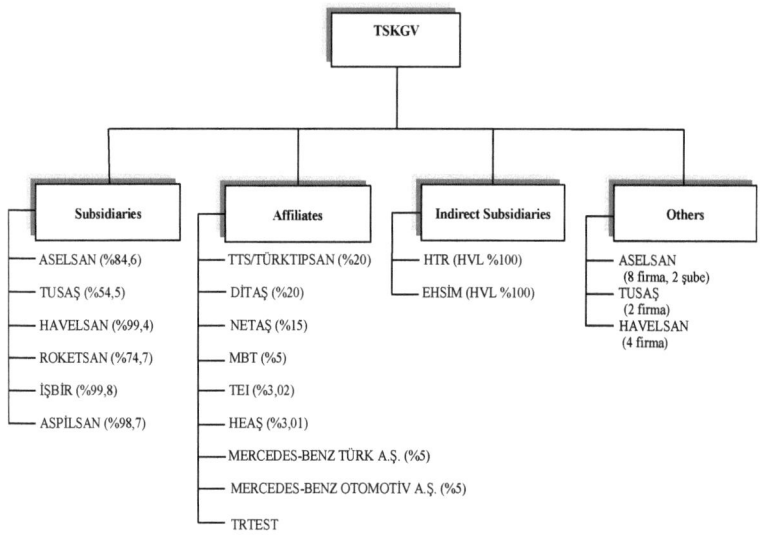

Fig. 1.
TSKGV-Affiliated Partnerships.

As it is previously mentioned, TSKGV was founded in 1987 upon the merger of foundations with similar missions. TSKGV (Turkish Armed Forces Foundation) can be described as a for-profit foundation, which is a common practice in Northern Europe, especially in Denmark (Turaboğlu and Yılmaz, 2017: 742). TSKGV allocates funds for equity increases and managerial expenditures of companies that it has founded and joined as well as for projects carried out for producing defense industry products (Yentürk, 2011: 34). From this point of view, TSKGV's contribution to the defense industry is not only about allocating funds but also making considerable contributions to the companies that it has founded or incorporated. The foundation has direct or indirect shares in 33 companies most of which offer defense industry products (Fig. 1, Turaboğlu, Yılmaz, 2017: 742).

80% of TSKGV's total revenue comprises profits and other financial revenues while 20% consists of donations, aids, rental and fair revenues. Management and other investment expenses account for 20% of its total expenditure while 28% is spent on investments in defense industry subsidiaries, with 52% on funds into projects of the Military Commands (Yentürk, 2011: 34).

The total assets of Foundation-Affiliated Partnerships (FAP), in which the Turkish Armed Forces Foundation had shares until 2016, grew by 76.000 times, with equities by 37.000 times, net profit for the financial year by 94.000 times, and it has morphed into one of the world's leading defense industry companies. FAPs within the body of the Turkish Armed Forces Foundation make up 45% of the total sales, 56% of the total exports, and 52% of total R&D spending for the defense industry, and employ 32% of the total number of staff members (Akbaş, 2016: 79-80).

Production by Learning and Purchasing Guarantee

It would not be wrong to say that the adoption and production of technology for defense industry products is the main strategy under this planned term kicked off by the foundation of SAGEB. This is because SSB runs defense industry projects coupled with technological gain liability, industrial participation/offset practices and programs to raise researchers. Within this framework, the supply of defense industry products takes the following route for development (ssb.gov.tr, 30.06.2020):

- Direct procurement until 1990s except for F-16 production,
- Co-production starting from 1990s,
- Partial design of main platforms starting from 2000s,
- Original design starting from 2010,
- Command over core and advanced technologies starting from 2020.

Within this framework, the strategy, currently adopted by the Presidency of Defense Industry, namely the "technological depth and global influence", is presented in Fig. 2 (ssb.gov.tr, 30.06.2020).

Fig. 2. Strategy of Technological Depth and Global Influence

System projects are carried out by the main contractors that assume responsibility of integration and ranked at the top of the pyramid. Sub-contractors report to main contractors, and they are responsible to develop, produce and test sub-systems and deliver them to the main contractors. Reporting to sub-contractors, small-sized enterprises serve as sub-industry organizations that provide parts and components. Universities and research institutes are tasked with providing qualified labor force through their studies, having access to technologies needed and offering technological depth.

Based on the strategic approaches that mentioned before, the turnover of the industry, which followed an upward trend except for 2009 and 2015, grew by almost 6 times from 2006 to 2019 (Fig. 3, ssm.gov.tr, 10.09.2019).

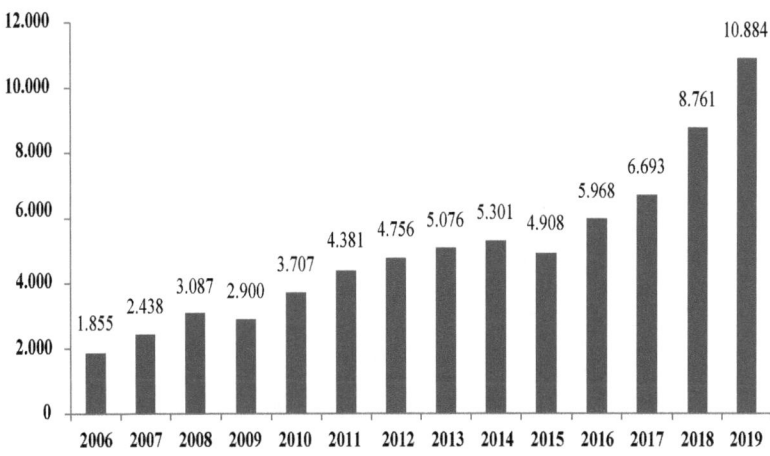

Fig. 3. Turnover of Defense and Aviation Industry ($ billion)

While the growth in exports is based on offset practices, the fact that products are as good as products of competitors in terms of price and quality and that they have established themselves in practice has played a role, too. This points to something similar in terms of the sum and number of projects run by SSB. The total contracted sum of defense industry projects amounted to $ 10.221 billion back in 2006 while it rose to nearly $ 60 billion in 2019. The number of the projects, which stood at 115 in 2006, rose to almost 700 in 2019 (ssb.gov.tr, 27.06.2020).

Despite, it is volatility compare to the total turnover, the exports of the defense and aviation industry tend to have an upward trend. The total sum of the defense industry's exports rose from $ 487 million in 2006 to $ 3.068 billion in 2019, which means a nearly 6-fold increase (Fig. 4, ssm.gov.tr, 10.09.2019).

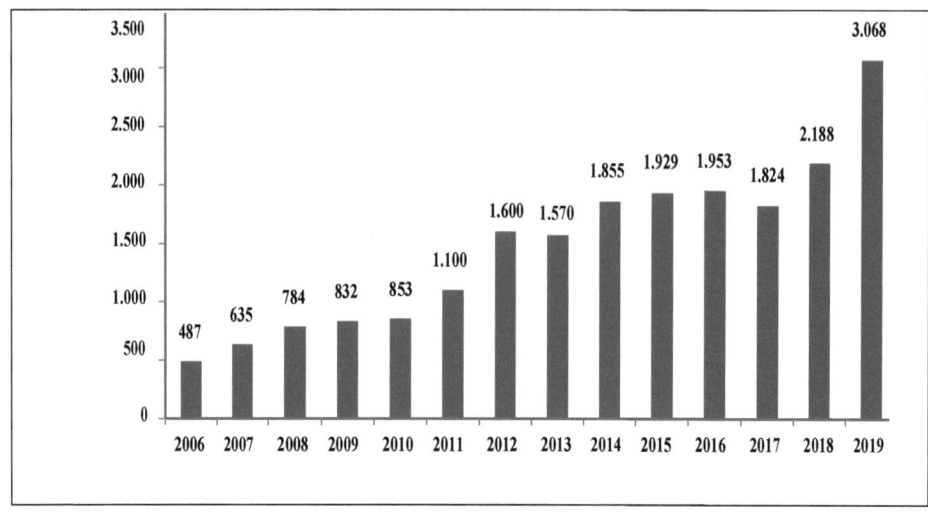

Fig. 4. Export Figures of Defense and Aviation Industry ($ billion)

As mentioned before, offsets play a major role in the growth trend. Offsets are intended to make sure that the money spent by a buyer as part of an exchange of commercial goods returns to the buyer's economy even if it is partial and in different forms (Altan, 1999: 15). They are implemented by companies of developed countries in developing countries to run high-technology projects that require large-sum payments in foreign currency. Such projects cover sales of aircrafts and defense industry products, or construction of petrochemical, industrial and power generating plants (Küçüközmen et al, 2009: 478). However, offset practices are not implemented for all trade agreements. This is because the idea of removing barriers to free trade, which has become more and more relevant upon the advent of globalization, is globally dominant. Defense industry products in particular are not part of it. This is because almost all countries would like to manufacture defense industry products for strategic purposes to the extent possible (Ayaz, 2003: 31).

Offsets, which are direct and indirect, are utilized by the Presidency of Defense Industry. As the number of original defense industry products rises, ever-growing exportation efforts gradually turn Turkey from a country of seeking offsets into a country of granting offsets. Direct offsets are intended to manufacture defense industry products within the country with a certain domestic input instead of direct procurement, and make sure that products have a guarantee of exports to a certain extent of production. Indirect offsets warrant the export of various products in certain proportion to any defense industry product supplied. Such various products could be defense and aviation industry products, as well as any other commercial goods. For offsets, the establishment of a new plant or company to manufacture export goods is one of the common gains.

Originally initiated by the supply of Ay class submarines and comprehensively put into effect for co-production of F-16 fighter aircrafts, offsets, one can argue, follow a three-stage course in Turkey (Gençtürk, 2008: 18).
- From 1984 to 2000 to serve as an instrument to raise funds,
- From 2000 to 2007 to improve the defense industry infrastructure,
- From 2007 to the present to boost the competitive edge of the defense industry and achieve strategic goals.

Operations that are considered under offsets in line with the aforementioned course are presented in Table 1 (ssb.gov.tr, 01.07.2020).

Table 1. Operations under Industrial Participation/Offsets (IP/O)

Group A	Deals for Turkish Defense Industry under supply contracts (domestic contribution)	
Group B	a.	Export of defense and aerospace products/services
	b.	Export of products/services under supply contracts
Group C	For defense and aerospace industries and others that require advanced technology,	
	a.	- Technological cooperation
	b.	- New and/or completion/expansion investment
	c.	- R&D operations

Over 100 companies make use of offsets carried by the Presidency of Defense Industry under a wide-scale legislation, and 40 companies have offset contracts. The gains out of offsets are as follows (Gençtürk, 2008: 21-22):
- Mitigating the adverse effect of direct procurement of defense industry products on the balance of payments,
- Increasing exports,
- Creating more jobs,
- Improving the manufacturing capacity and capabilities of the defense industry,
- Providing financial resources,
- Technology transfer.

A Suggestion of an Alternative Method of Growth for Turkish Companies: Industrial Foundations

It is obvious that financial resources are inadequate in the Turkish economy and capital accumulation shortages continue to be the main problem for private companies with domestic capital that have been favored and promoted over a long period of time. While many initiatives have been taken to overcome and diversify these shortages, it is still remained to be a considerable challenge. In fact, along with international organizations, the reforms introduced by the government directly and as a regulator (law-maker), a far reaching framework have been established. However, all these efforts fell short to offer a reliable solution. Some of the agencies and organizations that companies can apply to raise funds are as follows (Turaboğlu, 2018: 177-196):

- Istanbul Stock Exchange/BIST: -Equity Market, -Debt Securities Market, -Derivatives Market, -Precious Metals and Diamond Market,
- Banks (Development Banks, Commercial Banks, Participation Banks)
- Public Organizations (Turkish Ministry of Industry and Technology, -Scientific and Technological Research Council of Turkey (TUBITAK), Small and Medium Enterprises Development Organization (KOSGEB), -Regional Development Agencies, Turkish Ministry of Family, Labor and Social Services, -Turkish Employment Agency (İŞKUR), the Ministry of Trade, -Export Credit Bank of Turkey/TURK EXIMBANK, the Ministry of Energy and Natural Resources, the Ministry of Agriculture and Forestry, -Agriculture and Rural Development Support Institution (ARDSI), the Ministry of Culture and Tourism, the Ministry of Treasury and Finance, -Revenue Administration)
- Semi-Official Organizations (Credit Guarantee Fund/CGF, Union of Turkish Craftsmen and Tradesmen Credit Cooperatives (TESKOMB), Technology Development Foundation of Turkey (TTGV), Private Foundations),
- Venture Capital Trusts,
- Business Angels,
- Other Organizations and Corporations to Offer Entrepreneurship (Crowdfunding, Incubation Centers, Technology Development and Transfer Center, Microfinance/TGMP).

In addition to the aforementioned framework concerning to the supply of funds, a variety of organizations are referred, including joint-stock companies, holdings, labor companies, cooperatives and farmer trade unions with a legal status. The number of cases of success for options other than joint-stock companies and holdings is almost none. The lack of resources, and problems based on the agency theory such as differences in goals of partners, moral hazard, and inadequate monitoring and supervision lie behind it. Another challenge facing companies is that prospective expectations are established based on feelings rather than scientific methodologies. It is common that company founders expect the highest amount for gains and the lowest amount for costs. Therefore, most of the companies start production, somewhat bearing investment costs whereas they are forced to go out of business after a little while as they do not make a resource plan for working capital.

Based on how the defense industry is structured, this study is intended to offer an alternative for Turkish companies as a way for sustainable growth. As noted above, the structure, which is acknowledged to be successful, is built on three pillars: A planned effort, allocation of funds on a regular basis, production by learning and purchasing guarantee. Just like it is the case in defense and aviation industries, it is possible to establish a similar structure for industries with a high value added such as railway systems, shipbuilding and spacecrafts, engine and launching technologies, energy storage systems and software. To be established based on the know-how of the defense industry, such structures are more likely to succeed. However, it is obvious that such an effort would require the direct involvement of the government. Therefore, it would be much more feasible to offer recommendations based on not the entire structure of the defense industry but the Turkish Armed Forces Foundation that constitutes a considerable part of it.

It has been previously noted that industrial foundations, one of which is the Turkish Armed Forces Foundation, have a foothold in Northern European Countries, especially in Denmark. The reason why industrial foundations are common especially in Northern European countries is that their rather small and homogeneous structures allow everybody to get to know each other in any workplace, and reputation and social control stand out in such workplaces. Legislative reforms applicable in Northern European countries are reportedly another factor (Thomsen, 2016: 4-6). The main characteristics of the structure in question are as follows (Thomsen, 2012: 2-3; Bothello et al, 2020):

- Growth by raising funds,
- Having a legal entity,
- Attaching priority to social benefit (charitable purpose),
- Operating in line with the memorandum of association (bylaw),
- Having more principal shareholders in subsidiaries,

Analyzed within the framework of firm theory, industrial foundations are also named as corporate foundations or enterprise foundations (Thomsen, 2018: 3). They are mainly established in the form of charitable industrial foundations, business foundations and family foundations. Charitable industrial foundations are established for charitable reason, and they may also have one or more than one company. Business foundations are basically intended to make profit. A charity is of priority for charitable foundations while profit is the basic incentive for business foundations. Family foundations are intended to secure and promote the well-being of their founders and future generations. Depending on the applicable legislation, it could be possible to reduce the inheritance and succession duty to be paid whenever a foundation is handed over to the next generation (Thomsen, 2012: 6). One of the most important reasons behind the establishment of industrial foundations is touted as tax-related advantages (Fama and Jensen, 1983).

Denmark, where they are common, is home to nearly 1400 industrial foundations, and the top 100 of them have 93% of the total capital of industrial foundations (Thomsen, 2013: 4-5). 25% of top 100 companies in Denmark and 70% of publicly-traded companies are owned by foundations (Hansmann and

Thomsen, 2018: 4). Among companies that own a foundation are A.P. Moller-Maersk, Carlsberg, Hempel, Novo Nordisk, William Demant (Denmark); Aldi, Bertelsmann, Carl Zeiss, Robert Bosch (Germany); Tata Group (India); Ikea, Wallenberg Group (Sweden); Rolex (Switzerland); Heineken (The Netherlands); The Guardian (UK) and Hershey Company (US) (Thomsen, 2012: 13; Thomsen et al, 2018: 3; Bothello et al, 2020). The aforementioned ones are large-scale companies with global operations. For instance, Wallenberg Group owns Ericsson, Electrolux, ABB, SAAB, SAS Group, SKF, AIK and Atlas Capco (Henrekson et al, 2020: 174). It is a foundation that owns the controlling shares of Tata Sons Limited, which owns TATA Group operating in over 80 lines of work with 28 affiliated companies (Thomsen, 2011: 1-4). Carlsberg foundation has owned Carlsberg Breweries since 1882 (Hansmann and Thomsen, 2018: 6).

An industrial foundation is a structure that is usually formed by funds granted by their founders. The bylaw of such foundations cites charitable causes such as education, healthcare, art, research and social projects as their primary objectives. They have scores of companies within their body just like holdings do. While such foundations do not seek profit, companies they own seek to maximize profits. Profits of companies enable foundations to receive a share out of them and make use of them for their primary objectives (Dzansi, 2012: 62-64). A foundation board (board of trustees) serves as the managing body of foundations. Board members of foundations elect new members (self-elected). In some cases, they might be appointed by founders or organizations such as the Royal Academy of Arts and Sciences, and Ministries. Usually reporting to a ministry, a foundation authority is accountable to govern and supervise affairs concerning foundations on behalf of the state. Board members of foundations and companies might be either the same or totally different. When a foundation and a company board composed of different members, some opinion differences might arise about how to pay dividends. Founders who usually remain the owner of the foundation, lead the way in such cases. They are expected to attend board meetings like board members do, involve themselves in major decisions that concern the future of the company, and almost act as a CEO. Founders of foundations are briefed on a regular basis about the financial state of companies that foundations own, and any other major issues (Thomsen, 2018: 4).

Companies that own a foundation can make longer-term decisions, make longer-term investments, run operations on a stable basis, tend to contract debt less often, allocate more funds for R&D investments, and have a superior capability to survive compared to their competitors. They are more durable than competitors (Thomsen et al, 2018: 4). The fact that foundation-owned companies are long-lived, and their founders remain the owner of them in most cases helps avoiding family conflicts and nepotism in companies. In addition, political pressure and budgetary limitations are out of question in state-owned companies. While they have the same opportunities as their competitors in terms of supply of financial resources, they care about having majority of the votes. That is why holding Class A shares that allow for more voting rights and exporting Class B shares that grant fewer voting rights was a method that such foundations commonly referred to back in the day. It is a fact that foundation-owned companies are highly superior in terms of social responsibilities and they provide their employees with better conditions (Thomsen, 2018: 5).

Despite their superiority, foundation-owned companies suffer from managerial vulnerabilities. Therefore, the diminished drive of profitability can undermine cost-effectiveness efforts, and the reluctance of foundations to delegate the control of companies they own can make it difficult to have access to funds. Or they may end up being deprived of market monitoring and have limited risk diversification options. Board members of foundations may lack sufficient knowledge and experience about politics and administrative sciences (Thomsen, 2018: 6). Such problems that are relevant for companies owned by industrial foundations are usually addressed within the framework of agency theory (Franke and Draheim, 2015; Mühlbauer, 2016).

Empirical studies suggest that companies run by foundations are usually better managed than their competitors. Therefore, industrial foundations are described as a mesmerizing anomaly with a little bit of humor (Hansmann and Thomsen, 2018: 33). As reported by Hansmann (1980), the fact that they avoid opportunism protects them from failure. It is argued that the presence of managers who share the same goals as foundations can help a company succeed without any goal to maximize profits. This is because managers are further motivated by social control, morality and reputation effects (Thomsen, 2016: 5). A long-term ownership enables founders to do monitoring. Foundation-owned companies that heavily invest in R&D and have a range of products with a long profit life cycle tend to have the competitive edge (Thomsen et al, 2016: 29-33). If the following elements co-exist, foundation-owned companies tend to be more successful (Hansmann and Thomsen, 2010; Hansmann and Thomsen, 2018).

- Only some of the board members of industrial foundations and companies being the same,
- Publicly traded shares of foundation-owned companies,
- Foundations having a mission to both manage companies they own and do charity work,
- Foundations being a principal shareholder in multiple companies,
- Foundations and companies operating at different locations.

Conclusions

Grappling with financial crises very often and suffering from lack of funds and capital accumulation, failing to make effective and efficient use of the resources, and struggling with current deficit and inflation, the macro environment of the Turkish economy adversely affects the competitive edge of domestic private companies. While many instruments and organizational structures have been harnessed to overcome the lack of funds and accumulate capital, only few success stories have come to the fore.

The Turkish defense industry, which has achieved a major success in recent years, has attracted attention for its maneuvers to produce medical devices needed over the course of pandemic. The defense industry, which has reached a strong stands today, as a result of huge efforts exerted over a long period of time, has a different structure than other industries. The defense industry is based on three pillars: A planned effort, allocation of funds on a regular basis, and production by experience and purchasing guarantee. The structure has flourished with the domination of the Presidency of Defense Industry (SSB), the Turkish Armed Forces Foundation (TSKGV) and their subsidiaries (FAPs), and most of them now denote a vast ecosystem equipped with domestic and international SMEs with private capital, universities, tech-cities and clusters. One can consider the defense industry a role model as a whole and emulate it for industries with strategic priorities. However, one must remember that such vast structures require extensive funds, labor and time and, the direct involvement of the state the responsibilities of which are made to be mitigated. In fact, there are instruments and methods that the private industry can harness along with incentives and regulatory roles of the state. Based on the case of the Turkish Armed Forces Foundation (TSKGV) that plays a role in how the defense industry is structured, industrial foundations, best practices of which are common in Northern European countries in particular, might as well be one of those methods.

Foundations that are founded for various purposes including charity in particular, seek profit to achieve their goals are called industrial foundations. With the effects of tax and other legislative reforms, industrial foundations are commonly established in Northern European countries with a rather small and homogeneous demographic structure. Playing a major role in the Danish economy in particular such foundations are also named as corporate foundations or enterprise foundations and, they are established in three ways: Charitable industrial foundations, business foundations and family foundations. Foundations are run by boards whose members are usually replaced in a self-elected mode while companies they own are run by company boards. In both cases, board members could be the same or totally different. In any case, founders are expected to monitor actions of boards, and briefed about them on a regular basis.

While the literature is limited about this subject, it gives an idea about the superiority and vulnerabilities of foundation-owned companies compared to their competitors. As foundation-owned companies can have a more strategic perspective on the future, they are able to make long-term decisions and investments, and tend to become long-lived. Stable management, a lower leverage ratio and higher R&D spending are other superior aspects of foundation-owned companies. The properties of long-term ownership of foundations and monitoring by founders, could help avoiding any family conflict and nepotism in companies. In addition, political pressure and budgetary limitations are out of question in state-owned companies.

Despite their superior aspects, foundation-owned companies notably suffer from managerial vulnerabilities. Addressed within the framework of agency theory, these vulnerabilities are disruption of cost-effectiveness efforts by less significance attached to profit maximization, difficulty in having access to funds as a result of reluctance of foundations to delegate the control of companies they own, their deprivation of market monitoring, failure to diversify risks, and lack of knowledge and experience about political and administrative sciences on the part of foundation board members.

Empirical studies suggest that companies run by foundations have more strengths than vulnerabilities and, are usually better managed than their competitors. The fact that they are not opportunist as much as their competitors are protects them from risks and failures, and managers who embrace a foundation's mission tend to be successful. Companies with major R&D investments and a range of products with a long profit life cycle tend to be more competitive under the control of a foundation.

The afore-mentioned arguments suggest that industrial foundations can serve as a role model for Turkish companies in other industries. Such a structure can enable domestic private companies to turn the long-term perspective they would develop into an advantage. However, one must remember that Northern European countries, where foundations are common in practice, are positively affected by social, societal and economic varieties whereas cases such as TATA Group should not go unnoticed. Based on the benefits that it would offers; it is imperative to work on it and help entrepreneurs become familiar with it. This is because there is no sufficient studies over industrial foundations in the literature, and it is not widely recognized in both Turkey and rest of the world. The fact that foundations established for social purposes and own for-profit companies seems to be a research-worthy subject from the perspective of theory of the firm. Therefore, it would be much better to conduct such a study based on the agency theory.

References

Akbaş, O., (2016), 30. Yılında TSKGV: Gelişimi, Stratejik Önemi, Yönetim Esasları ve Gelecek Öngörüsü, Savunma ve Havacılık Dergisi, Cilt: 30, sayı:176, 2016, 75-80.

Altan, B., (1999), Türk Savunma Sanayinde "Offset" Uygulamaları, Türk Sanayicileri ve İşadamları Derneği, İstanbul, 1999.

Ayaz, A., (2003), Savunma Sanayi ve Dış Politika İlişkisi, Gazi Üniversitesi Sosyal Bilimler Enstitüsü Uluslararası İlişkiler Anabilim Dalı, Yayınlanmamış Yüksek Lisans Tezi, Ankara.

Beşinci Beş Yıllık Kalkınma Planı, Makine İmalat Sanayi Özel İhtisas Komisyon Raporu (1984), Devlet Planlama Teşkilatı, Ankara.

Bothello, J., Gautier, A., and Pache, A-C., (2020), "Families, Firms, and Philanthropy: Shareholder Foundation Responses to Competing Goals", 63-82, Ed: Lonneke, R., Bethmann, S., Meijs, L., Von Schnurbein, G., in Chapter 4 of Handbook on Corporate Foundations: Corporate and Civil Society Perspectives, Springer, Switzerland.

Dzansi, J., (2012), foundation Control and Investment Performance: Do Intrinsic Aspects of Ownership and Control Matter?, Global Economy and Financial Journal, 5/2, September 2012, 58-78.

Gençtürk, H., (2008), Finansman Yönetiminden Stratejik Hedeflere Giden Yol: Offset, Savunma Sanayi Gündemi, SSM Dergi, Nisan 2008.

Fama, E. F., and Jensen, M. C., (1983), Separation of Ownership and Control, Journal of Law Economics, 26/2, 301-325.

Franke, G., and Draheim, M., (2015), Foundation Owned Firms in Germany- A Field Experiment for Agency Theory, Conference Paper, Sessions: Financial Economics IV, No. D10-V2, Econstor, 1-52, http://hdl.handle.net/10419/113217.

Hansmann, H., (1980), The Role of Non-profit Enterprise, The Yale Law Journal, 89/5, April 1980, 835-901.

Hansmann, H., and Thomsen, S., (2018), The Governance of Foundation-Owned Firms, Center for Corporate Governance at Copenhagen Business School and ECGI, November 2018, pp. 1-50.

Henrekson, M., Johansson, D., and Stenkula, M., (2020), The Rise and Decline of Industrial Foundations as Controlling Owners of Swedish Listed Firms: The Role of Tax Incentives, Scandinavian Economic History Review, 68/2, 170-191.

Küçüközmen, C.,C., Ban, Ü., Güzel, A., Aypek, N., and İltaş, Y., (2009), Ekonomik Terimler Sözlüğü, Gazi Kitabevi, Ankara.

Mühlbauer, S., (2016), Foundation Owned Firms – A Delegation Approach, Conference Paper, Sessions: Firm Behavior: Theory and Evidence, No: B24-V1, Econstor, 1-27, http://hdl.handle.net/10419/145719.

Şenol, T., (2007), Uluslararası Boyutuyla Savunma Sanayi Stratejilerine Bir Bakış, Savunma Sanayi Gündemi, 1, Mayıs, 34-39.

Thomsen, S., (2011), Trust Ownership of the Tata Group, Center for Corporate Governance, Copenhagen Business School, First Draft, 26. December 2011, 1-15.

Thomsen, S., (2012), What Do We Know (and Not Know) about Industrial Foundations?, Discussion Paper, Center for Corporate Governance, Copenhagen Business School, August 8, 2012, 1-20.

Thomsen, S., (2013), Industrial Foundations in the Danish Economy, Discussion Paper, Center for Corporate Governance, Copenhagen Business School, February 19, 2013, 1-25.

Thomsen, S., (2016), Nordic Corporate Governance Revisited, Nordic Journal of Business (NJB), 65/1, Spring 2016, 4-12.

Thomsen, S., (2018), Foundation Ownership and Firm Performance A Review of the International Evidence, Part of The Research Project on Industrial Foundations at the Center for Corporate Govarnence, Copenhagen Business School, November 8, 2018, 1-30.

Thomsen, S., Poulsen, T., Borsting, C., and Kuhn, J., (2018), Industrial Foundations as Long-Term Owners, ECGI Working Paper Series in Finance, No: 556/2018, Nowember 2018, pp.1-60.

Turaboğlu, T.,T., and Yılmaz, C., (2017), Bağış ve Yardımlar: Türk Silahlı Kuvvetlerini Güçlendirme Vakfı (TSKGV) ve Vakıf Bağlı Ortaklıkları (VBO) Üzerinden Bir Değerlendirme, Uluslararası Sosyal Bilimler Kongresi-International SocialResearchCongress (USAK) 2017, Cilt. III, ISBN: 978-605-82729-0-3, İstanbul, 20-22 Nisan 2017, 738-747.

Turaboğlu, T., T., (2018), Girişimciler İçin Yatırım ve Proje Analizi, Ekin Basım Yayın Dağıtım, ISBN: 978-605-327-743-9, Yenilenmiş 2. Baskı, Bursa, 2018.

Yentürk, N., (2011), Askeri ve İç Güvenlik Harcamalarını İzleme Kılavuzu, İstanbul Üniversitesi Bilgi Üniversitesi Yayınları, Yayın No: 337, Kasım 2011, İstanbul.

Ziylan, A., (2001), Savunma Nereden Nereye? Türkiye'de Savunma Sanayii Tarihçesi, Ulusal Strateji Dergisi, Kasım/Aralık 2001, 1-7.

Savunma Sanayi Müsteşarlığı, https://www.ssm.gov.tr/, 10.09.2019.

Savunma Sanayi Başkanlığı, https://www.ssb.gov.tr/WebSite/contentlist.aspx?PageID=40&LangID=1, 23.06.2020.

Savunma Sanayi Başkanlığı, https://www.ssb.gov.tr/urunkatalog/tr, 27.06.2020.

Savunma Sanayi Başkanlığı, https://www.ssb.gov.tr, 29.06.2020.

Savunma Sanayi Başkanlığı, https://www.ssb.gov.tr/Images/Uploads/MyContents.pdf, 30.06.2020.

Savunma Sanayi Başkanlığı, https://www.ssb.gov.tr/Images/Uploads/MyContents/F.pdf, 30.06.2020.

Savunma Sanayi Başkanlığı, Sanayi Katılımı/Offset Uygulamaları Yönergesi, https://www.ssb.gov.tr/ Images/Uploads/MyContents/.pdf, 01.07.2020.

Savunma Sanayicileri Derneği, https://www.sasad.org.tr/uyelerimiz, 27.06.2020.

Saygılı, M. K., (2002), Türkiye'de Kamu Fonu Uygulaması, Uzmanlık Tezi, Devlet Planlama Teşkilatı, Yayın No: 2631. http://www.sbb.gov.tr/wp-content/uploads/2018/11/MehmetKaGanSAYGILI.pdf., 29.06.2020.

T.C. Resmi Gazete, 20 Haziran 1998 tarih ve 98/11173 sayılı Bakanlar Kurulu Kararı. http://www.resmigazete.gov.tr, 24.06.2020.

Türk Savunma Sanayi, İstanbul Aydın Üniversitesi, https://www.aydin.edu.tr/tr-tr/arastirma/arastirmamerkezleri/sstuam/Pages/tss.aspx, 23.06.2020

BACKGROUND

SEFER DARICI
Asst. Prof. Dr. Sefer Darıcı is one of Turkey's well-known writers. He is the head of the Marketing and Advertising Department at Sivas Cumhuriyet University. He has eight books written in total published by national and international publishing houses. One of Darıcı's book that "Subliminal Occupation" is the bestseller in Turkey. Besides, he has written scripts, articles, and newspaper columns. Darıcı is currently the president of the Perception Research Center which he founded.

AYŞE MERİÇ YAZICI
She was born on January 1, 1985 in Konya. She completed his master's degree at Istanbul Aydin University between 2013-2016. She continues his PhD in Business Administration at the same university. She works in the fields of space economy, astropolitics, biomimicry. She has articles published in international journals in the same fields. She is a research scientist at the Blue Marble Space Institute of Science. She is fluent in English and Russian.

SERHAT YANIK
Serhat Yanık, who grauated from the Public Administration Department of the Faculty of Political Sciences of Istanbul University in 1991, completed his master's degree at the Business Administration Department of the same university in 1994 and the doctorate program at the Business Administration Department in 2000. Mr. Yanık, started his career at the Ministry of Finance in 1991, respectively served as Research Assistant in 1992 and as Associate Proessor between 2008-2016 and has been carrying out his duties as Professor at Istanbul University since 2016. Mr. Yanık, who is Head of Crowfunding Center and Board Member at Expert Accounting, Finance, Auditing and Insurance in various universities and institutions. Having published various national international publications and articles, Mr. Yanık involved in many scientific research projects and activities around the world. Between 2012-2019, Serhat Yanık served as Independent Board Member at Garanti Factoring A.Ş. As of 2019, Mr. Yanık still has been serving as Independent Board Member of Güneş Sigorta A.Ş. Mr. Yanık has started to serve as Independent Board Member in ICBC Turkey Bank A.Ş. as of 24 February 2020. He also has Certified Public Accountant and Independent Auditor's Certificate issued by the Public Oversight and Accounting and Auditing Standards Authority.

CÜNEYD EBRAR LEVENT
Cuneyd Ebrar Levent is an Assistant Professor of Finance and Accounting at Istanbul Aydin University. He has served as a board or a committee member

of many research centers, including the Corporate Governance and Sustainability Research Center, Social Researches and Implementation Center at IAU. His research focus is on financial economy and financial markets with particular emphasis on the relationship between sustainability, corporate governance, corporate social responsibility and corporate financial performance. He has contributed many articles in academic, business and professional journals and conference proceedings. One of his latest awards is `Doctoral Studies Support Award` of the `International Conference on Eurasian Economies` held in Russia.

ERDAL ŞEN

Assoc. Prof. Dr. Erdal ŞEN, teaching professor in Faculty of Economics and Administrative Sciences, Department of Business Administration (Eng.) at İstanbul Aydın University. He has been working extensively on the contemporary issues of; Management and Strategy, Institutionalization, Corporate Governance, Leadership, Entrepreneurship, COVID-19 and Senism. Since 2000, many books, articles, papers, book chapters and project studies have been published, including his own theory "Senism". He has been a teaching professor for more than fifteen years within six different universities. Also, he has been working within different sectors as consultant and realized various social responsibility projects as a society volunteer.

ERDEM BAĞCI

Erdem BAĞCI has graduated from the Business Administration Department, Near East University, TRNC, in 2005. He received his master degree from Department of Economics at Marmara University, Turkey in 2009 and his PhD degree from same Department and University, in 2013. After working in TC. Halkbank for a while, He has trained and directed over 20,000 Certified Public Accountants in Deha Educational Institutions and has provided training and consultancy services to many companies. He is an assistant professor of economics at Istanbul Gelisim University since september 2014 and he is an adjunct academic staff at MEF University since september 2016. His academic research areas are Macro-Economics Issues, such as; inflation, rate of growth, national income, gross domestic product (GDP), changes in unemployment and income inequality.

LUTZ PESCHKE

Asst. Prof. Dr. Dr. Lutz Peschke earned his first PhD in chemistry in the Department of Environmental and Life Sciences at the Research Center Jülich and the Department of Physical Chemistry at University of Heidelberg, and his second PhD in media studies which is about visual communication and knowledge transfer with help of information graphics in the Department of

Media Studies at University of Bonn. Since 1999 he works in different high budget project in the field of Public Understanding of Science and Humanities in Germany and Turkey, e.g. on behalf of the German Federal Ministry of Education and Research, German Federal Ministry of Environment, Nature Conservation and Nuclear Safety. He creates and directs big science festivals and stage shows, e.g. the annual 'Highlights of Physics' in Germany with the Federal Ministry of Education and Research and the German Physical Society, and the daily stage show 'Wissen LIVE' (knowledge LIVE) on the big science festival 'IdeenExpo', which occurs every two years for nine days in Hanover/Germany with average 500.000 participants. In 2014 he organized and moderated the first science slam in Turkey within the scope of the Turkish-Germany Year of Research, Education and Innovation 2014, supported by the German Embassy in Turkey. In 2016 he organised and moderated the first Grand Turkey Science Slam in six different cities of Turkey and a final event in the summer residence of the German Ambassador in Tarabya/Istanbul, supported by the German Embassy in Turkey, Siemens, Bosch, Zeiss, Rhode & Schwarz and in partnership with Bilkent University. Since 2018 he is Assistant Professor in the Department of Communication and Design at Bilkent University. He is coordinator of the European Horizon 2020 project "PandeVITA - Pandemic Virus Trace Application for the Effective Knowledge Transfer Between Science and Society Inside the Quadruple Helix Collaboration"

MURAT ADİL SALEPÇİOĞLU

Murat Adil Salepçioğlu, who graduated from Istanbul University (IU) Faculty of Political Sciences Department of Public Administration in 1987, completed his Master's Degree in the same Faculty in 1991 and received his Ph.D. from the same University in 2000. He started his career in 1987 at Garanti Bank T.A.Ş. Salepçioğlu completed his military service as a Reserve Officer. In 1991, Koç Holding A.Ş. and FCA N.A. Dr. Salepçioğlu retired from Koç Group in 2017 as the Corporate Governance and Shareholder Relations Manager, after working in different positions and positions. Since 2002, he has been teaching undergraduate and graduate courses at different universities. Dr. Salepçioğlu has been teaching as a full-time Assistant Prof. at Istanbul Aydın University (IAU) since 2017, where he started to teach graduate courses on assignment since 2012. He started working with the title of Assistant Prof. Currently, in the field of Management and Organization at the Faculty of Economics and Administrative Sciences, Department of Business Administration of the same University. Continuing his duty as a faculty member, Dr. Salepçioğlu also works as the Manager of IAU Corporate Governance and Sustainability Application and Research Center. Besides the Central Directorate, he works as the Head of the Department of Quality

Management and Quality Assurance Systems within the Graduate Education Institute. Dr. Salepçioğlu is married with 2 children and speaks English.

TURGAY CEYHAN

Turgay Ceyhan, who graduated from Anadolu University Faculty of Economics and Administrative Sciences, Department of Economics in 2010, completed his Master's Degree in Anadolu University Social Sciences Institute in 2012 and received his Ph.D. from the same University in 2016. Dr. Ceyhan, who completed his military service as a Reserve Officer in 2017, started working with the title of Assistant Prof. at Istanbul Gelisim University, Faculty of Economics, Administrative and Social Sciences, Department of Economics and Finance in 2018 and taught various courses at undergraduate and graduate levels there until 2020. Currently, he continues his duty as Assistant Prof. at Burdur Mehmet Akif Ersoy University, Bucak Faculty of Business Administration, Department of Economics and Finance. Dr. Ceyhan, who continues his paper and research studies in the field of Economics within the university, speaks English.

MUSTAFA ÇANAKÇIOĞLU

Ast. Prof. Mustafa Canakcioglu Ph.D. is the member of the Faculty of Management at the Kadir Has University. He studies about finance and accounting management. He has a numerous scientific studies which related to accounting, cost and management accounting, and financial analysis. He received his Ph.D. in Institution Social Science at the Istanbul University. He has written scientific studies published by well-known publishers.

FİGEN ÖZYILDIZ

Dr. Ozyıldız has been working on anti-microbial agents including plant based materials and inorganic materials. She is a graduate of Biology Department, Ege University and she completed her PhD on Microbiology from the same university. She has been teaching biology and microbiology for long years.

ELİF ALYAMAÇ SEYDİBEYOĞLU

She is a Chemical Engineer with a PhD in Polymer Engineering. She is currently working at the Department of Petroleum and Natural Gas Engineering, Izmir Katip Celebi University as an Asst. Prof. She has been conducting research on anti-microbial suture materials and nanocomposites.

M. ÖZGÜR SEYDİBEYOĞLU

He is a Materials Scientist with a PhD on Polymer Nanocomposites. He is a Professor at Materials Science and Engineering Department, Izmir Katip Celebi

University. He has been working on biobased materials and biomedical materials for certain time. He has extensive experience on nanocomposites and nanotechnology.

SELDAĞ GÜNEŞ PESCHKE

Seldağ Güneş Peschke was graduated from Ankara University Faculty of Law. She finished her master and phd in Ankara University Institute of Social Sciences. In 1995 she started to work in Privatization Administration as a lawyer. She has started her academic career in Gazi University Faculty of Law as research assistant in 1997. By the scholarship of Italian Government between 2000-2001, she did research for her phd. in Roma La Sapienza University. She got scholarships from DAAD and Frankfurt Max Planck Institute several times and worked in different German Universities between 2006-2017. In 2009 she became associate professor in Gazi University Faculty of Law. Since February 2015 she is working as Head of Comparative Law as a professor in Ankara Yıldırım Beyazıt University Faculty of Law. She has taken part in many EU and Horizon 2020 projects on youth, education, migration, women issues, research integrity. She is fluent in English, German and Italian. She has five books and many articles in national and international journals. She works mainly on personality rights, ethics, data protection, social media and media law, comparative private law, family law, gender studies.

ÖMER FATİH SAYAN

Born in İstanbul in the year 1977, Dr. Ömer Fatih Sayan studied electronics engineering, law and diplomatic studies. He received his MSc in electronics and communications engineering as well as in biomedical engineering from the Technical University of Munich and his PhD degree in biomedical engineering. He also made studies in internet law and social media. Starting his career in İstanbul Metropolitan Municipality in 1995 and having worked in private companies in Turkey, Germany and USAin the fields of chip manufacturing, cell phone design and R&D, he has given many lectures in conferences and he has many articles published in scientific journals. He also carried out his duty as Advisor and Chief Advisor to the Prime Minister. He worked as the Chairman of the Board & President of the Information and Communications Technologies Authority (ICTA) between 2015 and 2018 and since then he is functioning as the Deputy Minister of the Ministry of Transport and Infrastructure. He is married and has 3 children. He speaks English, German and French.

ALİ OSMAN BALKANLI

The researcher finished his undergraduate education at Istanbul University, Faculty of Political Sciences. After bachelor education, he completed the master and doctorate in Economics, Istanbul University, Faculty of Economics-Social

Sciences Institute. He focused on industrialization in his master study, In doctorate study, he focused on the development of financial markets and state intervention in these markets. During his education, he started his assistantship in the economics department, Istanbul University, Faculty of Political Sciences. Further, the writer worked as a journalist and column-writer in the economic department of journals and newspapers (Milliyet Pub. Group and Sabah Pub. Group). The researcher is currently working as Associate Professor in the Faculty of Political Sciences, Istanbul University. The researcher focused on Economics Theory, International Economics, and Development Economics in his studies and published national and international books, articles, and reports in these fields.

TUNCAY TURAN TURABOĞLU

Tuncay Turan Turaboğlu is a scholar at Mersin University Faculty of Economic and Administrative Sciences, Department of Business Administration since 1995. He has been giving lectures about entrepreneurship, finance and quality managements at both undergraduate and graduate level. He published many scientific articles in refereed journals, books and book chapters, conference papers, proceedings and reports concerning his area of expertise. Moreover, he got many certificates and awards for his productive works in finance, entrepreneurship, project management, quality assurance and mentorship. He is also the founder and partner of Mersin Bilişim Danışmanlık Ltd. which is a consultancy firm located in Mersin Technopark.

Bei Fragen zur Produktsicherheit wenden Sie sich bitte an:
If you have any questions regarding product safety,
please contact:

Walter de Gruyter GmbH
Genthiner Straße 13
10785 Berlin
productsafety@degruyterbrill.com